FLASHBACKS

FLASHBACKS

EYEWITNESS ACCOUNTS OF THE ROCK REVOLUTION

1964–1974

MICHAEL LYDON

ROUTLEDGE
NEW YORK ★ LONDON

Published in 2003 by
Routledge
29 West 35th Street
New York, NY 10001
www.routledge-ny.com

Published in Great Britain by
Routledge
11 New Fetter Lane
London EC4P 4EE
www.routledge.co.uk

Routledge is an imprint of the Taylor & Francis Group.
Printed in the United States of America on acid-free paper.

The material listed in "Permissions" on pp. 241–42 constitutes a continuation of this copyright page. The B.B. King, Janis Joplin, Grateful Dead, and Rolling Stones chapters are drawn from the author's book *Rock Folk*; the Aretha Franklin chapter, from his book *Boogie Lightning*. All of the writings in this book are reprinted as they originally appeared, without emendation, except for small changes to regularize spelling.

10 9 8 7 6 5 4 3 2 1

Library of Congress Cataloging-in-Publication Data

Lydon, Michael.
    Flashbacks : eyewitness accounts of the rock revolution, 1964–1974 /
Michael Lydon.
        p.   cm.
Includes index.
    ISBN 0-415-96643-4 (hardbound : alk. paper) — ISBN 0-415-96644-2
(paperbound : alk. paper)
    1. Rock music—1961–1970—History and criticism. 2. Rock music—1971–1980—
History and criticism. I. Title.
    ML3534 .L88 2003
781.66'09—dc21

2002153660

For Bill and Kitty,
friends through thick and thin

CONTENTS

PREFACE AND ACKNOWLEDGMENTS

Interning at the *Dayton Daily News* in the summer of 1963, I learned a crucial lesson: to avoid dull days rewriting garden club press releases, a cub reporter must find a big story and get it on paper fast and right.

The following winter, when the Beatles invaded America, I found my big story: rock 'n' roll. Until then I'd been writing about politics in the student paper, the *Yale Daily News*, and no one seemed to care. When I wrote my first piece on rock 'n' roll, panning the moptop Beatles and praising Martha and the Vandellas, that struck a responsive chord. "Hey, Michael," pals called out to me in the dorm dining hall, "that column you wrote about rock 'n' roll was wild." Hmm, I said to myself, maybe I've got something here.

Putting writing and music together was new for me, but I'd loved pop music as far back as I could remember: Patti Page's "The Tennessee Waltz" and Tennessee Ernie Ford's "Sixteen Tons." In high school I wore out my Duke Ellington records and studied clarinet so I could play like Benny Goodman. But jazz proved too difficult, too distant, and I gave up, believing I'd never be as good as Bird and Diz and all my idols. The rock 'n' roll of the sixties, in contrast, seemed simpler, more immediate. This wild electric music, I felt in my bones, had the power to change millions of lives, my own included.

I joined *Newsweek* after graduating in 1965 and got assigned to swinging London, home of mods and rockers. There I began reporting on rock 'n' roll in earnest, interviewing John Lennon and Paul McCartney, following my ears to Soho's tiny clubs and Abbey Road's huge studios, learning as I went along, listening to the music and the emerging youth dialogue. *Newsweek* moved me to San Francisco in January 1967 just as hippies and the Haight-Ashbury became national news. The Fillmore and Avalon Ballrooms became my beat, Janis Joplin and Jerry Garcia my inside sources. Jann Wenner asked me to help him found *Rolling Stone.* At Monterey Pop I sat in the press section and let my mind be blown. At Altamont I felt lucky to escape with my skin.

They were exciting days: kids my own age beaming big ideas through electric music. In the early seventies the music got to me. I began playing guitar, worked my way through a Bob Dylan songbook, began writing my own songs, and climbed up on my first coffeehouse stages with my partner Ellen Mandel. After years of reporting on others, I discovered my own passionate determination to add my voice to pop's worldwide symphony. The last reports in this book, on Aretha Franklin and Bob Dylan, come from a new twin perspective: that of reporter and fellow musician.

Why did rock 'n' roll become my big story? Because sixties rock was a big story. The Beatles and the Stones, Janis and Jerry, Aretha and Dylan did change people's lives; their vibrant music resounds today as a major theme in the history of that dissonant decade. More personally, rock 'n' roll awoke my own abiding love of music. The music of the sixties opened me up to gorgeous sounds and challenging ideas: "All you need is love"; "He not busy being born is busy dying"; "R-E-S-P-E-C-T, find out what it means to me."

I'm still responding to those challenges. Every day and in every note I play, I'm trying to sum up all I learned from Jerry and Janis, Mick and Keith, B.B. and Aretha, and so many, many more, and, just like them, to send my music out to the world, to anyone who'll listen. When I get back silly grins from couples dancing to my beat and singing in on the chorus, I tell my inspirations, "Thanks, I'm doing now what I loved you for way back when."

Rereading these pieces while preparing this book did, I'll confess, stir bittersweet emotions. The nutty days and nights they record seemed at moments like yesterday; at others I felt the full weight of the intervening decades. My subjects and I were all so young, so self-important, so eager to race into a future we were sure we could shape as we wished. Now we know that life shapes us as much as we shape life, and that soon enough come along younger generations thrilled about their own lives and heroes, for whom our adventures are faraway tales from that misty time before they were born.

Yet writing can capture passing life's freshness and hold it suspended on the page so that, in thirty or three hundred or three thousand years, readers may realize, "Ah, as I live now, they lived then." These pieces, I hope, will bring the exciting days of sixties and seventies rock 'n' roll alive for you. For all that my words cannot supply, listen to the music!

Since the writing in this book stretches back nearly forty years, it's hard to remember all the friends and colleagues who gave me helpful suggestions and encouragement. I could let this list run for pages and it would still be incomplete. I hope these scattered few names, in rough chronological order, will stand for the many who made my writing then and this book now both possible and a pleasure: Peter Guralnick, Zick Rubin, Sheward Hagerty, Jann Wenner, Seymour Peck, Baron Wolman, Jo Bergman, Stanley Booth, Ethan Russell, Bob Cornfield, Paul Williams, Jim Payne, Bill Graham, Richard Kostelanetz, Reed Robins, and Richard Carlin—plus, of course, the many musicians whose portraits I tried to paint because their music inspired me. And, first, last, and always—my wife and musical partner, Ellen Mandel.

Ed Sullivan with the Beatles—Ringo Starr, George Harrison, John Lennon, and Paul McCartney, at a rehearsal for their first appearance on American television, February 9, 1964. © 2002 AP Wide World Photos

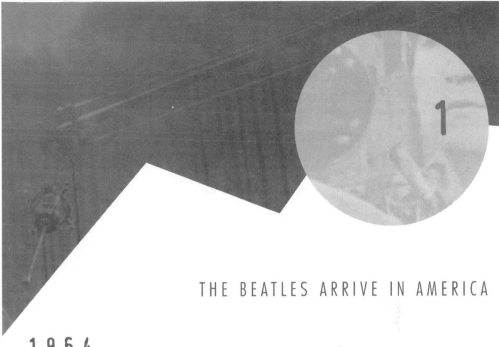

1964

When the Beatles hit America in February 1964, they created a pop music tidal wave
that for that moment at least drowned all the homegrown stars of rock 'n' roll. I was a
junior at Yale that winter, an ambitious writer on the *Yale Daily News*. Someone brought a
television over to the newsroom, and a bunch of us gathered to watch, transfixed, as the
moptop Beatles cavorted on the Ed Sullivan show. I remember most how their huge
smiles embarrassed and upset me; they were having more fun than I'd ever dreamed
was possible!

In a fit of jealous pique, I sat down to slam these audacious interlopers in my weekly
column (named "In A Mellow Tone" after the Duke Ellington song). This was my first piece
of "rock writing."

There is a scene in Jean Genet's *The Blacks* when the White Queen, cower-
ing in fear of revolution, recites a jumbled litany of Western accomplish-
ments and symbols to give herself strength. "Virgins of the Parthenon," she

1

cries, "stained glass of Chartres, Lord Byron, Chopin, French cooking, the Unknown Soldier, Tyrolean songs, Aristotelian principles, heroic couplets, poppies, sunflowers, a touch of coquetry, vicarage gardens. . . ." Her court responds with emotion, "Madam, we're here."

Confronted with the revolution caused by the four famed Liverpudlians, I can identify with the hapless queen. Whenever the first strains of "I Want to Hold Your Hand" begin to twitch my eardrums, I send out silent screams for help to Chuck Berry, Elvis Presley, Carl Perkins, Little Richard, the Orlons, the Impressions, Martha and the Vandellas, Major Lance, the Drifters, and those other greats who have long defended the American way of rock. With a heartwarmingly guttural "Yeaaah" of affirmation, they bring me peace again.

Thankfully the height of the storm has passed, but the memory of America's desertion of its homebred heroes galls me still. I weep for you, Drifters, creators of the lyric and moving "Up on the Roof," and for Ruby and her Romantics, who touched us all with "Our Day Will Come." I weep for the now lost chords of "Blue Suede Shoes" and "Jenny Jenny," for the unsold inventories of "Monkey Time" and "South Street." I weep for Little Stevie Wonder, plunged again into obscurity at the tender age of thirteen. I weep for all the artists and masters of the complex craft of rhythm and blues left stranded in sudden loneliness by the treacherous wave of adulation for a bunch of poor foreign imitations. I weep for America.

As Athens spurned Themistocles, we have spurned these dedicated and gifted interpreters of American soul. The rejection was not, of course, complete. "Talkin' 'Bout My Baby" can still be heard; "Good News," a refreshing fusion of traditional and modern blues and rhythm, is experiencing a well-deserved success. Murray The K's "Blasts from the Past" continue to celebrate legendary oldies like "Get a Job." But that does not lessen our guilt. And we must bear a double burden of guilt: some traitors have had the nerve to say that the English string and percussion quartet are a welcome return to the "classic" rock 'n' roll of the early fifties. Oh, rise up Wild Bill Haley and Gene Vincent with your Comets and Blue Caps, and lay low these smirking fools.

Let "Shake, Rattle, and Roll," "Blue Jean Bop," and "Be-bop-a Lula" be heard in the land once more. Show them what made our generation great.

That no one may think my passion misguided, I ask you to listen once again to that classic song, that transcendent evocation of adolescent love, "Heat Wave," by Martha and the Vandellas. Produced by a Motown Productions affiliate, Gordy Records, whose appropriate motto reads, "It's what's in the grooves that count," the disc combines perfect artistic form with rare insight into the world of today's youth.

Beginning with a complexly rhythmic combination of guitar, piano, drums, and clapping hands, "Heat Wave" wastes no time in setting a compelling mood. A deep and solemn sax soon adds more melodic content while adding body and depth to the rhythm (this solidity, essential to the form, is something the Britishers never achieve; note the fragmented and one-dimensional quality of their sound). Then we hear Martha's voice, backed by the lyric "oohs" of the Vandellas. The Vandellas repeat key idea words; Martha, whose range of tone and nuance is extraordinary, weaves her melody around the contrapuntal and contrasting background, at times leaving it for expressive vocal flights. After a short instrumental theme recapitulation, this time combined with gentle "oohs" and climactic shouts of "heat wave" from the Vandellas, Martha returns with even greater passion that finally overcomes her. She can no longer sing words, only the sublime "yeah" to the ecstatic shouting of "burning, burning" by her accompanists.

Few songs of any era have achieved such a synthesis of music and meaning. We become profoundly sympathetic with this girl who feels passion as a consuming fire, as something that destroys her as it gives her life. And all the while the inexorable beat carries her along against her will; she is caught in something larger than herself.

These few words show us how the song is revelatory of our times. Old orders have broken down, all is chaos. We can hear in "Heat Wave" the violence of breaking glass, dragsters, streets of neon lights, gang fights, screaming crowds. We can feel the fear of kids running from a petty crime, their fear of cops, school, of not being cool, of dark tenement stairs. In Martha's pathetic cry, "I don't understand it, can't explain it, ain't never felt this way before," we hear resentment and bewilderment. We hear young America.

This is the artistry we abandoned for the English synthetics so much admired by the Queen Mother. Me, I'll stick with the cool mothers and hope that the pain suffered by these musicians at our hands brings new profundity to their songs.

Paul McCartney and John Lennon on stage, circa 1965. © David Redfern/Retna Ltd.

LENNON AND McCARTNEY,
SONGWRITERS IN LONDON

1 9 6 6

After graduating from college in 1965, I went to work for *Newsweek* and wrangled an assignment in the London bureau. There I quickly became the youth reporter, covering the mods and rockers of Carnaby Street and hearing the Who at the Marquee. I remember hearing "(I Can't Get No) Satisfaction" at Biba, a hip boutique on the King's Road in Chelsea. The movie *Help!* converted me to the Beatles, and in March 1966, just after the release of *Rubber Soul*, I had the chance to meet John Lennon and Paul McCartney at Brian Epstein's London office for separate in-depth interviews about their songwriting. True to their reputations, Paul was a smoothie who put a public relations gloss on everything he said, and John was abrasive and sarcastic, speaking his mind and letting the chips fall where they may. *Newsweek*'s New York editors used the following piece as a research file, but it's never before been published as is.

It is now a dozen years since the pop music revolution, since Alan Freed began to play, instead of soupy white imitations, straight rhythm and blues   7 on New York radio and called it rock 'n' roll; since Wild Bill Haley and his Comets roared to the top of the Top 10 with "Shake, Rattle and Roll"; since the 45-rpm record and Ike's mid-fifties prosperity stretched that Top 10 into the Top 40, and even the Top 100. Despite adult accusations of the sameness of rock 'n' roll's bleating sounds, pop has changed many times in those years. Those indistinguishable songs from the teenager's transistors have in fact been the country rock sounds of Carl Perkins, Gene Vincent, or the Everly Brothers; the sweet harmonizing of the Platters, the Shirelles, the Drifters or the Five Satins; the plaintive blues orchestrations of Curtis Mayfield's Impressions; the guttural funny blues of Chuck Berry or the Coasters; and the jazzed-up beat of Motown's Miracles, the Marvelettes, and Martha and the Vandellas—even this list merely hints at the diversity. Many pop songs, however, are poor, quickly recorded imitations of a successful formula written by songwriters with a facile ear for discerning what sound has "teen feel." But for those few writers and performers like Mayfield, Keith Richards and Mick Jagger of the Rolling Stones, and the Beach Boys who attempt something new, rock 'n' roll's thirteen years of evolution and synthesis provide a rich tradition of themes, rhythms, harmonies, and effects to create upon. No one has mined this tradition more successfully or with more verve than Paul McCartney and John Lennon.

Lennon and McCartney's claim to immortality can be established purely by their commercial success. In the three-and-a-half years since "Love Me Do" became the first Beatles hit, they have published eighty-eight songs (not including another hundred or so, some dating back to the earliest days in Hamburg and Liverpool's Cavern Club, which have never been published or recorded). By February 1, 1966, the eighty-eight songs had been recorded in 2,921 versions, and by now the figure must be well over 3,000. They have been recorded by other beat performers like Billy J. Kramer, the Rolling Stones, Peter and Gordon; jazz singers like Ella Fitzgerald; rhythm and blues groups like the Supremes; ballad singers like Marianne Faithfull; dance orchestras of every variety and singers in every country of the world to which electricity has penetrated. Versions by the Beatles have by now sold close to two hundred million records; total sales of all Lennon-McCartney recorded compositions must be pushing half a billion. Only songwriters established for thirty years or more—giants like Cole Porter, Richard Rodgers and Lorenz Hart, Irving Berlin, and Jerome Kern—could hope to match the records set by these two boys in the past three years. And as their days as performing Beatles begin to die a natural death, their lives as writers become increasingly important.

The extraordinary response to Lennon and McCartney's songs, aside from their appeal as Beatles, indicates the writers' instinctive feel for the pop idiom developed from a lifetime immersion, to the exclusion of all else, in popular music. Growing up in Liverpool, they absorbed both the fruity tradition of music-hall ballads and the constant imports of popular records from America. John was a poet first, scribbling verses as soon as he could write, then writing his first song when he had learned one chord on a guitar at the age of fourteen. Paul met him in the mid-fifties when skiffle, an English adaptation of American folk music, was popular, and the team began to work together immediately. "When I first met John, he'd written the words to a skiffle song," Paul told me. "It still had a skiffley sound, but he'd changed the words to 'Come and go with me, Down at the Penitentiary' or something like that. Then I did one, 'When I Lost My Little Girl,' with the three chords I knew at the time. We got out of that stage and worked out chords together. We used to play truant and go to his house or mine and mess about all afternoon. It was a great feeling of escape. One song of that era was 'Love Me Do.' It wasn't good, but it was only a little bit worse than the kind of things on the hit parade then."

In those days when they were still the Quarreymen and then the Silver Beatles, Lennon and McCartney were fans of Little Richard, Buddy Holly, Elvis Presley, Carl Perkins, and Chuck Berry, and in four- or five-hour sessions at the Cavern Club they pounded out their versions of the American hits over and over again. The Liverpool scene, then swarming with groups, many now long disbanded, was also a formative influence. "If we hadn't played so long or so much, we never would have made it," John said in our interview last week. "It was a funny place, Liverpool then. You were half friends with the other groups, half rivals. In a way it was like a school of painting developing among a group, but people who see the school side forget there were jealousies and feuds. Sure, we learned from the others; you couldn't help it. But we were smart heads, we knew from the start we were better. We were the only group then writing songs, so we used to say we had written about a hundred, even though it was only thirty. Some of those are lost by now. We had one, 'That's My Woman Standing over There'; I've forgotten how it went."

The Beatles' first LP, *Please, Please Me*, includes several covers of songs by American groups, and its Lennon and McCartney originals reveal their American influences clearly. "P.S., I Love You" has a melody and harmony straight from the Shirelles; "I Saw Her Standing There" is a mixture of Chuck Berry's beat and Little Richard's falsetto. "Thank You Girl" has the ooh-ooh sound in the backup vocals that was a Buddy Holly trademark. But even there they were able to mix different sounds so that no song was simply an imitation. "P.S." has a calypso beat, John plays bluesy harmonica on many tracks, and some songs have a bit of Holly, a bit of Little Richard, plus the quick, driving beat and Liverpudlian "yeah, yeahs" that owe nothing to anyone but themselves.

"There's nothing wrong with pinching ideas from other people," Paul said, "everybody does it—Handel did it—but most people aren't as honest as Handel or us. It's the same thing as abstract art. Anybody can throw paint on canvas just like anybody can pinch bits from other songs, but not everybody can get the same result. You don't just stick it together. We go into the studio with a song, play it over, and talk about what other groups it sounds like. Then we see how we want to do it, and we end up with our interpretation of their style."

The second LP, *With the Beatles*, is still from the early days, but the Lennon-McCartney trademarks are stronger: the choppy rhythm section at beginning and end with a more melodic chorus section in between. Their arrangements are more complex, John introduces organ behind the drums, and they call in their producer George Martin to play piano. "Not A Second

Time" shows more concern with melody, and they try for the first time a heavy blues song, "I Wanna Be Your Man," which became the Rolling Stones' first hit record. According to Dick James, head of Northern Songs, which publishes all their music, by this time John and Paul were highly competent commercial songwriters. "Take 'From Me to You,'" James said last week. "It is a perfect Tin Pan Alley song, extremely commercial. It could have been written thirty years ago and will be listened to in another thirty years. It is simple, direct, repetitive, yet touching in an odd way. There are no frills, but it supports one idea. There is nothing special about it, but it is as good a standard pop song as has ever been written."

Each of these LPs was heavily interspersed with American songs, and the songs Lennon and McCartney wrote had for the most part been written long before they were famous. *A Hard Day's Night* marks the first real break with what John called "the cocoon of Liverpool. All the things there we dropped. It was like going to the next class in school."

The film of the same name began shooting in the winter of 1964, and for the first time they had to write on demand. "I remember during the filming we needed the title song," recalled producer Walter Shenson. "Dick James mentioned it to them, the title came from Ringo, the boys got to work, and they had written, arranged, rehearsed, and recorded the song in just over twenty-four hours." With their success they were more confident and more professional. The title song lets them express Liverpool slang for the first time, as does "Eight Days a Week." "I Should Have Known Better" is a chance to explore rhythm, while "Tell Me Why'" gets a Motown-style opening, another instance of them mixing styles. *A Hard Day's Night* also includes two of Paul's most beautiful ballads, "If I Fell" and "And I Love Her." Both match in the setting of a mood and the restrained sweetness of melody any of the older standards, and both are well on their way to becoming standards themselves, to be played at every dance along with "Smoke Gets in Your Eyes." The lyrics are not sophisticated; rather, they are as innocently direct as adolescent love: "I give her all my love, That's all I do / And if you saw my love / You'd love her too."

With *A Hard Day's Night*, Lennon and McCartney began their maturity. The fourth LP, *Beatles for Sale*, the single "I Feel Fine/She's a Woman"; and the *Help!* album continued their explorations. "We started off first with songs like 'Love Me Do,' with easy, stupid rhymes that didn't mean very much," Paul said, "then we moved to a middle bunch of songs which meant a little bit more. Not an awful lot more, but they were a little deeper. There was no mystery about our growth; it was only as mysterious as a flower is mysterious. There's no more point in charting it than charting how many teeth I had as a baby and how many I have now. Nobody thought that was miraculous, except perhaps my mother. We were just growing up."

All these songs are better than their early output. Their lyrics improve in the melancholy of "Please lock me away, and don't allow the day / here inside, where I hide, with my loneliness"; the Dylanesque rhymes of "Gather round all you clowns, let me hear you say / hey, you've got to hide your love away"; and the poignancy of "Suddenly I'm not half the man I used to be / There's a shadow hanging over me." The harmonies and counterpoint of "You're Going to Lose That Girl," the strings on "Yesterday," the rowdy cocksure mood of "Another Girl" all mark steps forward.

During the fall of 1965, in two weeks of constant writing and recording, they produced *Rubber Soul*, which, they feel, marks a total break with what they had done before. "You don't know us now if you don't know *Rubber Soul*," said John forcefully. "All our ideas are different now." "If someone saw a picture of you taken two years ago and said that was you, you'd say it was a load of rubbish and show them a new picture," said Paul. "That's how we feel about the early stuff and *Rubber Soul*. That's who we are now. People have always wanted us to stay the same, but we can't stay in a rut. No one else expects to hit a peak at twenty-three and never develop, so why should we? *Rubber Soul* for me is the beginning of my adult life. You can't be singing fifteen-year-old songs at twenty because you don't think fifteen-year-old thoughts at twenty—a fact that escapes a lot of people."

Part of this excitement is purely an excitement about the present, and both boys admit it. But the songs of *Rubber Soul* do mark a new maturity, both in music and lyrics. Steve Race, a well-known British jazz critic who has long been a Lennon and McCartney fan, admits he was astonished when he first heard the LP. "When I heard 'Michelle' I couldn't believe my ears,' he said in heated excitement recently. "The second chord is an A chord, while the note in the melody above is A-flat. This is an unforgivable clash, something no one brought up knowing older music could ever have done. It is entirely unique, a stroke of genius. In fact, when Billy Vaughan recorded it, his arranger was so attuned to the conventional way of thinking he didn't even hear what the boys had done, and wrote an A-flat into the chord below—taking all the sting out. I suppose it was sheer musical ignorance that allowed John and Paul to do it, but it took incredible daring. And 'Girl,' why, it's like a folk song from some undiscovered land, it's so new— the alternation from major to minor is fantastic. The use of the sitar on 'Norwegian Wood,' plus the involutions of the opening three phrases, is sheer brilliance."

Paul himself talked for two hours on *Rubber Soul* to journalist Francis Wyndham. On "The Word":

> This could be a Salvation Army song. The word is *love*, but it
> could be *Jesus* (it isn't, mind you, but it could be). "It's so fine,
> it's sunshine, it's the word." It's about nothing really, but it's
> about love. It's so much more original than our old stuff, less
> obvious. "Give the word a chance to say / That the word is just
> the way"—then the organ comes in, just like the Sally Army.

On "We Can Work It Out" (released as a separate single in Britain):

> The middle eight is the best—it changes the beat to a waltz in
> the middle. The original arrangement was terrible, very skiffley.
> Then at the session George Martin had the idea of splitting the
> beat completely. The words go on at a double speed against the
> slow waltz music.

13

On "Girl":

> John's been reading a book about pain and pleasure, about
> the idea behind Christianity—that to have pleasure you have
> to have pain. The book says that's all rubbish, it often happens
> that pain leads to pleasure, but you don't have to have it, that's
> all a drag. So we've written a song about it. "Was she told when
> she was young that pain would lead to pleasure? / Did she
> understand it when they said / that a man must break his back
> to earn his day of leisure / will she still believe it when he's
> dead?" Listen to John's breath on the word "girl": we asked the
> engineer to put it on treble, so you get this huge intake of
> breath and it sounds just like a percussion instrument.

All the lyrics are imaginative, either probing problems usually too serious for pop songs or having touches of the wildly inventive humor that
marks John's poetry. Part of "Norwegian Wood," written by John after a late
night and a hangover, goes, "I had a girl / or should I say she once had me;
. . . She asked me to stay and she told me to sit anywhere / I looked around
and I noticed there wasn't a chair."

Every song on the LP has something new. This time, instead of picking
up a country and western song for Ringo to sing, they wrote their own:
"What Goes On." In "Drive My Car," they fulfill an ambition of long
standing: a near perfect one-note song in which, strictly speaking, there is no
melody, only the rhythmic singing of a single note. "Melodic songs are in
fact quite easy to write," Paul told me, "To write a good song with just one
note in it—like 'Long Tall Sally'—is really very hard." Into the loping beat
of "I'm Looking through You" they stick riffs of what is known in England
as "rave-up" guitar until the song comes out as part country and western and
part blues shout. And yet, despite all the innovation and the radical expan-
sion of the pop idiom on *Rubber Soul,* the LP has become their biggest seller
to date. That is one of the advantages in being both a Beatle and a song-

writer, Paul said. "We are so well established that we can bring the fans along with us and stretch the limits of pop. We don't have to follow what everyone else is doing."

Like many artists, however, Lennon and McCartney find it both difficult and hardly relevant to explain in words what they are doing and how they do it. When a now famous January 1963 article in the *Times* referred flatteringly to their use of "Aeolian cadences" and "chains of pandiatonic clusters," "melismas," and "submediant switches," they were as baffled as the ordinary fan. They do not find extraordinary what they have done. In interviews there is hardly a trace of introspection or critical analysis of their work. If pressed they try to answer as truthfully as possible, but avoid getting involved in detailed discussion of how and why they have changed. "It all comes back to this," Paul said after an hour's talk. "We just happen to be songwriters. We write songs that people like. We wrote worse songs, we hope to write better songs."

They are almost as vague about the process of writing the songs. Paul has just begun to learn written notation, and for practice recently wrote a simple piece for his girlfriend, Jane Asher, who plays classical guitar. Otherwise they write in their heads or work out a tune on a guitar. "I've never sat down to write a simple song," John explained to me. "I might think the song won't be complex, but I'm not of those writers who chomp out songs to a formula. The beginning idea could be anything on earth. A bit of melody might come to me, and if it sticks, I'll find my guitar and play it into a tape recorder, try to fool with it and extend it. Maybe I'd call Paul up and tell him to come over and we'll work on it together. 'Norwegian Wood' started as a guitar bit. I was just fiddling when it came to me. It almost never got written, but then I found some time." In Liverpool ideas used to come from playing together, and a new song might have grown from improvisation on stage. Now, except for occasional late night sessions when they play for their own enjoyment, they tend to develop ideas on their own. Many songs, however, get written just by sitting down to write. "When we have an LP to do, we know we have to write twelve songs, so we will sit down to write a raver or a ballad on order," said John. "We want to write more this

15

way, I've never liked the idea of going to an office just to write, but we might do this soon. Otherwise a lot of ideas, good ones, get lost."

Many songs John and Paul write together, both doing words and music; others are done solo. But just as they are distinct personalities, their musical abilities differ. Paul, more open, gentle, and articulate, tends to write the "soppier" songs—"John doesn't like to show he's sentimental; I don't mind." John, a deeper, more explosive, and enigmatic person, is more willing to try less conventional sounds. John also tends toward a greater interest in lyrics; Paul toward music. But their tastes and personalities complement each other, and they are close and trusting friends, a rare thing in creative partnerships. "A perfect example of how we work is 'Drive My Car,'" Paul said. "I wrote it with the repetitive line being 'You can give me golden rings.' When I played it to John at the recording session, he said, 'Crap!' It was too soft. I thought about it and knew he was right, so we went on to other songs, then that night we spent hours trying to get a better idea. Finally we ended up with 'Baby, you can drive my car.' The idea of the bitchy girl was the same, but it gave the song a better story line, and made the key line much more effective."

Lyric ideas come on everywhere. They once wrote a song called "Thinking of Linking," picking up the phrase from the television commercial for the Link Furniture Company. Noting the ambiguous sexual meaning, however, they never recorded it. Some of John's ideas stay semiconscious for years before they come out as songs. As a child he was amused by a religious motto that hung in his home:

> However black the clouds may be,
> In time they'll pass away.
> Have faith and trust and you will see,
> God's light make bright your day.

This appeared in *Spaniard in the Works*, John's second book, as

> However Blackpool tower may be,
> In time they'll pass away

Have faith and trump and B.B.C.,
Griff's light make bright your day.

and in the song "Tell Me What You See" as

Big and black the clouds will be,
Time will pass away
If you put your trust in me,
I'll make bright your day.

Both John and Paul stress that since they do not write their songs down, the finished record is really the song they write. In the studio they do most of the arranging, but are aided by George Martin, who has produced every- thing they have done, and by the inventive playing of George Harrison and Ringo Starr. Though they would blanch at the comparison, they are rather like Duke Ellington, who writes and arranges with particular musicians in mind. "George Martin is important because he knows what we want," John told me. "He acts as a translator between us and Norman Smith, the engi- neer who actually runs the recording machines." Now they are interested in getting more complicated electronic effects, using more overdubbing, feed- back, and "hyping" their sounds. One of their biggest recent influences has been a newly popular British group, the Who, who use tremendous amounts of feedback. "They started us thinking again," Paul said. "We had that feed- back idea in 'I Feel Fine' but the Who went farther and made all kinds of weird new sounds. I suppose Donald Zec [a disparaging music critic at the *Daily Mirror*] would say, 'What would they do without amplifiers?' But that's as silly as saying, 'If God wanted us to smoke, he'd have given us chim- neys.' We haven't got chimneys, but we smoke—so what? What would the theater be without a stage and makeup, or movies without a camera?"

Both say that other influences are hard to pin down. "If we say we are influenced by someone or we like them, that will make them sound too important," said Paul. "Our best influences now are ourselves." "We listen to   17 records every day, a big mixture of stuff," said John. "You can't pick out any one person." But John did mention Steve Cropper, guitarist/writer with Booker T. and the M.G.'s, suggesting that they would like to have Cropper produce Beatle recording sessions. Paul mentioned a wide range of people he likes now: from groups like the Marvellettes and rhythm and blues singer Otis Redding through Karlheinz Stockhausen and John Cage and on to Albert Ayler, a pioneer of random jazz. Cage, he felt, is too random for his taste. "I like to get ideas randomly but then develop them within a frame." As an afterthought he put forward the Fugs, a New York group who sing wildly obscene songs, purposely using verbal shock as a musical technique. "It's like a new development in discordancy. Anyway, it's new and very funny," he explained.

Summed up, their musical achievements have been breathtaking. Cole Porter, Irving Berlin, and Richard Rodgers all had written songs, and good ones, by their early twenties, but none could have matched the sheer output, range, or originality of John Lennon and Paul McCartney, aged twenty-five and twenty-three, respectively. Yet they feel they have just begun, and fairly modestly at that. In interviews they stress repeatedly the obvious facts: that they have been at the game seriously just over six years; that much of their early work was adolescent and imitative; that they can hope to live and create for another forty years; and that they have total financial freedom to develop in any way they please. "None of us have barely started," Paul says. "At first we wanted to make money; now we've got it, a fantastic platform of money to dive off into anything. People say we've had a fantastic success and that is all. We don't look at it that way. We look at our lives as a whole, think in terms of forty more years of writing. I wouldn't mind being a whitehaired old man writing songs, but I'd hate to be a whitehaired old Beatle at the Empress Stadium, playing for people. We might write longer pieces, film scores—I know we want to write the whole score of our next film. We might write specifically for other people, write for different instruments—you name it, and it's possible we could do it." Their development has already, in fact, brought them fully around one circle: Marshall Chess, head of Chess

Records, which records Chuck Berry, has asked John and Paul to write songs for Berry, who until now has written all his songs himself. The boys now influence their influences.

John and Paul like to write songs, and so far they have hardly had to work at it. "I'd never struggle writing a song till it hurt," John says, "I'd just forget it and try something else." The direct sense of their own enjoyment comes through in the songs. Each one, from the first to the last, is a direct statement of a simple emotional idea. Perhaps in some cases the emotion is a juvenile one, and they would be the first to admit that. Yet each song is honest; none have the syrupy sentimentality of the songs written by adults for teenagers. This transparent honesty is the key to both the appeal and quality of their songs. In that way their work is a perfect mirror of themselves, the boys whose candid simplicity has baffled and annoyed their elders. "One thing that modern philosophy, existentialism and things like that, have taught people, is that you have to live now," said Paul. "You have to feel now. We live in the present, we don't have time to figure out whether we are right or wrong, whether we are immoral or not. We have to be honest, be straight, and then live, enjoying and taking what we can."

Each Lennon and McCartney song can stand as a statement of that idea. Thus, any comparison of their work with that of earlier generations of songwriters is beside the point, not just because the boys have been totally grounded in the idioms of rock 'n' roll, but because their rough and straightforward presentation has no more to do with Cole Porter's ironic sophistication than Levis and the direct fashions of today have to do with the gauzy silks of the thirties. To stretch a point, John and Paul's music is pop art, not just pop music; but unlike pop art, which with time is increasingly evidencing its sterility, their music shows every sign of deepening in meaning and mood. Their work to date has shown an unbounded, joyful inventiveness unparalleled in popular music. It has shown as well a deep, if not "serious," insight into the emotions of growing up. Nothing so far has curbed them. As Lennon and McCartney grow, they are losing none of their fey freedom or their youth, and with that, as they have proved, they can do anything.

Jimi Hendrix sets his guitar on fire. Still from *Monterey Pop!* directed by D. A. Pennebaker. Courtesy of Pennebaker-Hegedus Films, Inc.

THE MONTEREY INTERNATIONAL POP FESTIVAL

1 9 6 7

In January 1967, just as the sixties musical-social ball was bouncing westward, *Newsweek* transferred me to San Francisco. I arrived in time for the Human Be-In and soon was hanging out at the Avalon and the Fillmore, interviewing Jerry Garcia and Janis Joplin, and covering student demonstrations in Berkeley. In May I began to hear rumors of a huge hippie festival; all the best new bands were coming; this was going to be far fucking out!

Monterey *was* far fucking out. I drove back to San Francisco Monday morning, slept like a log, got up Tuesday, wrote the piece in one four-hour burst, and sent it to New York, where the editors boiled it down to ten paragraphs. The full piece's splattered prose, I think, does capture some of the magic and the music of those three days, but I couldn't get in everything that happened at Monterey. For example: Tiny Tim was at Monterey, not on the big stage, but back in the artist's lounge on a white folding chair, waves of brown hair falling over his face as he beamed smiles, strummed his ukulele, and sang old songs in his high-pitched voice for a little circle of bemused and amazed listeners. Brian Jones of the Rolling Stones thought Tiny Tim was "brilliant."

But who could get everything in? Times like that Monterey weekend are so intense that we can only measure their impact as they echo in our lives down through the years.

MICHAEL LYDON

Monterey still echoes for me as one of those signal events that set me on my adult path. D.A. Pennebaker's superb film *Monterey Pop* has kept the festival's sound and images from fading in memory, and this festival gave birth to generations of music festivals that blossom to this day. Many of Monterey's offspring outgrew their mother, but none had her tentative innocence, her blushing first-time exuberance.

The Monterey International Pop Festival is over, all over. And what was it? Was it one festival, many festivals, a festival at all? Does anything sum it up, did it mean anything, are there any themes? Was it just a collection of rock groups of varying levels of proficiency doing their bit for a crowd of thousands who got their fill of whatever pleasure or sensation they sought? Was it the most significant meeting of an avant-garde since the Armory show or some Dadaist happening in the 1920s? Was it, as the stage banner said, "Love, flowers, and music," or was it Jimi Hendrix playing his guitar as if it was an enormous penis and then burning it, smashing it, and flicking its pieces like holy water into a baffled, berserk audience? Was it a hundred screaming freak kids with war-painted faces howling and bashing turned-over oil-drum trash cans like North African trance dancers, or was it the thousands of sweet hippies who wandered, sat, and slept on the grass with flutes and bongos, beads and bubbles, laughing and loving softly?

Was its spirit Simon and Garfunkel, singing like little lost lambie-pie castrati, or was it Ravi Shankar, rocking over his sitar and beating a bare foot while opening up a musical world to seven thousand listeners who, at his request, did not smoke for his three-hour concert? Rolling Stone Brian Jones was part of it, wandering for three days, silent inside his blond hair and gossamer pink cape; so was a girl writhing on a bummer at the entrance to the press section; while no one helped, cameramen exhausted themselves recording her agony. Was it a nightmare and something beautiful existing together or a nightmare and many beautiful things existing side by side?

One is left only with questions that a mind besodden with sound and sound and sound and sound cannot answer. Saturday night, Jerry Garcia of the Grateful Dead commented, "There's a lot of heavy stuff going on." Whether he meant music or acid or emotion or everything, he was right. Something very heavy happened at Monterey last weekend.

Those very odd three days began in Friday's cool gray air as the first of the crowd began to circle through the booths of the fairground. The only word for it then was *groovy*. A giant Buddha stood in one corner, banners decorated with astrology signs waved, and everything the hippie needs to make his life beautiful was on sale: paper dresses, pins, earrings, buttons, amulets, crosses, posters, balloons, sandals, macrobiotic food, and flowers. There was a soul food stand, the Monterey Kiwanis had fresh corn on the cob, the Congregation Beth El had pastrami sandwiches, and hippies with the munchies snapped their fingers to the popping of the popcorn stand. In the festival offices, Mama Michelle Phillips of the Mamas and Papas was hard at work doing everything from typing to answering the phone. Papa John Phillips was keeping his cool in his gray fur hat, which he never once took off in the frantic chaos.

Nothing but chaos could have been expected. Two months earlier the whole festival had been nothing more than an idea in the head of publicist Derek Taylor, and in the rush of preparation that idea had changed many times.

At first it was to be a commercial proposition; then Taylor, unable to raise the money needed to pay advances to the invited groups, had gone to Phillips and Dunhill producer Lou Adler for bankrolling. Why not make it a charity and get everyone to come for free, they suggested, and suddenly it became not a money-spinning operation but a happening generated by the groups themselves, which hopefully would make some composite statement of pop music in June 1967.

The festival was incorporated, with a board of governors that included Donovan, Mick Jagger, Andrew Loog Oldham, Paul Simon, John Phillips, Smokey Robinson, Jim McGuinn, Brian Wilson, and Paul McCartney. "The Festival hopes to create an atmosphere wherein persons in the popular music field from all parts of the world will congregate, perform, and exchange ideas concerning popular music with each other and with the public at large," said a release. After paying the entertainers' expenses, the profits from ticket sales (seats ranged from $6.50 to $3.50; admission to the grounds without a seat was $1.00) were to go to charities and to fund fellowships in the pop field. Despite rumors that part of the money would go to the Diggers, an anarchist group based in both Los Angeles and San Francisco, to help them cope with the "hippie invasions," so far no decision has been made on where the money will go.

This vagueness and the high prices engendered charges of commercialism—"Does anybody really know where these L.A. types are at?" asked one San Francisco rock musician. And when the list of performers was released there was more confusion. Where were the Negro stars, the people who began it all? asked some. Where were the Lovin' Spoonful, the Stones, the Motown groups? Does a pop festival mean anything without Dylan, the Stones, and the Beatles?

"Here they are trying to do something new," said the Fillmore's Bill Graham, "and they end up with group after group, just like the jazz festivals. Will anybody have the chance to spread out if they feel like it?"

But as it unfolded it was clear that, if not perfect, the festival was as good as it could have been. The Spoonful could not come because of possible charges that could be brought on a pot bust they had helped to engineer to avoid a possession charge against themselves; it was rumored, moreover, that John Sebastian wants to spend all his time writing and that they are breaking up as a group. Two of the Stones are facing pot charges of their own in England. Smokey Robinson and Berry Gordy were enthusiastic about the festival at first, John Phillips said, but "then they never answered the phone. Smokey was completely inactive as a director. I think it might be a Crow Jim thing. A lot of people put Lou Rawls down for appearing. 'You're going to a whitey festival, man,' was the line. There is tension between the white groups who are getting their own ideas and the Negroes, who are just repeating theirs. The tension is lessening all the time, but it did crop up here, I am sure."

Phillips also reported that Chuck Berry was invited. "I told him on the phone, 'Chuck, it's for charity,' and he said to me, 'Chuck Berry has only one charity and that's Chuck Berry. $2,000.' We couldn't make an exception." Dylan is still keeping his isolation after the accident that broke his neck last summer, and though rumors persisted up to the last minute Sunday night that the Beatles would show, or at least were in Monterey, they decided to keep their "no more appearances" vow. Dionne Warwick made a last-minute bow out with a bad throat, and the Beach Boys, whose Carl Wilson faces a draft evasion charge, decided to lay low.

Yet as the sound poured out incessantly—the concerts with nary an intermission averaged five hours in length (can you imagine going to four uncut top-volume *Hamlets* in three days, or sitting in the Indianapolis pits while they reran the race eight times over a weekend?)—gaps were not noticed. One dealt with what was at hand, and what was there was very, very good indeed. There were a few disasters that can be written off from the start: Laura Nyro, a melodramatic singer accompanied by two dancing girls who pranced absurdly; Hugh Masakela, whose trumpet is only slightly better than his voice—he did, however, do some nice backing for the Byrds on "So You Want to Be a Rock 'n' Roll Star"; and Johnny Rivers, dressed like an L.A. hippie, who had the gall to sing the Beatles' "Help!" not once but twice. Others, like the Association, with their slick high-schooly humor, didn't fit in; still others, like Canned Heat, an L.A.-based blues band, had bad days. But the majority rose to new heights for the concert. There was the feeling that this was the place, that the vibrations were right, that one was performing for one's peers and superiors, that anything and everything that one was capable of was demanded. "I saw a community form and live together for three days," said Brian Jones Sunday night. "It is so sad that it has to break up."

That community was formed not only on the stage between the performers and the audience, but backstage, at the artists' retreat behind the arena called the Hunt Club, and in the motel rooms where parties went on till dawn. There was little offstage jamming (no motels had the space, proper

25

wall thickness, or power) except for a four-hour blast between the Grateful Dead, the Jefferson Airplane, and Jimi Hendrix that carried the members to breakfast Monday morning after everyone else had gone home, yet everyone talked, listened, and grooved with everyone else. The variety of music was tremendous: blues to folk to rock to freak. There were big stars, old stars, comers, and groups who avoid the whole star bag. If one was good, in whatever bag, one was accepted. Musical styles were not barriers; however disparate the criteria, there seemed to be some consensus on what was real music and what was not.

The festival had a sort of rhythm to it that was undoubtedly coincidental—the organizers swore that there was no implicit ranking in the order of the acts—but that worked. Friday night was variety night to get things moving, Saturday afternoon was blues, old and gutty and new and wild. Saturday night opened some of the new directions, then a return to peace with Shankar Sunday afternoon; and a final orgiastic freak out Sunday night.

The Association began it all in the cool gray of Friday night with a professional style and entertaining manner, doing a fine job on their sweetly raucous hit single, "Windy." Then the Paupers, a four-man group from Toronto, provided the first surprise. The almost unknown group, managed by Albert Grossman, Dylan's grandmotherly and shrewd mentor, was able to get a screaming volume and a racy quality unmatched by some of the bigger groups. "I found them at the Whisky a Go Go in New York," Grossman said. "They were cutting the Jefferson Airplane to pieces so I signed them up." Only together seven months, they are sure to get better. "We are trying to create a total environment with sound alone," said lead guitarist Chuck Beale. "Sound is enough. We don't use lights or any gimmicks. When we record we never double track or use any other instruments. What the four of us can do is the sound we make. That's all."

Lou Rawls, the blues singer whose "Dead End Street" is currently on the charts, came next and pulled the audience back to what he called "rock 'n' soul." Backed by a big band, he looked as if he would have been more at home in a night club, but his fine funky voice and from the heart monologues about the nitty-gritty of Negro life were soulful indeed. To watch him was to be back at the Apollo Theater, where rock is flashy, stylish, and flamboyant, but still communicating with the kids high in the balcony. "The blues," he said as he came offstage exhilarated, "is the way of the future. The fads come and go, but the blues remain. The blues is the music that makes a universal language." Other music at the festival seemed also to speak to all, but Rawls, a solid member of the professional black school of music, hit one major thread: the new music is still close to the blues, and most of the far-out sounds in the three days were but new blues ideas. He also had his finger on another key truth: "I'm trying to portray the facts as they stand. A few years ago rock was all facade, all doo-wah-diddy-diddy, all prettied up. I get the feeling that people now are trying their best to be where it's at."

After Johnny Rivers stayed on too long, Eric Burdon, one of the best white blues singers around, romped through a half-dozen numbers with his new Animals, the high point coming with "Paint It, Black," the Jagger-Richards masterpiece that Burden, unbelievably, improved upon, particularly with the zany screechings of an electric violin. Brian Jones, sitting in the dirt of an aisle, applauded wildly.

Simon and Garfunkel finished off the night, and what can one say about them? "Homeward Bound" brought back memories of the time when a sweet folk-rock seemed to be the new direction, but though the song sounded nice enough, they seemed sadly left behind. "Benedictus" had them harmonizing like choirboys, and they did an encore, a funny new nonsense song, "I Wish I Was a Kellogg Cornflake." When the last note floated out about 1:30 A.M., the first night was over and the peace was extraordinary. While the lucky (or unlucky?) few drove to their motels, the mass of the crowd drifted to the huge camping area near the arena and to the football field at Monterey Peninsula College nearby. There, with the sweet smell of pot drifting over sleeping bags, the music continued in singing and talking and in just being.

In the bright hot sun of Saturday afternoon the serious blues shouting began. Canned Heat led off with an uninspired set, and then came one of the most fantastic events of the whole shebang: the voice of Janis Joplin, singer of Big Brother and the Holding Company, a San Francisco group almost entirely unknown outside of the Bay Area. A former folk singer from Port Arthur, Texas, Janis was turned on a year ago by Otis Redding, and now she sings with equal energy and soul. In a gold knit pants suit with no bra underneath, Janis leapt, bent double, and screwed up her plain face as she sang like a demonic angel. It was the blues big-mama style, tough, raw, and gutsy, and with an aching that few singers reach. The group behind her drove her and fed from her, building the total volume sound that has become a San Francisco trademark. The final number, "Ball and Chain," which had Janis singing (singing?—talking, crying, moaning, howling) long solo sections, had the audience on their feet for the first time. "She is the best white blues singer I have ever heard," commented *San Francisco Examiner* jazz critic Phil Elwood.

Country Joe and the Fish, the acid-political group from Berkeley, came next, and while they did not reach their accustomed heights, their funny satirical words and oddly dissonant music went over well. They did two of their political songs, "Please Don't Drop that H-Bomb on Me, You Can Drop It on Yourself," whose title is the complete lyric, and "Whoopee, We're All Going to Die," which contains the memorable line, "Be the first on your block to have your boy come home in a box." These were among the very few explicit protest songs at the festival; nowadays rock musicians are musicians first and protestors a slow second. "There are two parts to music," said lead guitarist and music writer for Country Joe, Barry Melton, "the music and the lyrics. Music we have with everybody, but some say the lyrics shouldn't be political. Everybody agrees with us on the war, but we feel that in this society, you have to make your stands clear. Others don't want to speak up in songs, be right up front. That's why we put politics in." Melton's songs, particularly "Not So Sweet Martha Lorraine," a nightmarish song about a mysterious lady who "hides on a shelf filled with volumes of literature based on herself" and who gets high with death, have been called "pure acid," but Melton says all music is psychedelic. "One part of LSD is liberation, do what you want to do. I feel I do that, do what I want to do. When I hear a sound that is groovy I use it. I try to find music all over the place. Listening to anything can give you musical ideas. That's freedom, and maybe that's psychedelic." He spoke for most of the groups: it would be hard to find any of the musicians who has not taken LSD or at least smoked pot, but by now it has become so accepted that it it's nothing to be remarked on by itself. Acid opened minds to new images and new sounds, and made them embrace a wild eclecticism, but rather than being "acid" as such, it has become music.

Al Kooper, an organist who has often played with Dylan, took a half hour with some funky blues organ and vocal, but the action began again with the Paul Butterfield Blues Band, a newly constituted version of the group that, more than any other, has led the revival of white interest in blues bands. Led by Butterfield's fine voice and better harmonica, and with the strange melancholic whimsy of Elvin Bishop's guitar, the backup band of bass guitar, trumpet, sax, and drums rocketed through some very impressive work. They also returned for the Saturday night show, with Bishop showing off his odd voice on a gloomy blues, "Have Mercy this Morning." The Butterfield group, which began years ago gigging with Muddy Waters in Chicago—knew, unlike the Quicksilver Messenger Service and the Steve Miller Band who followed—precisely what it was doing. Without being uptight, Butterfield's band was precise. They swung deftly on a broad emotional range, but my strongest memory is the haunting, looping sound of Butterfield's harmonica as it broke a small solo of just a few notes into tiny bits and experimented with their regroupings.

The blues afternoon ended with a group that had no idea (apparently) what it was doing but did it with such a crazy yelping verve that it looked like in time it could do anything it wanted. Billed as the Electric Flag, it was the first time it had ever played together. Its leader, guitarist Mike Bloomfield, has been gradually building the band after leaving Butterfield's group a few months ago. Its set was an astounding masterpiece of chaos with

29

rapport. Drummer Buddy Miles, a big Negro with a wild "do" who looks like a tough soul brother from Detroit but who is actually a prep-school-educated son of a well-to-do Omaha family, sings and plays with TNT energy, knocking over cymbals as he plays. Barry Goldberg controls the organ, and Nick "the Greek" Gravenites writes the songs and does a lot of the singing. The group was, for the groups present as well as the audience, a smash success. The Byrds' David Crosby announced from the stage Saturday night, "Man, if you didn't hear Mike Bloomfield's group, man, you are out of it, so far out of it."

The afternoon concert rode out with the Electric Flag on a wave of excitement that faltered in the evening concert. There was a curious feeling around late Saturday: everything was still very groovy, but the sweetness was going. The excitement of the music was getting too high. That stalled Saturday night but the level did not diminish. San Francisco's Moby Grape led off the concert, overshadowed by the rumor, fed by the ambiguous statements of the festival management, that the Beatles would appear for the record arena audience of 8500. The Grape had a driving excitement and some very nice playing with the four guitars, but no particular impression stands out. Masakela was terrible; but Big Black, his conga player, was brilliant, holding up his reputation as the best conga player in the business. The Byrds were disappointing. Considered by many to be America's Beatles, they were good, doing several new songs, but they lacked the excitement to get things moving. Butterfield was not as good as he had been in the afternoon and went on too long, and the evening hit bottom with Laura Nyro.

From there on things got better. The Jefferson Airplane were fantastically good. Backed with a light show put on by Headlights, who do the lights at the Fillmore, they created a special magic. Before they came on, the question hung: are the Airplane as good as their reputation? They thoroughly proved themselves. As they played, hundreds of artists, stagehands, and hangers-on swarmed on to the stage, dancing. Grace Slick, in a long light-blue robe, sang as if possessed, her harshly fine voice filling the night.

In a new song, "The Ballad of You and Me and Pooneil," they surpassed themselves, playing largely in the dark, the light show looming above them, its multicolored blobs shaping and reshaping, primeval molecules eating up tiny bubbles like food then splitting into shimmering atoms. The guitar sounds came from outer space and inner mind, and while everything was going—drums, guitar, and the feedback sounds of the amplifiers—Marty Balin shouted over and over the closing line, "Will the moon still hang in the sky, when I die, when I die, when I die?" They were showered with orchids as they left the stage.

In no time Booker T. and the M.G.'s were on, rocking through some dynamic blues, and suddenly Otis Redding was there, singing the way Jimmy Brown charges in football. "Shake," he shouted, "Shake, everybody, shake," shaking himself like a madman in his electric green suit. What was it like? I wrote at the time, "ecstasy, madness, loss, total, screaming, fantastic." It started to rain and Redding sang two songs that started slow, "to bring the pace down a bit," he said, but in no time the energy was back up again, "Try a Little Tenderness," he closed with, and by the end it reached a new orgiastic pitch. A standing, screaming crowd brought him back and back and back.

Day two was over and Sunday came gray and cold, but the excitement was still there and growing. Could anyone believe what had happened, what might happen? Hours of noise had both deafened and opened thousands of minds. One had lived in sound for hours: the ears had come to dominate the senses. Ears rang as one slept; dreams were audible as well as visual.

Sunday afternoon was Shankar, and a return to peace. And yet there was an excitement in his purity, as well as in his face and body, and that of the tabla player whose face matched Charlie Chaplin's in its expressive range. For three hours they played music, and after the first strangeness, it was not Indian music, but *music*, a particular realization of what music could be. It was all brilliant, but in a long solo from the sixteenth century Shankar had the whole audience, including all the musicians at the festival, rapt. Before he played, he spoke briefly. The work, he said, was a very

31

spiritual one and he asked that no pictures be taken (the paparazzi lay down like lambs). He thanked everyone for not smoking, and said with feeling, "I love all of you, and how grateful I am for your love of me. What am I doing at a pop festival when my music is classical? I knew I'd be meeting you all at one place, you to whom music means so much. This is not pop but I am glad it is popular." With that he began the long melancholic piece. To all appearances he had seven thousand people with him, and when he finished, he stood, bowed with his hands clasped to his forehead, and then, smiling, threw back to the crowd the flowers that had been showered on him.

Sunday night the festival reached its only logical conclusion. The passion, anticipation, and adventure into sound had gone as far as any could have thought possible, and yet it had to go further. Flowers and a groovy kind of love may be elements in the hippie world, but they have little place in hippie rock. The hippie liberation is there; so is a personal kindness, openness, and pleasantness that make new rock musicians easy to talk to; but in their music there is a feeling of a stringent demand on the senses, an experimenting with the techniques of assault, a toying with the idea of beautiful ugliness, the creativeness of destruction, and the loss of self into whatever may come.

One of the major elements in this open-mindedness is feedback. Feedback is nothing new; anyone who has played an electric guitar has experienced it. Simply, feedback happens when a note from a vibrating string comes out of the amplifier louder than it went in and re-reverberates the string. The new vibration adds to the old, and thus the note comes out of the amp louder still. Theoretically the process could go on, the note getting louder and louder, until the amp blows out. In practice it can be controlled so that the continuing note is held as with a piano's sustain pedal. That means that behind their strumming and picking, the musicians can build up a level of pure electronic noise, which they can vary by turning to face the amp or face away, moving toward it or moving away. Feedback can tremen-

dously increase a group's volume, produce yelps, squeals, screams, pitches that rise and rise, that squeak, blare, or yodel wildly. If nothing else, this festival established feedback. One major test of each group was their ability in using feedback, and though it has many uses and effects, overall it creates a musical equivalent of madness. Every night featured feedback, but Sunday night was feedback night and a complete exploration of a new direction in pop music.

The night was foreshadowed by the first group, the Blues Project, the New York band that shares the new blues limelight with Paul Butterfield. Their first song featured electric flute in the hands of Andy Kolburg. It was part a blues, part a Scottish air, part weird phrases that became images of ambiguity. Big Brother and the Holding Company came back and were weaker than they had been, but one short number, "Hairy," was a minute composed of short bursts of utter electronic blare, chopped up into John Cage–like silences. A group too new to have a name—the Group with No Name was their billing—were terrible and may well not last long enough to get a name. Buffalo Springfield were totally professional, but largely undistinguished, except for a closing song, "Bluebird," which alternated from the sweet sound to the total sound.

And then came the Who. Long popular in England, where they have achieved a notoriety for their wild acts at London's Marquee Club, they had never been seen in America. They were dressed in a wild magnificence, like dandies from the seventeenth, nineteenth, and twenty-first centuries. They opened with one of their English hits, "Substitute" ("I'm just a substitute for another guy / I look pretty tall but my heels are high"), with singer Roger Daltrey swirling around the stage in a gothic shawl decorated with pink flowers, and Keith Moon defining berserk at the drums—he broke three drum sticks in the first song and overturned one of his snares. They had a good, very close sound, excellent lyrics, and the flashiest guitar presence of any group to appear.

Then John Entwistle, bass guitar, stepped to the mike and said, "This is where it all ends," and they began "My Generation," the song that made them famous. A violently arrogant demand for the supremacy of youth—

"Things, they say, look awful cold / Hope I die before I get old"—the song has Daltrey stammering on "my g-g-g-generation" as if overcome by hatred or by drugs. After about four minutes of the song, Daltrey began to swing his handheld mike over his head, Townsend smashed his guitar strings against the mike stand before him, building up the feedback. Then he ran and played the guitar directly into his amp. The feedback went wild, and then he lit a smoke bomb before the amp so it looked like it had blown up, and smoke billowed on the stage. He lifted his guitar from his neck and smashed it on the stage, again, again, again, and it broke, one piece sailing into the crowd. Moon went psychopathic at the drums, kicking them through with his feet, knocking them down, trampling on the mikes. The noise continued from the guitar as everything fell and crashed in the smoke. Then they stopped playing and walked off unconcerned, leaving only the hum of an amp turned on at full volume.

It was known to be a planned act, but like the similar scene in the film *Blow-Up* (inspired by the Who), had a fantastic dramatic intensity. And no meaning. No meaning whatsoever. There was no passion, no anger—just destruction. And it was over as it began. Stagehands came out and set up for the next act.

That was the Grateful Dead, and they were beautiful. They did at top volume what Shankar had done softly. They played pure music, some of the best music of the concert. I have never heard anything in music that could be said to be qualitatively better than the performance of the Dead Sunday night. The strangest of the San Francisco groups, the Dead live together in a big house on Ashbury Street, and living together seems to have made them totally together musically. Jerry Garcia, lead guitarist, and owner of the bushiest head at the festival, was the best guitarist of the whole show. The Dead's songs lasted twenty minutes and more, each a masterpiece of five-man improvisation. Beside Garcia there is Phil Lesh on bass, Bob Weir on rhythm guitar, Bill Kreutzmann on drums, and Ron "Pig Pen" McKernan (who seldom talks) on organ. Each man's part was isolated, yet the sound was solid as a rock. It is impossible to remember what it was like. I wrote down at the time: "accumulated sound like wild honey on a moving plate in gobs . . . three guitars together, music, music, pure, high and fancy . . . in it all a meditation by Jerry on a melancholy theme . . . the total in all parts . . . loud quiets as they go on and on and on . . . sounds get there then hold while new ones float up, Jerry to Pig Pen, then to drums, then to Lesh, talking, playing, laughing, exulting."

That sounds crazy now, but that's how it seemed. The Dead built a driving, unshakable rhythm that acted not just as rhythm, but as a wall of noise on which the solos were etched. The solos were barely perceptible in the din, yet they were there like fine scrolls on granite. At moments Garcia and Weir played like one instrument, rocking toward each other. Garcia could do anything: one moment he hunched over, totally intent on his strings, and then he would pull away and prance with his fat ungainly body, then play directly to some face he picked out in the crowd straining up to the stage. Phil Lesh called to the audience as they began, "Anybody who wants to dance, dance. You're sitting on folding chairs, and folding chairs are for folding up and dancing on." But the crowds were restrained by ushers, and those who danced on stage were stopped by nervous stagehands. It was one of the few times that the loose reins of the festival were tightened. Was it necessary? Who knows? But without dancing, the Dead didn't know how well they had done. Lesh was dripping with sweat and nervous as he came off, but each word of praise from onlookers opened him up: "Man, it was impossible to know how we were doing without seeing people moving. We feed on that, we need it, but, oh, man, we did our thing, we did our thing."

They certainly did. The Dead on Sunday night were the definition of virtuoso performance. Could anybody come on after the Dead? Could anyone or anything top them? Yes, one man: Jimi Hendrix, introduced by Brian Jones as "the most exciting guitar player I've ever heard." Hendrix is a strange-looking fellow. Very thin, with a big head and a protuberant jaw, he has a tremendous bush of hair held in place carelessly by an Apache-style headband. He is both curiously beautiful and as wildly grotesque as

35

the proverbial Wild Man of Borneo. He wore scarlet pants and a scarlet boa, a pink jacket over a yellow and black vest over a white ruffled shirt. He played his guitar left-handed, if in Hendrix's hands it was still a guitar. It was, in symbolic fact, a weapon that he brandished, his own penis that he paraded before the crowd and masturbated; it was a woman whom he made love to by straddling and by eating it while playing the strings with his teeth, and in the end it was a torch that he destroyed. In a way the heavily erotic feeling of his act was absurd. A guitarist of long experience with Little Richard, Ike and Tina Turner, and the like, he had learned most of his tricks from the masters in endless series of club gigs on the southern chitlin circuit.

But dressed as he was and playing with a savage wildness—again, how to describe it? I wrote at the time, "total scream . . . I suppose there are people who enjoy bum trips . . . end of everything . . . decay . . . nothing louder exists, 2000 instruments (in fact there were three: guitar, bass, and drums) . . . five tons of glass falling over a cliff and landing on dynamite." The act became more than an extension of Elvis's gyrations, it became an extension of that to infinity, an orgy of noise so wound up that I feared that the dynamo that powered it would fail and fission into its primordial atomic state. Hendrix did not only pick the strings, he bashed them with the flat of his hand, he ripped at them, rubbed them against the mike, and pushed them with his groin into his amplifier. And when he knelt before the guitar as if it were a victim to be sacrificed, sprayed it with lighter fluid, and ignited it, it was exactly a sacrifice: the offering of the perfect, most beloved thing, so its destruction could ennoble him further.

But what do you play when your instrument is burnt? Where can you go next? "I don't know, man," said Hendrix with a laugh after the show. "I think this has gone about as far as it can go." "In England they've reached a dead end in destruction," said Brian Jones. "Groups like the Move and the Creation are destroying whole cars on stage." Asked what it all meant, Andrew Loog Oldham, whose Rolling Stones have pushed far into their own violence kick, said, "If you enjoy it, it's okay," and the screaming, frightened, but aroused audience apparently enjoyed it very much.

After a short and only mildly recuperative silence, on came the Mamas and the Papas, backed by vibes, drums, tympani, piano, and John Phillips's guitar. They were great, everything the Mamas and Papas should be. Mama Cass Elliot was in fine form, joking, laughing, and hamming it up like a camp Queen Victoria. Introducing "California Dreaming," she said, "We're gonna do this song because we like it and because it is responsible for our great wealth." When they finished, a wave of applause swept from the farthest reaches of the crowd up to the stage and the hundred or more musicians, stagehands, and hangers-on dancing and shouting in the wings. "We're gonna have this festival every year," said Mama Cass, "so you can stay if you want." The roar of renewed applause almost convinced me that the crowd would wait patiently through the summer, fall, and winter, never stirring until next June.

Now that the Monterey Pop Festival is a day in the past, what did it prove about pop music? In a way, it proved little. Pop has few of the formal identifying qualities of jazz or folk, and so it did not prove that pop music is now here or there or anyplace. It did show that pop is still in a continuum with the blues, still loves and gets inspiration from the blues. It also showed that LSD and the psychedelics have tremendously broadened the minds of the young people making the new music.

It also demonstrated the continuing influence of the Beatles. Dozens of the other Monterey performers owe their being there to the Beatles. John Phillips was a folksinger until he heard the Beatles. "They were not so much a musical influence," he said, "as an influence because they showed that intelligent people could work in rock and make their intelligence show." Moreover, Monterey Pop ratified the shift away from folk music that has been going on for over two years. The festival was, among other things, the largest collection of former folksingers and guitarists ever gathered in one place. Musicians trained in folk make up the bulk of the new rockers. This means that they came to rock 'n' roll not as the only form, not the one they were trained in, but as an experiment, as a form they looked at first from the outside and rather distantly considered its possibilities.

That sense of experiment is what makes rock so lively today. The years of folk training, in which the two marks of status were knowledge of esoterica and the quality of performance, mean that the new rockers feel a need to push farther and farther ahead, and also that they are excellent players. The general level of musical competence was extremely high, and the heights hit by Mike Bloomfield and Jerry Garcia were as high as those reached by Chuck Berry, Bo Diddley, Doc Watson, and other immortal folk and rock guitarists.

In some ways it was surprising that there was little experimentation in some directions. No group went far afield from the basic instrumental lineup, staging, song lengths, or musical forms. This indicates that rock is still rather traditional, that it is still a commercial art, that the public will not take leaps forward that are too wild, that the performers are still young and unsure of themselves, and that the rock revolution is still new.

This may all change, and if it does the festival will have played an important role. Brian Jones was right: for three days a community formed. Rock musicians, whatever their bag, came together, heard each other, praised each other, and saw that the scene was open enough for them to play as they liked and still get an audience. They will return to their own scenes refreshed and confident. The whole rock-hippie scene was vindicated. Even the police thought it was groovy. Monterey police chief Frank Marinello was so ecstatic that Saturday afternoon he sent half his force home. "I'm beginning to like these hippies," he told reporters. "When I go up to that Haight-Ashbury, I'm going to see a lot of friends." The fairgrounds, which at times held 40,000 people, far more than any other time in its history, were utterly peaceful. The tacit arrangement that there would be no busts for anything less than a blatant pot orgy was respected by both sides. When Mama Cass introduced "California Dreamin'" at 12:30 Monday morning, she said, "This whole weekend was a dream come true."

The first (and it later turned out, only) Monterey International Pop Festival was a dream come true—an odd, baffling, and at times threatening dream, but one whose main theme was the creation and further growth of rock 'n' roll music, a music as young, vital, and beautiful as any being made today.

A dapper B.B. King, 1968. © Baron Wolman

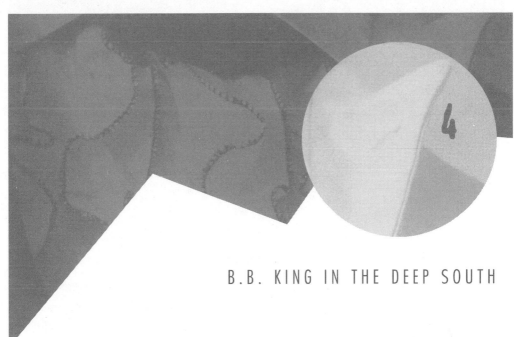

1968

B.B. King played the Fillmore many times in the fifties and early sixties when the auditorium was San Francisco's premiere venue for touring black bands—the Fillmore district was the city's Harlem. When he showed up in February 1967, B.B. expected the same old same old, but to his astonishment was greeted by a sea of white faces: promoter Bill Graham had recently taken over the Fillmore for his psychedelic dances and, heeding the advice of long-haired blues guitarist Mike Bloomfield, had booked B.B. so the emerging hippie audience would hear the real blues, straight from the source.

The hippies, naturally enough, loved his music, and over the next three years, B.B. became prosperous and famous. Dozens of magazines interviewed him, he appeared on all the late-night television talk shows, his albums became best-sellers, and his singles began edging into the charts. In 1968, when he played the Fillmore again, he still stayed at the Oakland Holiday Inn because his next gig was at Oakland's black Club Showcase. But in 1969 he stayed at the Mark Hopkins, and his next date was a concert in the Hollywood Bowl. The chitlin circuit wasn't behind him forever ("I still want to play for the people who were so loyal to me," he said), but the need to do that endless grind was over. He had

41

made it, and was on his way to becoming what he is now, the true king, the Duke Ellington of the blues.

In 1969 B.B. was playing and singing better than ever before, his control tighter and his emotional range wider. Where he might once have fallen back on surefire routines, he was experimenting. A year before he had said how he envied the melodic inventiveness of guitarists Charley Byrd and Kenny Burrell. "I just don't know where they get all those little notes, then string 'em together in pretty tunes," he said. "Oh, man, I'd like to play like that." Now he was still playing the blues, but opening up its structure to a new lyricism. His singing could be no more rich than it always had been, but now it had a flamboyant zest that made him seem to sparkle in the spotlight. Most extraordinary was that his process, the straightened hair which virtually no black entertainer over thirty is ever without, was gone. He wore his hair in a short Afro cut. He looked younger, and when he smiled, he looked like a ten-year-old at a carnival. Every crowd gave him long standing ovations.

"Yes, I'm liking success, all of it," he said one night in the dressing room. "My music is getting out, and I'm not having to worry where the next dollar is coming from no more. I'm not rich, understand, but farther from the edge than ever before."

In the fall of 1968, I had traveled with B.B. in the Deep South; there and then the edge was a lot closer.

A cool night breeze blew outside, across the Mississippi and the cane fields that press against the town of Port Allen, Louisiana. Inside the Club Streamline—a bare cinder-block box crowded with chipped, linoleum-topped cafeteria tables—it was noisy, stifling, and rank with sweat. B.B. King was an hour late. He was coming from Mobile, where he had played the night before, and the customers—field workers in collarless shirts, city dudes from Baton Rouge across the river, orange-haired beauticians, oil refinery workers with their wives—were grumbling. "We want B.B.!" shouted a lady with a heavy sprinkling of gold teeth.

"'Deed we do," answered someone, but Sonny Freeman and the Unusuals, King's six-piece touring band, kept rolling through "Eleanor Rigby." Then, from a side door B.B.'s valet carried in a big red guitar, plugged it into a waiting amplifier, and left it gleaming on a chair in the dim yellow light.

"Lucille is here; B.B. can't be far behind," said the gold-toothed lady.

The tenor sax player took the mike. "Ladies and gentlemen, it's show time, and we're happy to present the star of the show, the King of the Blues, Mr. B.B. King." A wave of clapping washed back to the bar, and a heavyset man in a shiny maroon suit stepped lightly to the stage and picked up the guitar. The band started "Every Day I Have the Blues," and B.B. King, eyes screwed shut and body bent forward, hit a quick chord.

From that instant the very molecules of the air seemed alive; King and his guitar were a magic source of energy from which came fine glistening notes that drew the whole club into their tremulous, hesitant intensity. "Put the hurt on me," a man yelled. Women jumped up and stood twisting their hips, heads bowed, hands held high in witness. "Evra day, evra day I have the blues," B.B. sang, rocking back and forth, both fists clenched beside his head, and the shouting went on.

"Thank you, ladies and gennulmen," King said smoothly when he finished, the band riffing gently behind him. "So sorry I'm late, but we're so glad to have you with us and we hope to he'p you have a good time. If you like the blues, I think you will. Are you ready to get in the alley?"

A deafening roar said yes. He hit a high note that he bent sharp as it faded, then another, then another, the crowd erupted, and he was off again. For an hour he played the blues, rough and smooth, exultant and down-hearted, blues that are fresh every time: "Rock Me, Baby," "Three O'Clock Blues," "Don't Answer the Door," and his classic "Sweet Little Angel": "I got a sweet little angel, . . . When she puts her wings around me, I get joy and everything."

But at the break B.B. wasn't so happy. Splashing his thick neck with Fabergé Brut cologne and touching up his roughly processed hair with

UltraSheen, both proffered by Wilson, his valet, he moaned about his gas pains. He'd been going to a doctor for his stomach, he told the knot of hangers-on gathered around his dressing-room chair like retainers at a friendly throne, but that doctor hadn't meant nothing but misery.

"'No fried or fatty foods,' he tells me, 'no salad dressing, no liquor, and no women.' I told him, I said, 'Doc, those first things maybe, even liquor, but the last, forget it.' And he said to me, 'B., you can say forget it, but the pills I'm givin' you for your stomach, they gonna make you forget it.'"

He paused to get a chuckle of appreciation from the admirers. It came, and B.B. smiled too. "I'm not through yet, lemme go on.

"Now I didn't believe the doctor that some pill was gonna make me forget lovin', and for three weeks it didn't, I was goin' just like always. And then this morning, I was with a sweet gal I been trying to make for fifteen years. She finally said the time was right, so there we was, trying to get something done before I had to get up and drive all the way here, and, you know what? Wouldn't do a thing! Not a blame thing," and he slapped his thigh, laughter bubbling out of him. "I played with it, she played with it, but it just lay there like a hound," and he held his index finger out, limply crooked. Everyone backstage broke up laughing, and B.B. sat there basking in his own joke, his grin wide and loose.

He went back onstage, chuckling, this time in a light green suit, purple turtleneck, and gold pendant. It was one o'clock, late for working people on a weekday night, and the club was emptying. But B.B. played on, oblivious of the tables deserted but for bottles and overturned glasses. "Look at him, man," said Elmore Morris, B.B.'s entr'acte singer for eleven years. "The greatest. It's the depths he gets to—he knows what they are and how to get to 'em. A mean man or a small man couldn't do that; takes a real man like B. to penetrate like he does."

Born Riley B. ("I never knew what that B. was for") King in Itta Bena, Mississippi, he became Riley King, the Blues Boy from Beale Street, when he got his first radio job in Memphis in 1948; in time that got shortened to Blues Boy King and then to B.B. "It still means Blues Boy," he says. "That's what I am. It's too late to change." Now forty-four, he looks his age but not a day older; there is no stoop in his stance, no gray in his hair, and no tiredness in his bright eyes and lively mouth. His face most often has a calmly mournful quality but can break up in laughter and suddenly have an impishness that just as suddenly disappears. At times, particularly in his Cadillac, he looks like a sober Negro doctor, exuding quiet success, but even then you see in his eyes that he is a bluesman, a man for whom the blues are his sorrow, his power, his essence. "I always start my show with 'Every Day I Have the Blues,'" he says simply, "because it's true."

The blues—"American music," says B.B.—are hard to define. "If you have to ask, you'll never know," some say, others adding more aggressively, "If you ain't got 'em, don't mess with 'em." The passion expressed in blues is, however strong, so subtle that great debates have always raged over which musicians and fans could really (or really really) play or feel them. Purists believe that the true bluesmen (all black) could be counted on two hands; blues democrats argue that Moses, Beethoven, Ghandi, and all disappointed lovers know the blues.

The evidence is on the side of the democrats. As a musical form, the blues emerged less than a hundred years ago out of the peculiar institution of slavery of Africans in America; they are now a metaphor for emotions felt by people all over the globe. Blues are at the essence of a wide range of American musics, and have influenced all modern composers. Whatever bastardized or attenuated idiom or style they get shoved into, they always maintain their integrity against depredation.

The blues are first the music of black Americans. Their technical basics evolved in the meeting of black slave and white master cultures; in time they have accumulated a vast range of meanings, subjects, and styles, becoming the aggregate expression of black Americans, detailing every facet of their lives, reflecting every change in their fortunes, and speaking, often obliquely,

45

their self-assertion in a world that tries to trap them in invisibility. The fundamental requirement of the blues is absolute honesty, and they are accurate to the last nuance of black life in America. Aesthetically, the blues are black America, and to love them, to find expression of oneself in them, is to identify with the black American experience.

That experience is as diverse as the blues, but its unifying fact is displacement—simply not being at home. The blues are the music of a people profoundly alienated, a people making their way in a foreign land—Babylon, Eldridge Cleaver calls it—to which they were brought as captives. On one hand attempting to deal with the cruel or absurd reality facing them as best they can, they are also searching for a surer, more essential reality: their past, their historical, racial, and primal selves, the web from which they were ripped. One feels the earnestness of that search, its yearning and frustration, in every blues chorus with its Sisyphean climb away from the tonic chord, the brief reaching of an instable peak, and the inevitable fall back to the tonic.

But so powerful is the world black Americans live in that the search must be carried on within its terms. The blues are played on Western instruments, but the notes that give blues their emotional tonality are not the do-re-mi that white Americans call "the scale." Guitars are not fretted to include them; "blue notes" lie between the keys, as pianists say. A blues musician can only reach them by distorting the sound their instruments were built for: bending a guitar string, fading open trumpet valves, "overblowing" a harmonica, or grace-noting across several piano keys. He must twist and restructure the reality he is given to find his way to those tones that soothe and inspire him. Using the tools of the West, he repeatedly re-creates those haunting tones that seem to be an elusive key to a past and self that is remembered only enough to make its disappearance agonizing. The tragedy of the blues is that you can't go home again; their hope is that through them, maybe someday, somehow, you can. And with them, right now, you can make wherever you are a lot more homey.

The dialectic of displacement and the yearning for home is universal, a theme as old as man's expulsion from Eden, new as our own births; yet the popularity of the blues indicates that it has particular relevance today. If we knew it no other way, the worldwide acceptance of the blues would prove that millions of humans now feel robbed of their homes, cheated of their birthrights, lost and oppressed. A lot of people in this world, of all colors and cultures, have the blues.

In a century the blues may be a form like the sonata form, something to be learned from a book. Today they are living truth. And an American one; while the world is being Americanized (i.e., accepting the technology of the white master culture), it is also (maybe therefore?) learning the other side of life, the loneliness of displacement. Blues truth runs counter to hysterical confidence in progress, machines, and human power. It is a darker, more fateful, though ultimately more relaxed and humorous truth that has its own sober and sensual comfort. "When it all comes down," say the blues (here in the words of Memphis Slim), "you gotta go back to Mother Earth." The blues tell that truth with the ease and grace of folktales, as well as raunchiness, anger, and despair. This simple music bears that truth's burden because it is not quite an "art," but the vital creation of men and women of very human genius.

B.B. is one of those men. He has been on the road for almost twenty years, but the day when he was a James Brown sex symbol with Top 10 songs has been over for a decade. Soul music, with a heavy beat, gospel influences, and glamorous stars, is the staple of the best-selling charts, not the blues as played by older men who won't change the rhythm to suit the latest dance steps. Blues are "roots," recognized as the basic source but ignored because they merge into the cultural background. It is the Otis Reddings, Bob Dylans, Rolling Stones, and Janis Joplins who, working changes on the blues, get the hits. Even when folk enthusiasts in the late fifties and early sixties were "discovering" blues singers like Son House and Mississippi John Hurt, B.B. was passed over as too urban and sophisticated.

47

His blues are all music created by city artists in the past twenty years; few date directly from the oral tradition of the country blues singers. But B.B., long caught in the middle, is now getting full attention.

On one hand, educated blacks who had scorned the blues as dirty music, an opiate of the people, the result of an oppressed past, are turning to the blues to express their blackness; B.B. is both funky enough and modern enough for them to dig. For a Negro to say, "B.B. is my main man," Charles Keil wrote in *Urban Blues*, "is to say, 'I take pride in who I am.'" On the other, the millions of white kids going deeply into rock 'n' roll, led by young white guitarists like Eric Clapton, began to discover the blues in the mid-sixties. The touted "new rock" is as much a blues revival as it is electronic psychedelia. What the Beatles are to the latter, B.B. is to the former. For blues fans, black and white, he is not only a beautiful musician, but the essence of the lead guitarist, the soul man alone with his guitar, a breed that for cultists has all the misterioso allure of the cowboy, racing driver, or bull-fighter. Both audiences recognize B.B. as a proud and intelligent man, an artist who presents himself with no apologies and no put-ons.

"I'm different from the old blues people," he says. "I don't smoke or drink on stage. And unlike the new ones, I don't dance. I'm just not electri-fying. I figure that it's the singing and the playing the people come for and that's what I give 'em. My only ambition is to be recognized as one of the great blues singers. If Frank Sinatra can be tops in his field, Nat Cole in his, Bach and Beethoven and those guys in theirs, why can't I be great and known for it in blues? It's been a long time, and the fellas that made it before me with the Twist and rock—I'm not saying they don't deserve it, but I think I do, too."

In Port Allen recognition seemed a long way away. The group had just started forty-five straight one-nighters on the chitlin circuit that would have them crisscrossing the Deep South. They would get good crowds because it's blues country, but they knew they'd been doing it for years and that you don't make money from people who don't have it themselves. And that night, right after the Club Streamline promoter said he didn't have the $650 promised and B.B. wearily accepted four hundred dollars, there was trouble.

They left the club at 3:00 A.M.—B.B., his road manager Frank Brown, and valet Wilson in the green Cadillac Fleetwood Brougham, the band in a Ford Econovan (a disparity exactly expressive of their business relationship to B.B.; despite it, they are all friends).

They planned to drive the two hundred miles to the motel in Mobile by morning, sleep until early afternoon, then drive to Montgomery for the date that night. While they gassed up in Baton Rouge, Wilson and two of the guys in the band, all wearing dashikis, walked over to a café for sandwiches and sat down at the counter. No eating at the counter, said the counterman as a dozen white toughs watched over their beers; no takeouts either. "We're Wallaces here," shouted a tough. The guys shrugged and started out. "Great, man," sneered Wilson from the door.

"Whah, you nigger," said a tough, coming out after him and punching him to the gravel. "Git 'em!" cried another, and suddenly a half dozen whites came outside, one swinging a heavy chain.

The three fought back, and when Frank, a giant, came running and grabbed away the chain, the whites scattered. But tenor sax man Lee Gatling had been stabbed in the arm, and trumpeter Pat Williams was bleeding from a chain wound on the forehead. The police who gathered asked a few questions, said they couldn't find any suspects, and stood under the blue-white gas station lights eyeing the band suspiciously.

B.B., who had missed the action because he was in the men's room, quickly took charge, ordering an ambulance, calming his men, and talking to the police—but his mind was somewhere else.

"Wanted something to eat, just something to eat, and a man'll hate you so bad he'd kill you. You think things are getting better," he said to no one in particular, staring at the "I Have a Dream" stickers on his bumper. "Thought you knew how to get along, never anything like this happen before. Oh, man, this hurts so bad. And they tease me when I sing the blues. Hah! What else can I sing?"

They all waited at the hospital until six before a doctor appeared and said Gatling and Williams were all right. As the sun rose they started for Mobile, getting there, sleepless, in the glare of early afternoon.

B.B. got a few hours' sleep before they started out for Montgomery. The anger of the night before was beginning to recede, and as the Cadillac swept north, he talked about his life. He had told his story before to other interviewers, often in the same words, as if he had saved it all up, knowing it would one day be worth telling. His mother had left his father when he was four, he said, taking B.B. to the Mississippi hills and her churchgoing family. She died a few years later, and he spent his boyhood as a fifteen-dollar-a-month hired hand for a white tenant farmer until his father found him and took him back to the delta, where he chopped cotton and drove a tractor on a plantation.

Young Riley King had sung in church since he was tiny, and learned guitar from a minister uncle, first sneaking the guitar off the bed where the uncle put it while he ate dinner. In the delta he started singing and playing regularly in a gospel quartet.

At eighteen he was drafted and then deferred: the plantation owners wanted good workers on the home front. This is something that B.B., who misses having no formal musical education, is still bitter about: "If I had been let stay in, I could have gone to music school on the G.I. Bill." But deferment meant getting Army equivalent pay instead of fieldhand wages and having money in his pocket. "I'd take the extra and buy a bus ticket for as far as it would take me—Jackson, Oxford, even Hattiesburg—and play the blues on street corners, making more on a weekend than I could all week. 'Course, I was sneaking away; playing blues if you were in a sanctified singing group was evil, consorting with the devil. But I didn't mind 'cause of the money, and all those people cheering me as I played—that made it worth it."

After the war he moved to Memphis, determined to make it. He lived with his cousin, the great bluesman Bukka White, and landed a ten-minute spot on WDIA, one of the first radio stations anywhere with Negro personnel, advertising Pepticon Tonic and playing his blues. He was immediately popular; by 1949 he had the best-known blues trio in Memphis, his own show as a disc jockey, and his first big record, "Three O'Clock Blues," which stayed at the Number 1 spot in the rhythm and blues charts for eighteen weeks.

"I was a star from then on, getting good guarantees, making every record—'Sweet Sixteen,' 'Rock Me, Baby,' 'You Know I Love You'—a hit. Always traveling, too. One year we did 342 one-nighters, me and Lucille," he said, patting the guitar case behind his head. The present Lucille, a red Gibson with gold frets and mother-of-pearl inlay, is Lucille number 7; a label on the case reads, "My name is Lucille, I am a guitar. My boss is B.B. King. Please Handle Me With Care."

Lucille got her name in a nothing town by the name of Twist, Arkansas: "We were playing some club, and some guys were fightin' and they knocked over a kerosene barrel and burned the place down. I was almost killed going back in to save my guitar, and when I found out the fight was over a gal named Lucille, I named my guitar that to tell me to keep her close and treat her right."

The car now slipped through miles of forest; Frank had the radio on jazz softly.

Harder times came in the late fifties and early sixties. When Top 40 programming swept radio everywhere, replacing specialty shows like blues hours with solid pop, B.B. didn't get much airplay. Most bluesmen either moved to rock or went off the road; blues became the music of country people, the old and the poor. He always had work, but the clubs and money weren't good, especially compared to the standards set by black stars making it in white markets. He still recorded, but the albums sold for $1.99 on drugstore racks. One car crash wiped out his savings; another almost took off his right arm.

"Then my second wife left me and it like to killed me. I really loved that gal, but she wanted me off the road. I wanted to, too, but I was behind to the government so I couldn't. She didn't understand. Just being a blues singer was

B.B. King and Lucille, 1968. © Baron Wolman

hard. People thought they were all illiterate, drinking and beating their women every Saturday night. I'd fight for the blues, but they wouldn't listen, and since I didn't have school past ninth grade I didn't feel too confident of myself. I'm still a country boy, a little scared of people who can make you feel bad. It's like since I was a boy going to bed with no lights 'cause there was no electricity, I've been afraid of the dark."

That night B.B. was magnificent. The Montgomery Elks Club, Southern Pride Lodge No. 431, was packed to the walls with a good-time crowd, and he worked for them. His face beaded with sweat, Lucille brought up under his chin, his eyebrows going up and down, B.B. pulled out the notes, starting solos with just the rhythm of organ and drums, and building slowly to the full power of the band behind him, Lucille always showing the way; when you thought she had said it all, B.B. sang, his voice both tough and vulnerable. Young white audiences marvel at his guitar playing, but for black audiences he is a blues singer, first and last. "I've been downhearted, baby, ever since the day we met," he began one song softly, ending in full-blown shouting:

> Ah gave you a bran' new Ford,
> You said, "Ah wanna Cadillac!"

B.B. vamping, hand on hip, gave the girl's response:

> Ah bought you a ten-dollar dinner,
> You said, "Thanks for the snack."
> I let you live in my penthouse,
> You said it was just a shack.
> I gave you seven children,
> An' now you wanna give 'em back!

With that women were jumping up and down; men were rolling back in their chairs, all howling at the joke of it, when B.B. finished, "Our love is nothing but the blues, woman; baby, how blue can you get?" Before the cheering had died down he was into a slow and very funky "Don't Answer the Door," which ended in more screaming. And then the next song and the next—fast ones, slow ones, setting up moods and dissolving them for new ones; everything real and true. "There's no signifyin' jive with B.!" shouted one delirious listener, his glass held up in salute, as B.B. left the stage.

"I wish they had something could measure the pressure inside a person," B.B. said in the cramped dressing room. He spoke softly but intensely. "Like at times when you're in a strong mood, if you've been hurt bad by a gal or your best friend. It's like that when I'm playing and I know exactly what I want to play, it's a goal I'm trying to reach, and the pressure is like a spell—oh man, I don't have the words.

"But I know this, I've never made it. I've never played what I hear inside. I get close but not there. If I did, I'd play the melody so you'd know what it was saying even if you didn't know the words. You wouldn't know when Lucille stopped and my voice began."

A beautiful woman with a wig of rust-colored curls came in. "Hello, B., how are you?" she said.

"Happy to see you, beautiful," he said with a big smile, and kissed her.

"Haven't seen you for a year, B. Are you staying over?" she said, rearranging her curls.

"No, baby, we're going to Atlanta soon as we're ready."

She looked crestfallen. They chatted a few minutes and she left.

"Man," said B.B., wiping his brow. "Gonna have to do something about those pills!"

Out at the car the guys in the band were talking about the fight; they hadn't stopped talking about it. They couldn't figure out the why of it. Nothing like it had ever happened to any of them; its ferocity had astonished them. B.B. joined them.

"You never saw anything like it before, B.?" asked one.

Never, and he couldn't explain it for them, he said, but things are better now. You didn't stay at Holiday Inns when he started, but in black fleabags;

you kept food in the car and relieved yourself beside the road. "If you had that fight a while back, you'd be in jail now. Only one thing I regret about that fight: you fellas didn't put one of them in the hospital."

"Next time, B.," said Lee.

It was a long drive to Atlanta and B.B. felt like talking. T-Bone Walker's clean sound and Elmore James's swing were his big guitar influences; church preaching for his singing. But he always loved jazz, especially Count Basie. "I just love to swing, man," he said, "and nobody swings like the Count." Charlie Christian's guitar was an inspiration, but "the man who won my heart" was Django Reinhardt. "He had a singing guitar, gypsy Spanish, soulful. It really filled my soul."

Classical works are too long for B.B., but there's no music that, if he listens to it, he can't see what it's getting at—even Japanese koto music. When he retires he'd like to have a disc-jockey show again and play whatever he feels like. "All music is beautiful. Man, I got twenty thousand records and I never buy ones I don't like. I even have a record of Gene Autry singing 'T. B. Blues.' He's a rich man now, but there was a time when he was saying something.

"Old bluesmen, they didn't listen to anything but blues; I do and I'm more polished than them. But blues can't be too polished; they have to be raw and soulful. They started with a fella singing to you like he was telling you a story; if he kept up the tempo, he could make a chorus fifteen, even twenty bars long if he wanted to say his piece. I was like that, but when I got a band I had to stay within twelve bars to keep with the other fellas. And man, those bars went flyin' by! But blues can't be perfect. A lotta white people can't sing the blues because their English is too good. Blues and correct English don't sound right. You gotta break the verbs for it to be blues.

"Some say the blues are backward, but I think they can he'p black people now. If something is bothering you and you got a friend, it he'ps if you can talk about it. It may not solve it, but it he'ps. You can talk about your problems in the blues and you find people have the same problems, and then you can do something. Blues words are usually about men and women, because that's where it all starts—men do most things on account of women—but if you hear the blues, you know it's about a lot more."

B.B. doesn't have a home; Memphis is home base, and he has a farm there that his father lives on, but in Memphis, as elsewhere, home is the motel room he's in. The one in Atlanta looked it. Spilled over the bed, tables, floor, and sink were briefcases full of contracts, letters, unfinished songs, notes for a book to be called *How I Play the Blues*; an electric pan in which he makes oatmeal for his ailing stomach; a tape recorder, a tape-cassette-radio, a dozen changes of street clothes and another dozen stage out-fits, books about flying (B.B. is almost qualified as a pilot), two big red volumes of *Joseph Schillinger's System of Musical Composition*, from which he is learning to write his own arrangements, copies of *Billboard* and soul music magazines, and empty packs of Kools. "I've been doing this a while," he said, padding around the piles in his black silk underwear. "I own an apart-ment building in Memphis, wouldn't mind moving in, but whites live there, and if I moved in, they'd move out and my property wouldn't be worth a thing. That's the truth."

He found what he was looking for, a sheaf of unfinished songs. "This one I've been working on. It says what I think about myself. 'I ain't no preacher, Not trying to be no saint. Because I don't get high every day, don't mean I don't take a drink.' That's all now, but it's gonna be a song, saying I'm just B.B., take me as I am.

"Maybe soon I'll just work weekends, maybe even have a club of my own. I got four kids by various women; they're all grown and have chil-dren. Maybe I'll enjoy my grandchildren like I never had a chance to with my own. But I'll never stop playing. As long as people'll hear me, I'll keep playing."

The next date was at the Lithonia Country Club, a place at the end of a dirt-road maze twenty miles from Atlanta. "This is a real funk," said Sonny Freeman, unbelievingly. The club, a shack, was half empty, and the decor made the Club Streamline look like the Stork Club; there were bare wooden chairs and tables, a cracked cement floor, and a stage, incongruously lined with ripped tin foil and lit by one fixed spotlight.

It was a tough night; the audience seemed to like the blues but just wouldn't clap. "You know we're working hard for you," B.B. pleaded several times. "Whyncha beat your hands together for us," but all he got was desultory applause.

"Man, you see what it's been like for us all these years," he said at the break. "It's so hard when people ain't with you. But if they can't be satisfied, man, I play for my own satisfaction."

He did. Coming back on at midnight, the club even emptier than when he had begun, he played roughly, slashing his pick across the strings in harshly vibrant chords, even breaking two strings. But as he was bringing the show to a close, he changed moods. Singing in a pure falsetto, leaving the roughness behind, he made his voice all sweet pleading.

"Worry, worry, worry; worry's all I can do," he sang, his head up tilted, the light glinting off the diamond B.B. ring on his left hand. "My life is so miserable, baby, and it's all on account of you."

The riffing of the band built through the second chorus and exploded as he started the third. "Someday, baby," he sang, his voice almost squeaking, "someday, baby, someday, baby." He stood there, a big, powerful man on a sagging stage lost in the scrub woods of Georgia, singing to thirty people, all black, poor, middle-aged or old, a little drunk, and only a few hours away from work the next day, singing "Someday, baby," as high as he could over and over again. One knew that for every "Someday, baby" he sang, there were many somedays on his mind. Finally, he came to the last one: "Someday baby, when the Blindman calls my name / You won't be able to hurt me no more, woman / 'Cause my heart won't feel no more pain."

He said his thank yous, left the stage, changed, thanked the band for playing well (as he does every night), and got into the Cadillac, turning on the portable television he keeps plugged into the cigarette lighter.

"What's happening?" he asked Frank, who has been driving for him for ten years, as they pulled out."

"Another day done passed by," said Frank.

It was a fine social night backstage at the Fillmore West after a year of days passed by.

B.B.'s stomach troubles were long gone. Two lovely young women had dropped by especially to see him; a huge black man named Ernie who he had once played with in Memphis was there and had brought a fifth of scotch. B.B. sent out for some beer. Someone else was passing around a goatskin flask of red wine.

When everyone was pretty high, three young black men came to the door and shyly asked if they could enter. B.B. waved them in and offered one his seat. No, they said, they didn't want to take up his time, but they were representatives of the San Francisco State Black Students Union (BSU), and they wanted to tell B.B. that they thought he was the greatest, a real soul brother who told it without any jive. He thanked them, but their manner somehow implied a "but," and he waited for them to go on.

"I hope this isn't rude," said one, "but I wanted to ask you, if it's not too personal, why you now wear your hair natural."

"I'll tell you," said B.B. "Because I'm beginning to get a feeling for who I am. I had a process for years, partly because it was the fashion and 'cause I thought it looked good, but I always knew it wasn't quite right; it was a mask I wore to hide something. Now I don't feel I need it anymore."

Another one said it was still pretty short, but B.B. said he had it the way he wanted it. The tall thin student, whose name was Tony and who seemed to be the leader, asked if B.B. would play for the BSU. Not this trip, he said, and they'd have to wait until he was in California again, but he'd be glad to do it free. Tony didn't quite seem to trust him; B.B. said he was a man of his word; Tony looked doubtful, and then the conversation started to get a little ugly.

It was hard to tell what the students wanted. They kept needling him with questions, often all three speaking at the same time, bursting out with an impatience both nervous and angry. What was success, why did he play for whites, did he think whites understood the blues, what was the blues, did everyone have them or only black people, did he think black people had suffered more than any other race, did he believe in violence? They were at once apologetically self-abasing, acting as if their questions were unloaded, and openly antagonistic. B.B. was remarkably polite. He knew a lot of white people who were worse off than blacks, he said, and what the students knew from books about plantation life he knew from his own life. He had walked, he reckoned, about 60,000 miles behind a mule plowing cotton. But they cut him off before he could finish, and he pleaded in vain to speak his mind.

"You say you lived on a plantation," screamed one student, "but was your mother and wife raped before your eyes?"

"You know they weren't because I'm still alive," said B.B., "and that would only happen over my dead body."

"But that's the blues," shouted another student, "and that never happened to no white man."

"You come here to ask me about the blues, and then you tell me what they are?" B.B. asked in disbelief.

"But how can you really have 'em if you say anybody can have 'em?" said Tony.

"I didn't say anybody, I just said no race got a monopoly on suffering," said B.B.

They continued at an impasse for twenty minutes, a strange spectacle: young men whose own sense of pride and dignity as humans and blacks had in large measure been awakened by B.B.'s artistry having to reinforce that still shaky confidence by attacking him. Finally they were almost calling him an Uncle Tom. For the first time, he showed anger.

"Listen," he said. "I've got only one more thing to say. You're upset now, but it don't bother me. You know a lot more about who you are than I did at your age, and I'm proud of you. You are going to be leaders, and we need leaders. But there's one word I don't want you to forget, and that's *justice*. Be just. Please be just. That's the lesson of suffering and it's the lesson of the blues. I try to be just when I play my song, and if you can't be just, that's when you don't really know the blues."

"But, but . . . " Tony started to stammer.

"No buts," said B.B. "Now let's shake hands and don't bother me no more."

Pete Townsend, in full flight, 1967. © Baron Wolman

5

THREE SHORT PORTRAITS:
PETE TOWNSEND, JIMI HENDRIX, AND JIM MORRISON

1968

These three short pieces were written for the drama section of the *New York Times*. In those days rock bands touring America often started on the West Coast and worked their way east, so the Sunday Arts section editor, the late, great Seymour Peck, would assign me to catch a band at the Fillmore West and then run my piece the Sunday before the band opened at the Fillmore East. The art of writing miniprofiles is to cram as many facts as possible into the fewest words, and I vividly remember the agony (and the fun) of trimming these pieces to the bone. Now they read like snapshots frozen in a moment of time: the "rock opera" that was then only a gleam in Pete Townsend's eye soon became *Tommy*, his magnum opus.

PETE TOWNSEND AND THE WHO

The Who play rock 'n' roll music ("it's got a back beat, you can't lose it," says Chuck Berry). Not art rock, acid rock, or any type of rock, but an unornamented wall of noise that, while modern and electronic, has that "golden oldies" feeling. Four mod kids who started in 1963 as the High-numbers in London's scruffy Shepherd's Bush, the Who play a tight driving music that is a descendant of the rock of Elvis Presley, Bill Haley, Gene Vincent, and even the early Beatles.

In San Francisco near the end of a ten-week, fifty-city tour, the Who were at their best, packing the Fillmore West three nights straight, their single show nightly an hour and a half of brilliantly intense excitement capped by the climactic smashing of the guitar and drums that is their trademark. They played old songs and new, drawing each out into long rocking statements that had wild but economical power. The smashing is by now almost offhand, and gone is their audience hatred (almost: Pete Townsend did kick the fans who scrambled too eagerly for his broken guitar). Jumping around with smiling hilarity and dressed in street clothes rather than their former outfits—pop-art suits and Regency lace—the Who just played the music.

"We're getting used to the fact that to play more music we have to sacrifice some of the visual bit," said Townsend. "The costumes used to get in my way, and I don't want to look like James Brown anymore. The whole violent style happened because we couldn't play—it covered that up and expressed our frustrations. Now we're getting more musical, so we don't need the anger like we did."

He scratched his neck for a moment, grinned dourly, and continued in thick cockney. "But we still like the smashing. If some creep yells for it, we'll do it and be happy. Whatever there is in our systems we don't get out playing, we get out with the smashing. It's inherent to us. It is the Who."

But the Who are more than their nihilistic ritual (from which Michelangelo Antonioni built the nightclub riot scene in *Blow-Up*). In their five years they have toured England endlessly, done five American tours, and produced several polished albums and a series of hits. Though without the overwhelming success in America that makes pop stars millionaires who can retire from public life while still adolescents, the Who are in a secure middle status: not as big as the Beatles or Rolling Stones, but with a demonstrated staying power, both creative and popular, lacked by such as Cream and Jimi Hendrix.

The men Who are: saucy-faced Keith Moon, presiding madman at the drums; the painfully skinny and bleached blond Roger Daltrey, who sings lead and writhes for the ladies; stolid bassist John Entwistle, who writes a few songs, including the group's most requested number, "Boris the Spider"; and Townsend, a pleasantly moody twenty-three-year-old who, besides playing lead guitar, is the group's leader, main songwriter, spokesman, and theorist. "Talk to Peter," said Entwistle, "he'll spin out the rubbish as long as you're willing to listen."

Townsend did, sprawled out bonily on a sofa in his motel room. "Maybe we play rock 'n' roll, but if we play it, it's because we're in the one big rock 'n' roll movement. There's not Chuck Berry and Fats Domino and the Beatles and the Who, all playing different music. There's just rock 'n' roll, full stop. We're in it, it's not in us."

He stopped and sneered a classic Townsend sneer. "Rock's just about dead in England, the scene there has had it. England is a European country filled with boring people who like boring things. It must have been an accident that the Beatles got their sound together there. Do you know that Engelbert Humperdinck"—he almost spat out the name of the currently popular English ballad singer—"is a bigger property now than anybody? Rock 'n' roll is happening in America like it always did. We love it here. The Byrds, Steppenwolf, Booker T., Moby Grape—that's rock 'n' roll.

"You can tell what is and what isn't rock 'n' roll. To be the real thing, a song has to have an awareness of rock history. It has to have the beat, that undulating rhythm. Even while it feels history, it has to say something new. And, most important, it has to have crammed into it all the poignancy and excitement of youth because that's what it's really all about."

The Who live the definition. Their biggest early hit was "My Generation," with the lines, "Things, they say, look awful cold / Hope I die before I get old." "Summertime Blues," a hit of singer Eddie Cochrane's from the mid-fifties, is still in their repertoire. Townsend carries tapes of Cochrane (killed in a car crash in 1960) wherever he goes. All four are big fans of what English pop fans call "flash," the hard-edged charisma of fame, sex, power, and lavishly spent money. While in San Francisco, Townsend bought a Lincoln Continental Mark II and will have it shipped to London. "I love American cars, and this one's a classic," he said. "All gold paint, leather seats, and the engine is painted bright blue." They tour not just for the money—they make up to $7,500 a night—but because grueling one-night stands are part of rock tradition.

"We're traveling on our own now, but I'd rather tour with a lot of groups, a couple of dozen blokes jammed into a bus having the time of their lives. If we stopped touring, we'd go off. Dead.

"Playing onstage, though, we're playing history. New ideas come from sitting down by yourself and working. That's where the spark is, work. I don't respect groups who won't work. And the spark, you have to get that on the records. So we don't mess around with all the fancy studio stuff, tracking and tracking a thing into obscurity. We want to make sure that on record the impact of the idea is captured in all its vibrancy and dynamite—that's what we're after. We've never put out a record that didn't say what it was supposed to."

What Townsend and the group want to say has changed. From the first days of pure aggression, they have moved through the humor of "Happy Jack" and "Tattoo" to the zinging unearthliness of "I Can See for Miles" and "Magic Bus," their latest release. Some of the anger is still there, in part because Townsend grew up hating people who laughed at his enormous nose; his songs often feature deformed little boys who get back at the cruel world. Now Townsend is testing new directions for the album the group will record in the fall.

"I am incredibly excited. I know people want something new. They want a new reason to go to a rock 'n' roll concert. What we are going to try is opera, not something trashy like the pompous arty types do. They do fancy things because they can't play. We've done mini-operas, now we want a long thing around a theme—I've been thinking about a story about a blind, deaf kid—with dialogue, songs, and an incredible finale. I want to get into stuff that will leave the smashing way, way behind."

Townsend started to pace the room. "We'll be into impressionistic music, music like Wagner and Mahler, music that conjures up things more powerful than you can handle. Music can create fantastic high points in people's minds. We want to take those minds," and as he spoke, he raised his hands high above his head, then whipped them down as though hurling a boulder into the innocent sofa, "and bomb them open!"

JIMI HENDRIX

"Will he burn it tonight?" a neat blonde asked of her boyfriend, squashed in beside her on the packed floor of the Fillmore auditorium. "He did at Monterey," the boyfriend said, recalling the pop festival where the guitarist, in a moment of elation, actually put a match to his guitar. The blonde and her boyfriend went on watching the stage, crammed with huge silver-fronted Fender amps, a double drum set, and whispering stage hands. Mitch Mitchell, the drummer, came on first, sat down, smiled, and adjusted his cymbals. Then came bassist Noel Redding, gold glasses glinting on his fair delicate face, and plugged into his amp.

"There he is," said the blonde, and yes, said the applause, there he was: Jimi Hendrix, a cigarette slouched in his mouth, dressed in tight black pants draped with a silver belt, and a pale rainbow shirt half hidden by a black leather vest.

"Dig this, baby," he mumbled into the mike. His left hand swung high over his frizz-bouffant hair, making a shadow on the exploding-sun light show, then down onto his guitar, and the Jimi Hendrix Experience roared into "Red House." It was the first night of the group's second American tour. During the first tour, last summer, they were almost unknown. But this time two LPs and eight months of legend preceded them.

Jimi Hendrix in performance, 1968. © Baron Wolman

The crowds in San Francisco—Hendrix's three February nights there were the biggest in the Fillmore's history—were drooling for Hendrix in the flesh. They got him. This time he didn't burn his guitar ("I was feeling mild") but, with the blatantly erotic arrogance that is his trademark, he gave them what they wanted.

He played all the favorites, "Purple Haze," "Foxy Lady," "Let Me Stand Next to Your Fire," and "The Wind Cries Mary." He played flicking his gleaming white Stratocaster between his legs and propelling it out of his groin with a nimble grind of his hips. Bending his head over the strings, he plucked them with his teeth as if eating them, occasionally pulling away to take deep breaths. Falling back and lying almost prone, he pumped the guitar neck as it stood high on his belly.

He made sound by swinging the guitar before him and just tapping the body. He played with no hands at all, letting the wah-wah pedal bend and break the noise into madly distorted melodic lines. And all at top volume, the bass and drums building a wall of black noise heard as much by pressure on the eyeballs as with the ears.

The black Elvis? He is that in England. In America James Brown is, but only for Negroes; could Hendrix become that for American whites? The title, rich in potential imagery, is a mantle waiting to be bestowed. Within his wildness, Hendrix plays on the audience's reaction to his sexual violence with an ironic and even gentle humor. The Daughters of the American Revolution sensed what he is up to: they managed to block one appearance when he toured with the Monkees last summer, because he was too "erotic." But if Jimi knows about his erotic appeal, he won't admit it.

"Man, it's the music, that's what comes first," he said, taking a quick swig of Johnny Walker Black in his motel room. "People who put down our performance, they're people who can't use their eyes and ears at the same time. They've got a button on their shoulder blades that keeps only one working at a time. Look, man, we might play sometimes just standing there; sometimes we do the whole diabolical bit when we're in the studio and there's nobody to watch. It's how we feel. How we feel and getting the music out, that's all. As soon as people understand that, the better."

The Jimi Hendrix Experience, now doing a two-month tour, was formed in October 1966, just weeks after Hendrix came to London from Greenwich Village, encouraged by former Animal Chas Chandler. Mitchell, twenty-one, came from Georgie Fame's band, a top English rhythm and blues group, and twenty-two-year-old Redding switched to bass from guitar, which he had played with several small-time bands. Their first job, after only a few weeks of rehearsal, was at the Paris Olympia on a bill with Johnny Hallyday.

Their first record, "Hey Joe," got to Number 4 on the English charts; a tour of England and steady dates at in London clubs, plus a follow-up hit with "Purple Haze," made them the hottest name around. Men's hairdressers started featuring the "Experience style." Paul McCartney got them invited to the Monterey Pop Festival and they were a smash hit.

But Jimi Hendrix, born James Marshall Hendrix twenty-two years ago in Seattle, Washington, goes a lot further back. Now hip rock's enfant terrible, he quit high school for the paratroopers at sixteen ("Anybody could be in the army; I had to do it special, but, man, I was bored"). Musically he came up the black route, learning guitar by playing along with Muddy Waters records on his back porch, playing in Negro clubs in Nashville, begging his way onto Harlem bandstands, and touring for two years in the bands of rhythm and blues headliners: the Isley Brothers, Little Richard, and King Curtis. He even played the Fillmore once, but that was backing Ike and Tina Turner before the Haight-Ashbury scene.

"I always wanted more than that," he said. "I had these dreams that something was gonna happen, seeing the numbers 1966 in my sleep, so I was just passing time till then. I wanted my own scene, making my music, not playing the same riffs. Like once with Little Richard, me and another guy got fancy shirts 'cause we were tired of wearing the uniform. Richard called a meeting. 'I am Little Richard, I am Little Richard,' he said, 'the King, the King of Rock and Rhythm. I am the only one allowed to be pretty. Take off those shirts.' Man, it was all like that. Bad pay, lousy living, and getting burned."

Early in 1966 he finally got to Greenwich Village where, as Jimmy James, he played the Café Wha? with his own hastily formed group, the Blue Flames. It was his break, and the bridge to today's Hendrix. He started to write songs—he has written hundreds—and play what he calls his "rock-blues-funky-freak" sound.

"Dylan really turned me on—not the words or his guitar, but as a way to get myself together. A cat like that can do it to you. Race, that was okay. In the Village people were more friendly than in Harlem, where it's all cold and mean. Your own people hurt you more. Anyway, I had always wanted a more integrated sound. Top 40 stuff is all out of gospel, so they try to get everybody up and clapping, shouting, 'yeah, yeah.' We don't want everybody up. They should just sit there and dig it. And they must dig it, or we wouldn't be here."

A John Wayne movie played silently on the television set in the stale and disordered room, and Hendrix started alternating slugs of scotch and Courvoisier. He stopped and turned toward the window, looking out over San Francisco. "This looks like Brussels, all built on hills. Beautiful. But no city I've ever seen is as pretty as Seattle, all that water and mountains. I couldn't live there, but it was beautiful."

Besides his music, Hendrix doesn't do much. He wants to retire young and buy a lot of motels and real estate with his money. Sometimes he thinks of producing records or going to the Juilliard School of Music to learn theory and composition. In London he lives with his manager, but plans to buy a house in a mews. In his spare time he reads Isaac Asimov's science fiction. His musical favorites as he listed them are Charles Mingus, Roland Kirk, Bach, Muddy Waters, Bukka White, Albert Collins, Albert King, and Elmore James.

"Where do you stop? There are so many, oh, man, so many more, all good. Sound, and being good, that's important. Like, we're trying to find out what we really dig. We got plans for a play-type scene with people moving on stage and everything pertaining to the song and every song a story. We'll keep moving. It gets tiring doing the same thing, coming out and saying, 'Now we'll play this song,' and 'Now we'll play that one.' People take us in strange ways, but I don't care how they take us. Man, we'll be moving. 'Cause man, in this life, you gotta do what you want, you gotta let your mind and fancy flow, flow, flow free."

JIM MORRISON AND THE DOORS

"Play 'Light My Fire'!" "Yeah, 'Light My Fire'!" Out of the vastness of the Los Angeles Forum, its 18,000 seats filled on a December Saturday night with the cream of L.A.'s teenybopper set, came the insolent cry. The Doors didn't want to do their 1967 hit; not only had they just finished their first number, but on stage with them and their thirty-two amplifiers were a string sextet and a brass section ready to perform new Doors music.

Jim Morrison, the Lizard King, 1969. © Baron Wolman

They got through a few more numbers, but then with the yelling getting louder, they acquiesced. A roar of cheers and instantly the arena was aglow with sparklers lit in literal tribute. The song over, and the kids shouting for the band to play it again, lead singer Jim Morrison, in a loose black shirt and clinging black leather pants, came to the edge of the stage.

"Hey, man," he said, his voice booming from the speakers on the ceiling. "Cut that shit." The crowd giggled.

"What are you all doing here?" he went on. No response.

"You want music?" A rousing Yeah.

"Well, man, we can play music all night, but that's not what you really want, you want something more, something greater than you've ever seen, right?"

"We want Mick Jagger!" someone shouted. "'Light My Fire'!" said someone else, to laughter.

It was a direct affront, and the Doors hadn't seen it coming. That afternoon before the concert Morrison had said, "We're into what these kids are into." Driving home from rehearsal in his Mustang Shelby Cobra GT 500, he swept his arm wide to take in the low houses that stretched miles from the freeway to the Hollywood Hills. "We're into L.A. Here kids live more freely and more powerfully than anywhere else, but it's also where old people come to die. Kids know both, and we express both."

The teens had belonged to the Doors; their amalgam of sensuality and asceticism, mysticism and machine-like power had won these lushly beautiful children heart and soul, and the kids had made them the biggest American group in rock music. Now, at one of their biggest concerts, prelude to the biggest ever at New York's Madison Square Garden in January, the kids dared laugh, even at Morrison. Not much, but they had begun.

The Doors started out in L.A.'s early hip scene in 1965. Morrison, then twenty-two, son of a high-ranking Navy official, met organist-pianist Ray Manzarek on the beach at Santa Monica while both were making experimental films at UCLA. Drummer John Densmore and guitarist Robby Krieger became friends of Manzarek's at one of the Maharishi Mahesh

73

Yogi's first meditation centers in southern California. Named from a line of Morrison's poetry—"There are things that are known and things that are unknown; in between are doors"—by early 1966 they had their first date, playing for $35 a week at a tiny and now defunct club on Sunset Strip.

While on their second job as the house band at the Whisky a Go Go, working behind dozens of groups they have now eclipsed, they began to build a following, playing blues and classic rock songs with a harsh and eerie stringency. "We were creating our music, ourselves, every night," Morrison said, "starting with a few outlines, maybe a few words for a song that gradually accrued particles of meaning and movement. Sometimes we worked out in Venice, looking at the surf. We were together and it was good times."

Their best songs, "Crystal Ship," the diabolical "The End," and "Light My Fire" took shape in those early days while Morrison was developing the erotic style that has made him the group's star and rock's biggest sex symbol. He doesn't fall off stages any more, but he writhes against the microphone stand, leaps from eyes-closed passivity into shrieking aggression, and moans sweet pain like a modern St. Sebastian pierced by the arrows of angst and revelation.

Just about everybody takes him seriously: the New Haven, Connecticut, police, who last year arrested him for "giving an indecent or immoral exhibition"; the girls who rush the stage, sometimes only to get ashes flicked from his cigarette; and critics who rave in detail about "rock as ritual." But no one takes Morrison as seriously as Morrison takes Morrison.

His stage manner, he said, unlike the acts of Elvis Presley, Otis Redding, and Mick Jagger, with whom he is often compared, has a conscious purpose. Shyly, almost sleepily soft-spoken in private, he sees his public self as that of a new kind of poet-politician. "I'm not a new Elvis, though he's my second favorite singer—Frank Sinatra is first. I just think I'm lucky I've found a perfect medium to express myself in," he said during a rehearsal break, slouched tiredly in one of the Forum's violently orange seats. Though handsome with his pale green eyes and Renaissance prince hair, he has none of the decadent power captured in the spotlight.

"Music, writing, theater, action—I'm doing all those things. I like to write, I'm even publishing a book of my poems pretty soon, stuff I had that I realized wasn't for music. But songs are special. I find that music liberates my imagination. When I sing my songs in public, that's a dramatic act, not just acting as in theater, but a social act, real action.

"Maybe you could call us erotic politicians. We're a rock 'n' roll band, a blues band, just a band, but that's not all. A Doors concert is a public meeting called by us for a special kind of dramatic discussion and entertainment. When we perform, we're participating in the creation of a world, and we celebrate that creation with the audience. It becomes the sculpture of bodies in action.

"That's politics, but our power is sexual. We make concerts sexual politics. The sex starts out with just me, then moves out to include the charmed circle of musicians on stage. The music we make goes out to the audience and interacts with them, they go home and interact with the rest of reality, then I get it back by interacting with that reality, so the whole sex thing works out to be one big ball of fire."

That analytical abandon was just right for the serious rock of the post–*Sergeant Pepper* era. After the album version of "Light My Fire" got heavy airplay on FM rock stations, Elektra released a shorter single that became a Top 40 Number 1. The Doors have followed it with a series of singles and two more albums. They have a quickly identifiable instrumental sound based on blues topped with Morrison's strong voice and lyrics. Manzarek plays a rather dry organ, but Krieger is an aggressive guitarist and Densmore a solid and inventive drummer.

Yet as the kids in the Forum knew, they've never topped "Light My Fire." The abandon has gotten more and more cerebral, the demonic pose more strained. The new music they wanted the crowd to like at the concert was abstract noise crashing behind a Morrison poem of meandering verbosity.

After the show Morrison said it had been "great fun," but the backstage party had a funereal air. And at times that afternoon, he showed that he knew their first rush of energy was running out. Success, he said, looking   75 beat in the orange chair, had been nice. "When we had to carry our own equipment everywhere, we had no time to be creative. Now we can focus our energies more intensely."

He squirmed a bit. "The trouble is that now we don't see much of each other. We're big time, we go on tours, record, and in our free time, everybody splits off into their own scenes. When we record, we have to get all our ideas then, we can't build them night after night like the club days. In the studio creation is not so natural.

"I don't know what will happen. I guess we'll continue like this for a while. Then to get our vitality back, maybe we'll have to get out of the whole business. Maybe we'll all go off to an island by ourselves and start creating again."

Janis Joplin sings the blues, 1969. © Baron Wolman

6

JANIS JOPLIN

1 9 6 9

A few days after doing the interviews for this article, I was at the Avalon Ballroom when Janis came in, wrapped in a fur coat and fur hat, scarves and beads flying. She was by herself, and when she saw me, she gave me a big "Hello, Michael," and came over to chat. I felt extremely embarrassed. Janis Joplin wanted to talk to me? Impossible! She was a star, me a lowly reporter, she an uninhibited sex symbol, me a quiet guy, nervous with girls.

So I mumbled something and tried to look cool. In the face of my apparent indifference, Janis's enthusiasm sank into disappointment. "Oh," she said, with a look that said, "Boy, you're a washout," and walked away.

I certainly hadn't meant to close Janis out, but that was the sum effect of my awkwardness. Over the years I've often looked back on those few seconds with regret, realizing that this scene must have been repeated for Janis many times: her approaching strangers and fans with her down-home bubbly charm and then feeling let down by their retreating into awkward confusion.

Lit by the bright lights of the pool table, Janis Joplin was resplendent. Her wild brown hair, touched with gold, hung in untamed waves down her back and over her lavender silk shirt and blue velvet vest. Gold sandals and bright blue stockings were on her feet, on her wrists dozens of bracelets in flaming acrylic colors; a blue and red kerchief was tied loosely into her immense fur hat; silver Indian bell rings were on every finger, and she was laughing, dancing, and singing, her eyes, mouth, and body never still.

It was late afternoon in a San Francisco Irish bar, the B&G Club, in the miserably rainy San Francisco winter of 1969, and Janis was grooving. The night before she had been "feeling oh so good with this beautiful cat." An afternoon of drinking sweet vermouth in deep tumblers full of ice had put her in a zingy-mellow mood, and right then she was playing 8-ball with a little tattooed guy, and all the luck was coming her way.

"Shoot easy, girl, and you'll either make it or leave him stuck," suggested a gaunt old barfly.

Janis, once (she says proudly) was "8-ball champion of 6th Street in New York between Avenue A and First Avenue," looked over the table with a practiced eye, her face set and deadly serious. With a sharp tug at the pink ribbon that belted her skintight purple bell-bottoms, she bent to shoot.

"Oh, no, man, I don't play like that. Being that chickenshit is tacky, man," she said and blasted away. The shot she wanted she missed, but out of the clattering rebounds, the 6 ball dribbled into a side pocket. "MMEEEEE-OOH!" she cried, giving a quick shimmy with the cue stick high over her head, then spinning to the bar for a long gulp of her double vermouth. "I told ya, I told ya," she cackled with a grin that almost closed her eyes.

Everyone in the bar roared with laughter—even the guys in her band. Rehearsal should have started a half-hour earlier, but unlike the dank practice room in a warehouse attic next door, the bar was warm, and Janis was a pleasure to watch.

Bammo went the 4 ball. Click-zizz-clunk went the 2; only the 8 was left. Janis chalked her cue with nonchalance.

"The side, girl, the side," whispered the barfly.

"Eight ball in the corner," she called and, pushing her bracelets up to her elbow, shot, missed by inches. "Oh, *day*-um," she said with a good Texas accent, instantly forlorn. But the little guy missed, too, and with her glee fully replenished, Janis finished off the game with a lightning stroke.

"Too much!" she crowed. Knocking back her drink, she slipped inside her massive Russian lynx fur coat and announced, "Okay, boys, let's go rehearse."

"Pep," said the barfly, lifting his glass in tribute, "that girl sure has pep."

That rainy winter Janis Joplin was, by all the rules of show-biz myth, at a truly crucial point in a star's career. As lead singer with the freak rock-blues group Big Brother and the Holding Company, riding the wave of music out of the whole hippie movement, Janis had become the biggest female star of rock 'n' roll. Yet that winter, with her fame still growing, she had quit to go solo and sing heavier rhythm and blues.

Within a month she would be starting the first tour with the new band. The money would be better than with Big Brother, well into five figures for most dates; her name alone, Janis Joplin, would have top billing. Would the great fan hordes, even those who felt personally betrayed when she quit Big Brother, hang with her? Would they dig what she was doing? Could she do it? The questions were hanging in the air like the rain—possible to ignore but persistently annoying.

At rehearsal, the groove started to go. It took ten minutes for everybody to get there, another fifteen to get down to work, and even then things were a little too loose.

"Will you guys for Chrissakes stop moving around and talking when I'm singing?" Janis shouted in fury, breaking off the song mid-chorus.

The band stopped and watched her warily. "Hey, Janis, calm . . . " one of the musicians began.

"Calm? Listen, man, when I'm out there singing, I'm the one, right? I don't need you guys upstaging me. It's my act, man, I'm the one they paid to see, dig?"

81

"Janis, oh Janis, we promise to be good boys," said the drummer with a broadly mock mollification that made her laugh.

"Okay, man, I'm sorry, too. I don't wanna be a bitch about it. But y'know, we got three"—she held up three fingers—"*three* weeks before we open in New York, and we don't have one tune really down." The tension was seeping out. "Let's start from the top." Her voice was a bit weary.

She's doing the hardest thing you can do—carrying a whole band on her shoulders, all the personalities, plus doing her own thing. But it's worth it. The benefits are mystical; it's a compulsion, nothing to do with logic. See, first and foremost, Janis is a blues singer. Think what that means. The tradition of hardship, tragedy, early death. Bessie Smith. Robert Johnson died at twenty-one. A blues singer isn't a performer, doesn't need an audience. Can sing to the ocean, the moon. Even when there are 10,000 people out there, there still might be no audience. But the blues sustain you. Blues are a faith in beauty and peace, coupled with extreme worldly knowledge; the ultimate decision is always positive.

—Nick Gravenites, blues guitarist-singer-
producer and Janis's friend.

"Oh, yeah, I'm scared," Janis had said earlier that afternoon. "I think, 'Oh, it's so close, can I make it?' If I fail, I'll fail in front of the whole world. If I miss, I'll never have a second chance on nothing. But I gotta risk it. I never hold back, man. I'm always on the outer limits of probability."

She put down her drink and pointed to a newspaper clipping on her kitchen wall, her answer to a reporter who stopped her one day to ask, "What are you doing with life?" "Getting stoned, staying happy, and having a good time," her answer read. "I'm doing just what I want with my life, enjoying it. I don't think you can ask more of life than that."

"My credo," Janis said laughing and looking suddenly like a little girl. "When I get scared and worried, I tell myself, 'Janis, just have a good time.' So I juice up real good and that's just what I have."

Go after good times and you'll have some bad times; but for Janis, anything is better than a life of average times, all the peaks cautiously leveled out for stability and longevity. "I have to be incredibly there, man. Whatever I do, I do a lot, and whatever it is, it's a damn sight better than being bored. Took a vacation when I thought it would be nice to do nothing after the road. Man, I just about went out of my head.

"Yeah, I know I might be going too fast. That's what a doctor said. He looked at me and said my liver is a little big, swollen, y'know? Got all melodramatic—'What's a good talented girl doing with yourself' and all that blah. I don't go back to him anymore. Man, I'd rather have ten years of super-hyper-most than live to be seventy by sitting in some goddam chair watching TV. Right now is where you are, how can you wait?"

Janis—such a strange, unsettled mix of defiance and hesitancy, vulnerability and strength—doesn't wait; every moment she is what she feels—mean or loving, up or down, stone sober or drunk out of her skull. The intensity makes her always magical, and makes radiant her unpretty face, with its too big nose, too wide mouth, and rough complexion. She consumes vast quantities of energy from some well inside herself that she believes is bottomless, and the heat of it warms everyone who meets her. When she sings, all that terrible energy is brutally compressed into the moment.

She sings jumping and dancing, her fists alternately clenching and breaking open to clap; the corners of her marvelous mouth turning down in the fierceness of joy breaking through anguish; her hair covering her eyes until swept back with a meaty hand. In great shouts that send her strings of beads flying and knot her face into grimaces, the energy explodes and

83

explodes again, sending out waves of electrical excitement. Some say she can sing more than one note at a time; maybe, but does it matter? In her every note there are infinite meanings.

Janis is a rock 'n' roll woman, perhaps the greatest that ever lived. There have been great woman singers of rock 'n' roll, but only a few have dared take full place in the essentially masculine world of rock stardom. Diana Ross, Martha of the Vandellas, Grace Slick, Tracy Nelson, and even Aretha Franklin are in the end female singers in the long "chantoosie" tradition; they can sing tough if they want to, but they never risk losing their essential femininity on or off stage. But Janis and a few of her sisters—Etta James, Little Eva, Sugar Pie DeSanto, Gladys Knight, and of course Big Mama Willie Mae Thornton (no one else white comes to mind except Mae West, a fine blues singer herself)—express their womanness with a raunchy boldness that is magnificently sexy though not one bit ladylike. Janis is a girl who has always wanted to be one of the guys, though she has always known she is a woman, and a tender one, inside. She has a masculine scorn for the politely devious wiles of acceptable femininity, yet losing a good man can break her heart. The ambiguity of brashness and softness is at the heart of her appeal; on stage, second to second, she is one and then the other, so you first glory in her strength and then want to reach out and soothe her sorrow.

Her almost inhuman devotion to the exploration of the moment has made her not just a star but the inamorata of the hip rock generation. She is not the symbol of its philosophy, but the thing itself: everything comes to those who don't wait. For the millions of kids who know that *now* is more important than the deferred gratification their parents and "the system" are pushing, Janis is the belle ideal.

"Everybody I know—" Janis says, "—what they're good at is being themselves. I've been doing it for twenty-six years, and all the people who were trying to compromise me are now coming to me, man. You better not compromise yourself, it's all you've got. And you don't have to, I'm a goddam living example of that.

"People aren't supposed to be like me, sing like me, ball like me, drink like me, live like me; but now they're paying me fifty thousand dollars a year for me to be like me. That's what I hope I mean to those kids out there. After they see me, when their mothers are feeding them all that cashmere sweater and girdle bullshit, maybe they'll have second thoughts—that they can be themselves and win. You just have to start thinking that way, being that righteous with yourself, and you've won already."

Janis has won big—not everyone trying to be themselves ends up a rock star—but it hasn't been luck. Sustaining the confidence to keep upright and moving without the support of patterned respectability demands a mixture of selfishness, cynicism, faith, and desperate yearning. Janis has them all, plus a rock-bottom toughness. Her toughness scares her; sometimes she'd give it all up to get the cozy love and life sweet girls get, but the time for that is long since past. "I guess it's lucky people like me as I am," she said, briefly disconsolate. "If they didn't, I wouldn't know how to change."

I guess I'm just like a turtle, hiding underneath its horny shell,
I guess I'm just like a turtle, hiding underneath its horny shell,
But you know I'm very well protected, I know this goddam life
    too well.

                —Janis Joplin, "Turtle Blues"

The oldest child of a refinery executive in the gulf town of Port Arthur, Janis is a Texas girl not cut out for Texas. "I always wanted to be an artist, whatever that was, like other chicks want to be stewardesses. Port Arthur people thought I was a beatnik, and they didn't like beatniks, though they'd never seen one and neither had I. I read, I painted, I thought, I didn't hate niggers. There was nobody like me in Port Arthur. It was lonely, those feelings welling up and nobody to talk to. I was just 'silly crazy Janis.' Man, those people hurt me. It makes me happy to know I'm making it and they're back there, plumbers just like they were."

85

Hearing Huddie Ledbetter (Leadbelly) records started her singing; a trip to Los Angeles's Venice showed her she wasn't the only beatnik in the world, and at the University of Texas in Austin she fell in with the folk-music beats who lived in a rundown apartment house dubbed the Ghetto.

"She was a wild girl," recalls Travis Rivers, a Texas friend who is now manager of an excellent rock group, Mother Earth. "One time a bunch of us went to some clip joint over in Louisiana, college kids with all the toughs. Janis started dancing with some of the toughs, they started pawing her, and she bashed one of 'em on the head with a bottle. Man, did that start a fight! We were lucky to get out with our lives."

Janis sang folk music of all kinds in those days, but got her local reputation as a blues singer. "Even then, if you heard her once, you never forgot her," said another Texas friend. She wrote a few songs, including "Turtle Blues." But while she's written a few more since, songwriting has never become a major concern. College didn't either; after a few terms she dropped out and for five years she drifted in the folk-beat world in Texas, New York, and finally San Francisco, singing when she could, getting odd jobs or unemployment compensation when she couldn't.

By 1965, after two years in San Francisco, it had strung her out; the years of hitchhiking, going hungry, too much drugs, and finally a dead-end romance had created a crushing burden. She ran back to Texas for a final try at being the teacher her parents wanted her to be. For a year she lived at home, dressed like a good Texas girl, and studied hard at the Lamar State College of Technology at Beaumont. Her family was happy, and her grades were good, but Janis was restless and edgy with the strain of being proper.

San Francisco, however scary, was by then her home. North Beach and the emergent hippie community in the Haight-Ashbury were filled with people like her, wild kids (many of them—musicians, particularly—from Texas) who had broken out of small towns. Like a new kind of frontiersmen, looking for psychic space and adventure, they moved west to a city traditionally the last haven for American outcasts, bringing with them a good-humored vitality, a backwoods taste for the bizarre, and an uncouth and ribald sophistication.

Those kids in 1965–66 were discovering rock 'n' roll, learning happily that, with a few freaky injections, rock could be the perfect expression-celebration of their community life style. One mover in the trend was Chet Helms, a displaced Texan who as head of the Family Dog put on San Francisco's first hippie-rock dances and ran the "psychedelic" Avalon ballroom. Helms also encouraged the founding of a band called Big Brother and the Holding Company, which became the Avalon's unofficial house band.

Helms was an old friend and hitchhiking pal of Janis's from their Austin days; when Travis Rivers, also a friend of Helms, got to San Francisco and heard Big Brother, he knew that Janis would be perfect for them, and that this new rock would be perfect for her. He convinced Helms and in the spring of 1966 went back to Texas and told Janis about the music and the new scene; without one look back she quit Lamar State College, left her family, and drove with Rivers back to the Haight.

Plunged without introduction into the crazily vibrant world of music, posters, and LSD, she sang her first dance in June 1966. "All the Avalon regulars used to stand at the back not listening to the music and playing it cool," remembers one who was there, "but Janis sang one note, and they dropped their drinks and flocked to the front."

"It was the most thrilling time in my life," Janis recalls. "I mean, I had never seen a hippie dance before, man, and then I was up there in the middle of one. I couldn't believe it, all that rhythm and power. I got stoned just feeling it, like it was the best dope in the world. It was so sensual, so vibrant, loud, crazy! I couldn't stay still; I had never danced when I sang, just the old sit-and-pluck blues thing, but there I was moving and jumping. I couldn't hear myself, so I sang louder and louder; by the end I was wild."

The wildness was contagious. With her, Big Brother—until then fairly low in the city's rock pecking order—moved into the Big Three with the Jefferson Airplane and the Grateful Dead. The word of "the band with the

87

incredible chick singer"—white girl singers were then a very rare commodity in rock—spread quickly. When Janis moaned the last notes of Big Mama Willie Mae Thornton's "Ball and Chain" at the Monterey Pop Festival in June 1967, the stunned audience suddenly went berserk, and Janis, insane with joy, sweat dripping through the open lace of her clinging gold knit pant suit, was big time.

She's a very sweet little girl. I think of her as my sister, and I love her. Everybody who's ever known Janis loves her. They have to, and she needs it. Her problem is, that she knows she's good, but she can't really believe it, so she's reaching out all the time. A very human thing to do.

—Powell St. John, Austin friend formerly with the band Mother Earth.

"I can't talk about my singing, I'm inside of it. How can you describe something you're inside of. I can't know what I'm doing; if I knew it, I'd have lost it. When I sing, I feel, oh, I feel, well, like when you're first in love. It's more than sex, I know that. It's that point two people can get to they call love, like when you really touch someone for the first time, but it's gigantic, multiplied by the whole audience. I feel chills, weird feelings slipping all over my body, it's a supreme emotional and physical experience." Janis paused briefly. "I read a story about some old opera singer once, and when a guy asked her to marry him, she took him backstage after she had sung a real triumph, with all the people calling for her, made him see what it was like, then asked, 'Do you think you could give me that?' That story hit me right, man. I know no guy ever made me feel as good as an audience. I'm really far into this now, really committed. Like, I don't think I'd go off the road for love now, for life with a guy no matter how good. Yeah, it's the truth. Scary thing to say, though, isn't it?"

She shuddered at the unpleasant thought, then, looking down at her feet, gave a squeal of delight. "You dig my gold shoes?"—lifting one high— "I love 'em. I love wearing gold shoes, it's like a breakthrough. It demands a whole kind of attitude for a chick to wear gold shoes. I went down to I. Magnin's one day, man, and was sitting in the shoe place with all these chic, modely girls and all these chic, modely shoes, and I bought two pairs of gold sandals. It was a very strong thing, a very affirmative trip. Maybe only girls would understand, but it felt almost as good as singing."

Janis was in her apartment, a cramped four-roomer high on a hill in the Mission District. She and her roommate Linda, a strikingly handsome dark-haired girl who prefers to be last name–less, have decorated it with a loving carelessness, covering walls with posters and photographs and cartoons, the floor with Oriental rugs, and every available space with Victoriana and assorted bric-a-brac, including Charlie (the Siamese fighting fish in a wine bottle), Gabriel (the waist-high statue of a penis), and George (Janis's dog and best friend). Fittingly, most care has been lavished on Janis's bedroom, which, swathed in Indian canopies, scented by incense, and lit by bulbs with purple flowers as filaments, has a romantic bordello ambience.

Working with the new band has meant two solid months in San Francisco, and Janis likes that. She gets to make her own brown rice and salads (she's proudly dieted off fifteen pounds); shops; tools around in her Porsche, which a friend painted like a flowing mural of the universe, with rainbows, astrological signs, a bloody American flag, and Big Brother included; sees old friends; gets free drinks at the Coffee Gallery on Grant Avenue (a hangout since her North Beach days); and parties until she can't stand up anymore. Linda makes her more new clothes, and her gentle seriousness has a calming, restful effect on Janis.

The last time Janis really lived in San Francisco was over a year ago. She lived in the Haight, had a listed phone number, and was only starting to become a star. Now the city, her apartment, and friends are like a retreat, her only real world.

"The whole success thing has been weird," she said. "I had never said, 'I am a singer.' I was just Janis; singing was something groovy I could do without compromising myself. But now I look around after the violent changes I've been through in the last year, and I see how surreal it's gotten.

"See the *Playboy* poll? Best chick singers: Aretha Franklin, Dionne Warwick, then me. Too much! Flying around in airplanes, kids screaming, a lot of money and people buying me drinks. I can understand $100, but not $10,000. Money was always what I had in my pocket. What's that stuff in the banks?

"There's a fantasy at work that can suddenly click in. Like I went to this neighborhood fish store, and the girl at the counter said, 'Aren't you somebody, that singer, that . . . ' and then she got red and started babbling about how she went to Las Vegas and L.A. and she never saw anybody and now right in her store, et cetera, and it was *me* she was talking about! Or like making it at the Newport Folk Festival. Back in Texas I was always looking for somebody to hitch with me to it, and last year, the first time I go, Janis is the star. I dug it, man.

"That fur coat, too. Know how I got that? Southern Comfort! Far out! I had Miriam, the lady in my manager's office, photostat every goddam clipping that ever had me mentioning Southern Comfort, and I sent them to the company, and they sent me a whole lotta money. How could anybody in their right mind want *me* for their image? Oh man, that was the best hustle I ever pulled—can you imagine getting paid for passing out for two years?"

By this time she was laughing so hard that she was jumping up and down, but in a minute she had subsided enough to start rapping again—Janis in full swing is one of the great, all-time word-tumbling-on-word rappers.

"'Course there's reality, too. Fantasy and reality, that's how I see things. That's why I called my company—a company, dig that, man—Fantality, to get both in. Reality is cold dressing rooms, lousy food, sitting alone in motel rooms having to watch TV, stewardesses and people on airplanes treating you like a freak, lousy halls and bad sound, playing for people you don't feel you can relate to, people out there in Kokomo who just look at you, at your outsides, like, curious. Guys on the road at least have girls they can pick up, but who are the boys who come to see me—thirteen years old, man."

Go on the road, she said, and the only thing that can keep you going is the music. The rap slowed down; she had to explain why she left Big Brother, and that was hard.

Long before it happened, the breakup had been no secret and, in fact, had been considered inevitable. From Monterey onward Janis was increasingly singled out until promoters were advertising "Janis Joplin with Big Brother and the Holding Company." Reviewers lauded Janis consistently and had put down the band almost as consistently. The band, many said, was not good enough for her and she was wasting energy pulling them along. On record, without the electricity of live performance, the group sounded amateurish. But the band, which had more drive and originality than they were given credit for, didn't want to be her backing group. Janis, insecure about her own position and ambitions, thought they were trying to make her feel guilty for having more talent. Fights, at first discreet, broke out in dressing rooms and then on stage; the very fact of uncontrollable fighting, which seemed a failure of the whole hip spirit, added to the bitterness.

"It was a very sad thing, man," Janis said. "I love those guys more than anybody else in the whole world; they know that. But if I had any serious idea of myself as a musician, I had to leave. Getting off, real feeling, like Otis Redding had, like Tina Turner, that's the whole thing of music for me.

"But by the end we were shucking. We worked four, six nights a week for two years, man, doing the same tunes, and we'd put everything into them we could. I was jumping and dancing and all, but I was lying, and I'd go off stage and feel like the world's biggest bullshitter. I don't mind selling pleasure if people want to pay for it, but who wants to get paid ten grand for acting like you're having a good time? That's shameful, and I saw it before the band saw it. That's what happened."

"The shucking thing, that's her judgment," says Peter Albin, Big Brother's bass player, but otherwise, he sees much the same picture: the claustrophobic effects of long tours with no rehearsal time, delivering the formula songs the audience demanded. "Janis was the best musician; she could experiment on stage; we needed time and rest to do new things. So for us it got to the point where all we wanted to do was play our tunes and split the stage.

"It was a hard time," Albin says. "For a while there, for us all even being in the same room was a total stone drag. But after we knew it was over, it started to get good again, and now all of us are working hard and moving."

It was another evening back at rehearsal and worries. The whole process of assembling a new band had been frustrating; Janis had help—her manager, Albert Grossman, the sharp-eyed grandfather of new rock management, collected and auditioned some of the musicians, and Nick Gravenites and guitarist Mike Bloomfield suggested arrangements and worked the band into shape—but the pressure was on her.

A few days before their first date (not counting the disappointing preview at the Stax-Volt Christmas Show in Memphis) they didn't even have a name. Janis and Charlie, Janis Joplin Blues Church, Janis Joplin's Pleasure Principle, even Janis Joplin and the Sordid Flavors—nothing was quite right.

But that was minor. First the organ player got drafted. Another was found and then the trumpet player left. The new musicians had to learn everything from scratch while the others tried to think of new ideas, what riffs to use, where to put vocal backups, how to get drama into each song, how to vary beginnings and endings. New material had to be found; old material, like "Ball and Chain," had to be reworked to set it off from Big Brother's versions.

And Janis was trying to work on her voice, but she was recovering from her twenty-sixth birthday party ("Me and Linda and two guys for two days, man, best party I ever had"). "I've been as much a folk hero as a singer so far," she said as the musicians were tuning up.

"I wanna sing now. I'm exciting, but I'm not too subtle yet. Those people who say I'm like Billie Holiday—man, I'm nowhere near her; hear her once and you know that. But my voice is getting better. People like to say I'm ruining it. Maybe it's getting rougher, but I still can reach all the notes I ever could. I don't know how long it will last. As long as *I* do, probably."

"Hey, Janis, what should we start with?" asked drummer Roy Markowitz.

"Nick's tune, okay?" There was general assent. The room was so cold they could see their breath.

Markowitz called the beat, the organist started with some quick chords, the bass came in, then the drums, the sax and trumpet.

"As good as you've been to the whole wide world, baby, as good ... " Janis sang, her heels doing little hops, her mouth almost biting the mike. Then she cut it off. Something was wrong, she said, and the others agreed, and they all suggested changes—an added chorus here, a tighter bass line, the drums a little flashier to start the ending crescendo.

They started again. Two more false starts, and then it was right, the beginning slow, then getting intense; the middle softer but still holding the new level of intensity until it broke away into the finale.

"That's how good I'm gonna be to you," Janis shouted, working as hard as she ever worked on stage for the empty attic. The music was like a river, cushioning her, carrying her, pushing her on. George, the dog, got up from his sleep and started to moan and uncannily he seemed to blend in.

"As good as you've been, as good as you've been,"—bam, bam, bam from the trumpet and sax—"oh baby, I'm gonna be just that good, oh so good to you!" Bam-bam-bam-ba-ba-ba-aaaAPP! went the band, and the song was over.

The Grateful Dead on the steps of 710 Ashbury Street. Standing, left to right: Bill Kreutzmann, Jerry Garcia, Ron "Pigpen" McKernan, Bob Weir; seated, left to right, managers Rock Skully and Danny Rifkin, and Phil Lesh. 1969. © Baron Wolman

7

THE GRATEFUL DEAD

1969

When the news came in August 1995 that Jerry Garcia had died at fifty-three of illnesses caused by years of heroin addiction, I and several generations of Deadheads felt shocked and saddened. We had all known that Jerry and his bandmates enjoyed taking wild risks with LSD and other drugs, but the overall effect of their experimenting, as I had seen it back in 1969, was healthy, youthful adventuring. Jerry was such a cheery, affectionate fellow who gave off a palpable glow of good vibes. How could my Jerry—everybody's Jerry—have been giving such encouragement to musicians, fans, and total strangers while simultaneously destroying himself?

I have no answer to the question. I knew Jerry briefly and then only as a reporter, following him and the band with a notepad in my hand. When he died, I hadn't seen him or listened to the Grateful Dead for over twenty years. I can only wish in vain that somehow he could have turned his own good vibes onto himself in time to save his life.

But I do know this: Jerry Garcia had a most positive effect on my life and the lives of millions. Jerry knew he had extraordinary talent—how could he not know?—but music for him was a universal force that anyone and everyone could share. When I confessed to him my own musical hopes, his instant, smiling response was, "Yeah, man, do it! Whatever I am doing, you can do it too!" Thank you, Jerry Garcia, and wherever you are today, God bless you.

> But I reckon I got to light out for the Territory ahead of the
> rest, because Aunt Sally she's going to adopt me and sivilize me
> and I can't stand it. I been there before.
>
> —Mark Twain, *Huckleberry Finn*

The Grateful Dead didn't get it going Wednesday night at Winterland, and that was too bad. The gig was a bail fund benefit for the People's Park in Berkeley, and the giant ice-skating cavern was packed with heads. The whole park hassle—the benefit was for the 450 busted a few days earlier—had been a Berkeley political trip all the way down, but the issue was a good-timey park, so the crowd, though older and more radical than most San Francisco rock crowds, was a fine one, in a good dancing mood, watery mouths waiting for the groove to come. The Jefferson Airplane were on the bill too; so were Santana, the Ace of Cups, Aum, and a few others. It was a San Francisco all-star night, the bands making homegrown music for homegrown folks gathered for a homegrown cause.

But the Dead stumbled that night. They led off with a warm-up tune that they did neatly enough, and the crowd, swarmed in luminescent darkness, sent up "good old Grateful Dead, we're so glad you're here" vibrations. The band didn't catch them. Maybe they were a bit tired of being taken for granted as surefire deliverers of good vibes, drained by constant expectations. Or they might have been cynical: a benefit for those Berkeley dudes who finally learned what a park is but are still hung up on confrontation and cops and bricks and spokesmen giving TV interviews and all that bullshit. The Dead were glad to do it, but it was one more benefit to bail out the politicos.

Maybe they were too stoned on one of the Bear's custom-brewed elixirs, or maybe the long meeting that afternoon—with the usual fights about salaries and debt priorities and travel plans for the upcoming tour that they'd be making without a road manager, and all the work of being, in the end, a rock 'n' roll band—had left them pissed off. After abortive stabs at "Doing That Rag" and "St. Stephen," they fell into "Lovelight" as a last resort, putting Ron "Pigpen" McKernan out in front to lay on his special brand of oily rag pig-ism while they funked around behind. It usually works; but not this night. Mickey Hart and Bill Kreutzman, the drummers, couldn't find anything to settle on, and the others kept trying ways out of the mess, only to create new tangles of bumpy rhythms and dislocated melodies. For the briefest of seconds a nice phrase would pop out, and the crowd would cheer, thinking maybe this was it, but before the cheer died, the moment had also perished.

After about twenty minutes they decided to call it quits, ended with a long building crescendo, topping that with a belching cannon blast (which fell right on the beat, the only luck they found that night), and split the stage. "But, y'know, I dug it, man," said Jerry Garcia the next night. "I can get behind falling to pieces before an audience sometimes. We're not performers; we are who we are for those moments we're before the public, and that's not always at the peak."

He was backstage at the Robertson Gymnasium at the University of California at Santa Barbara, backstage being a curtained-off quarter of the gym, the other three quarters being stage and crowd. His red solid body Gibson, with its "Red, White, and Blue Power" sticker was in place across his belly and he caressed/played it without stopping. Rock Scully, their manager was scrunched in a corner dispensing Tequila complete with salt and lemon to the band and all comers—particularly to bassist Phil Lesh who left his Eurasian groupie alone and forlorn every time he dashed back to the bottle.

"Sure, I'll fuck up for an audience," said Mickey from behind his sardonic beard, bowing. "My pleasure, we'll take you as low and mean as you want to go."

"See, it's like good and evil," Jerry went on, his yellow glasses glinting above his eager smile. "They exist together in their little game, each with its special place and special humors. I dig 'em both. What is life but being conscious? And good and evil are manifestations of consciousness. If you reject one, you're not getting the whole thing that's there to be had. So I had a good time last night."

His good humor was enormous, even though it had been a bitch of a day. The travel agent had given them the wrong flight time and, being one day before the Memorial Day weekend, there was no space on any other flight for all fourteen of them. So they had hustled over to National Rent a Car, gotten two matched Pontiacs and driven the 350 miles down the coast. Phil drove one, and since he didn't have his license and had six stoned backseat drivers for company, he had gotten pretty paranoid. The promoter, a slick Hollywood type, had told them at five in the afternoon that he wouldn't let them set up their own P.A. "If it's good enough for Lee Michaels, it's good enough for you," he said, and they were too tired to fight it.

The Bear, who handles the sound system as well as the chemicals, was out of it anyway. When the band got to the gym, he was flat on his back, curled up among the drum cases. Phil shook him to his feet and asked if there was anything he could do, but Bear's pale eyes were as sightless as fog. By that time the emcee was announcing them. With a final "Fuck it, man," they trouped up to the stage through the massed groupies.

Robertson Gym stank like every gym in history. The light show, the big-name band, and the hippie ambience faded before that smell, unchanged since the days when the student council hung a few million paper snowflakes from the ceiling and tried to pass it off as Winter Wonderland. Now it was Psychedelic Wonderland, but the potent spirits of long departed sweat socks still owned the place. That was okay—another rock 'n' roll dance in the old school gym.

They brought out "Lovelight" again; this time the groove was there, and for forty minutes they laid it down, working hard and getting that bob-and-weave interplay of seven-man improvisation that can take you right out of your head. But Jerry kept looking more and more pained, then suddenly signaled to bring it to a close. They did, abruptly, and Jerry stepped to a mike.

"Sorry, he shouted, "but we're gonna split for a while and set up our own P.A. so we can hear what the fuck is happening." He ripped his cord out of his amp and walked off. Rock took charge.

"The Dead will be back, folks, so everybody go outside, take off your clothes, cool down, and come back. This was just an introduction."

Backstage was a brawl. "We should give the money back if we don't do it righteous," Jerry was shouting. "Where's Bear?"

Bear wandered over, still lost in some intercerebral space.

"Listen, man, are you in this group, are you one of us?" Jerry screamed, "Are you gonna set up that P.A.? Their monitors suck. I can't hear a goddam thing out there. How can I play if I can't hear the drums?"

Bear mumbled something about taking two hours to set up the P.A., then wandered off. Rock was explaining to the knot of curious onlookers.

"This is the Grateful Dead, man; we play with twice the intensity of anybody else; we gotta have our own system. The promoter screwed us, and we tried to make it, but we just can't. It's gotta be our way, man."

Ramrod and the other quippies were already dismantling the original P.A.

"Let's just go ahead," said Pigpen. "I can fake it."

"I can't," said Jerry.

"It's your decision," said Pigpen.

"Yeah," said Phil. "If you and nobody else gives a good goddam."

But it was all over. Bear had disappeared, the original P.A. was gone, someone had turned up the houselights, and the audience was melting away. A good night, a potentially great night had been shot by a combination of promoter burn and Dead incompetence, and at 1:00 A.M. it didn't matter who was to blame or where it had started to go wrong. It was too far gone to save that night.

"We're really sorry," Phil kept saying to the few who still lingered by the gym's back door. "We burned you of a night of music, and we'll come back and make it up."

"If we dare show our faces in this town again," said rhythm guitarist Bob Weir as they walked to the cars. The others laughed, but it wasn't really funny. They rode back to the Ocean Palms Motel in near silence.

"When we missed that plane we should have known," said Bill Kreutzmann. "An ill-advised trip."

Jerry said it was more than that. They took the date because their new manager, Lenny Hart, Mickey's father, while new at the job, had accepted it from Bill Graham. The group had already decided to leave Millard, Graham's booking agency, and didn't want anymore of his jobs, but went ahead with it rather than making Hart go back on his word.

"That's the lesson: take a gig to save face, and you end up with a shitty P.A. and a well-burned audience."

"Show biz, that's what it was tonight," Mickey Hart said softly, "and show biz is the shits."

The others nodded and the car fell silent. Road markers flicked by the car in solemn procession as the mist rolled in off the muffled ocean.

It's now five years since the acid tests, the first Family Dog dances, the Mime Troupe benefits, and the Trips Festival; almost the same since Donovan sang about flying Jefferson Airplane and a London discotheque called Sibylla's became the in club because it had the first light show in Europe; three years since the Human Be-In, since *Newsweek* and then the nation discovered the Haight-Ashbury, hippies, and "the San Francisco Sound." The Monterey Pop Festival, which confirmed and culminated the insanely explosive spring of 1967, is now two years gone. The biggest rock 'n' roll event of its time, that three-day weekend marked the beginning of a new era. The Beatles (who sent their regards), the Stones, Dylan, even the Beach Boys—the giants who had opened things up from 1963 to '67—were all absent, and the stage was open for the first generation of the still continuing rock profusion.

Though Monterey was, significantly, conceived in and directed from Los Angeles, its inspiration, style, and much of its substance was San Francisco's. The quantum of energy that pushed rock 'n' roll to the level on which it resided until the time of Woodstock had come from San Francisco.

The city, once absurdly overrated, is now underrated. The process of absorption has been so smoothly quick that it is hard to remember when it was all new, when Wes Wilson posters were appearing fresh every week, when Owsley acid was not just a legend or mythical standard, when only real freaks had hair down past their shoulders, when forty-minute songs were revolutionary, and when a dance was not a concert but a stoned-out bacchanal. But it was real; had it not been so vital it would not have been so quickly universalized. After 1966 rock 'n' roll came to San Francisco like the mountain to Mohammed. Its only two rivals have been Memphis and Nashville—like San Francisco, small cities with local musicians who, relatively isolated (by choice), are creating distinctive music that expresses their own and their cities' lifestyles. Musicians everywhere have been drawn to both the music and ambience of the three cities, just as jazzmen were once drawn to New Orleans, St. Louis, and Kansas City. Rock 'n' roll has always been regional music on the lower levels, but success, as much for the Beatles and Dylan as for Elvis or James Brown, always meant going to the big city, to the music industry machine. That machine, whether in London, New York, or Los Angeles, dictated that the rock 'n' roll life was a remote one of stardom which, with a complex structure of fan mags and fan clubs, personal aides, publicity men, limited tours, and carefully spaced singles, controlled the stars' availability to the public for maximum titillation and maximum profit. The fan identified with his stars (idols), but across an uncrossable chasm. The machine also tended either to downplay the regional characteristics of a style or exaggerate them into a gimmick. A lucky or tough artist might keep his musical roots intact, but few were able to transfer the closeness they had with their first audience to their mass audience. To be a rock 'n' roll star, went the unwritten law, you had to go downtown.

San Francisco's major contribution to rock was the flaunting of that rule. The Beatles had really started it; on one hand the most isolated and revered group, they were also the most personal; you knew the image, of course, not the real them, but the image was lively and changing. The same is true for Dylan, but San Francisco made it real. The early days at the Fillmore and Avalon were not unlike the months that the Rolling Stones played the Crawdaddy Club in Richmond, but for the first time there was the hope that those days would never have to end. The one-to-one performer-audience relationship was what the music was about. San Francisco's secret was not the dancing, the light shows, the posters, the long sets, or the complete lack of stage act, but the idea that all of them together were the creation and recreation of a community. Everybody did their thing and all things were equal. The city had a hip community, one of bizarrely various people who all on their own had decided that they'd have to find their own way through the universe; the old ways wouldn't work anymore.

In that community everybody looked like a rock star, and rock stars began to look and act and live like people, not gods on the make. The way to go big time was to encourage more people to join the community or to make their own; not to enlarge oneself out of it into the machine's big time. San Francisco said that rock 'n' roll could be making your own music for your friends—folk music in a special sense.

Sort of; because it didn't really work. Dances did become concerts, groups eagerly signed with big record companies from L.A. to New York; did do long tours; did get promo men, secluded retreats, and Top 40 singles; and did become stars. Thousands took up the trappings of community with none of its spirit; the community itself lost hope and direction, fought bitterly within itself, and scattered. San Francisco had not been deserted for the machine as Liverpool had been, but the machine managed to make San Francisco an outpost of itself. Janis Joplin is still the city's one superstar, but the unity of the musical-social community has effectively been broken; musicians play for pay, audiences pay to listen. There is now a rock musician's community that is international, and it is closer to the audience community than ever before in rock's history, but the San Francisco vision has died, or at least hibernated, unfulfilled.

There are many reasons: bad and/or greedy management, the swamping effect of sudden success, desperation, lack of viable alternatives, and the combined flatteries of fame, money, and ridiculous adulation on young egos. But the central reason is that rock is not folk music in that special sense. The machine, with all its flashy fraudulences, is not a foreign growth on rock, but its very essence. One cannot be a good rock musician and either psychically or in fact be an amateur, because professionalism is part of the term's definition. Rock 'n' roll, rather than some other art, became the prime expression of that community because it was, machine and all, a miracle beauty of American mass production, a mythic past, a global fantasy, an instantaneous communications network, and a maker of superheroes. There's no way to combine wanting that and wanting "just folks," too.

The excitement of San Francisco was the attempt to synthesize these two contradictory positions. To pull it off would have been a revolution; at best, San Francisco made a reform. In the long haul its creators, tired of fighting the paradox, chose modified rock over folk music.

All except the Grateful Dead, who've been battling it out with that mother of a paradox for years. Sometimes they lose, sometimes they win.

> True fellowship among men must be based upon a concern that
> is universal. It is not the private interests of the individual that
> create lasting fellowship among men, but rather the goals of
> humanity.
> . . . If unity of this kind prevails, even difficult and danger-
> ous tasks, such as crossing the great water, can be accomplished.
> —The *I Ching*, 13th hexagram: "Fellowship with Men"

The Grateful Dead are not the original San Francisco band—the Charlatans, the Great Society, and the Airplane all predate them, even in their Warlocks stage—and whether they are the best, whatever that would mean, is irrelevant. Probably they are the loudest—someone once described them as "living thunder." Certainly they are the weirdest—black satanic weird and white archangel weird. As weird as anything you can imagine, like some horror comic monster who besides being green and slimy happens also to have seven different heads, a 190 IQ, countless decibels of liquid fire noise communication, and is coming right down to where you are to gobble you up. But if you can dig the monster, bammo, he's a giant puppy to play with. Grateful Dead—weird, ultimately, and what an image that name is. John Lennon joked about the flaming hand that made them the Beatles, but Jerry Garcia is serious: "Back in the late days of the Acid Tests, we were looking for a name. We'd abandoned the Warlocks; it didn't fit anymore. One day we were all over at Phil's house smoking DMT. He had a big Oxford dictionary, I opened it, and there was 'grateful dead,' those words juxtaposed. It was one of those moments, y'know, like everything else on the page went blank, diffuse, just sorta oozed away, and there was GRATEFUL DEAD, big black letters edged all around in gold, man, blasting out at me, such a stunning combination. So I said, 'How about Grateful Dead?' and that was it."

The image still resonates for the Dead; they are, or desire to become, the grateful dead. Grateful Dead may mean whatever you like it to mean: life-in-death, ego death, reincarnation, the joy of the mystic vision. Maybe it is artist Rick Griffin's grinning skull balancing on the axis of an organic universe that is the cover of *Aoxomoxoa*, their third record. It doesn't matter how you read it, for the Dead, as people, musicians, and a group are in that place where the meanings of a name or event can be as infinite as the imagination, and yet mean precisely what they are and no more.

In the beginning they were nothing spectacular, just another rock 'n' roll band made up of suburban ex-folkies who, in 1964 and 1965, with Kennedy dead, the civil rights movement split into black and white, Vietnam taking over from ban-the-bomb, and with the Beatles, Stones, and

Dylan, were finding out that the sit-and-pluck number had run its course. Jerry had gone the whole route: digging rock in the mid-fifties, dropping into folk by 1959, getting deep into traditional country music as a purist scholar, reemerging as a brilliant bluegrass banjo player, and then, in 1964, starting Mother McCree's Uptown Jug Champions with Pigpen and Bob Weir. Pigpen is the son of an early white rhythm-and-blues disc jockey, and from his early teens had made the "spade" scene, playing harp and piano at parties, digging Lightning Hopkins, and nursing a remarkable talent for spinning out juiced blues raps. Bob Weir had skipped from boarding school to boarding school before quitting entirely, and got his real education doing folk gigs and lying about his age. "I was seventeen," he says, "looked fifteen, and said I was twenty-one." All three were misfits; Jerry had dropped out of high school to join the army, which kicked him out after a few months as unfit for service. "How true, how true," he says now.

But the Jug Champions couldn't get any gigs, and when a Palo Alto music store owner offered to front them with equipment to start a rock band, they said yes. Bill Kreutzmann, then Bill Sommers to fit his fake ID, became the drummer. A fan of rhythm-and-blues stylists, he was the only one with rock experience. At first the music store man's son was the bass player, but concurrently Phil Lesh, an old friend of Jerry's, was coming to a dead end in formal electronic music, finding less and less to say and fewer people to say it to. A child violinist, then a Stan Kenton–style jazz trumpeter and arranger, Phil went to a Warlocks gig on impulse and the group knocked him out. "Jerry came over to where I was sitting and said, 'Guess what, you're gonna be our bass player.' I had never played bass, but I learned sort of, and in July, 1965, the five of us played our first gig, some club in Fremont."

For about six months the Warlocks were a straight rock 'n' roll band; but no longer. "The only scene then was the Hollywood hype scene; booking agents in flashy suits, gigs in booze clubs, six nights a week, five sets a night, doing R and B rock standards. We did it all," Jerry recalls. "Then we got a regular job at a Belmont club, and developed a whole malicious thing, playing songs longer and weirder, and louder, man. For those days it was loud, and for a bar it was ridiculous. People had to scream at each other to talk, and pretty soon we had driven out all the regular clientele. They'd run out clutching their ears. We isolated them, put 'em through a real number, yeah."

The only people who dug it were the "heads" around Ken Kesey up at his place in La Honda. All the Warlocks had taken acid ("We were already on the crazy-eyed fanatic trip," says Bob Weir), and, given dozens of mutual friends, it was inevitable that the Warlocks would play at La Honda. There they began again.

"One day the idea was there," Jerry remembers. "Why don't we have a big party and you guys bring your instruments and play, and us Merry Pranksters will set up all our tape recorders and bullshit, and we'll all get stoned. That was the first acid test. The idea was of its essence formless. There was nothin' going on. We'd just go up there and make something of it. Right away we dropped completely out of the straight music scene and just played the tests. Six months; San Francisco, Muir Beach, Trips Festival, then L.A."

Jerry strained to describe what those days were like, because, just as it says in Tom Wolfe's *Electric Kool-Aid Acid Test*, the Dead got on the bus, and made that irrevocable decision that the only place to go was further into the land of infinite recession that acid opened up. They were not to be psychedelic dabblers, painting pretty pictures, but true explorers. "And just how far would you like to go in?" Frank asks the three kings on the back of Bob Dylan's *John Wesley Harding*. "Not too far but just far enough so's we can say that we've been there," answer the kings. Far enough for most, but not for the Dead; they decided to try and cross the great water and bring back the good news from the other side.

Jerry continued:

> What the Kesey thing was depended on who you were when
> you were there. It was open, a tapestry, a mandala—it was

whatever you made it. Okay, so you take LSD and suddenly you are aware of another plane, or several other planes, and the quest is to extend that limit, to go as far as you can go. In the acid tests that meant to do away with old forms, with old ideas, try something new.

When it was moving right, you could dig that there was something that it was getting toward, something like ordered chaos, or some region of chaos. The test would start off and then there would be chaos. Everybody would be high and flashing and going through insane changes during which everything would be demolished, man, and spilled and broken and affected, and after that, another thing would happen, maybe smoothing out the chaos, then another, and it'd go all night till morning.

Just people being there, and being responsive. Like, there were microphones all over. If you were wandering around there would be a mike you could talk into. And there would be somebody somewhere else in the building at the end of some wire with a tape recorder and a mixing board and earphones listening in on the mikes and all of a sudden something would come in and he'd turn it up because it seemed appropriate at that moment.

What you said might come out a minute later on a tape loop in some other part of the place. So there would be this odd interchange going on, electroneural connections of weird sorts. And it was people, just people, doing it all. Kesey would be writing messages about what he was seeing on an opaque projector and they'd be projected up on the wall, and someone would comment about it on a mike somewhere and that would be singing out of a speaker somewhere else.

And we'd be playing, or, when we were playing we were playing. When we weren't, we'd be doing other stuff. There were no sets, sometimes we'd get up and play for ten minutes and all freak out and split. We'd just do it however it would happen. It wasn't a gig, it was the acid tests, where anything was okay. Thousands of people, man, all helplessly stoned, all finding themselves in a roomful of other thousands of people, none of whom any of them were afraid of. It was magic, far out, beautiful magic.

Since then the search for that magic has been as important for the Dead as music—or rather, music for the Dead has to capture that magic. All of them share the vision to one degree or another, but its source is essentially Jerry Garcia. "Fellowship with man" stresses the need of "a persevering and enlightened leader . . . a man with clear, convincing and inspired aims, and the strength to carry them out." Some call Jerry a guru, but that doesn't mean much; he is just one of those extraordinary human beings who looks you right in the eyes, smiles encouragement, and waits for you to become yourself. He can be vain, self-assertive, and even pompous, but he doesn't fool around with false apology. More than anything else he is cheery; mordant and ironic at times, but undauntedly optimistic. Probably ugly as a kid—lumpy, fat-faced, and frizzy haired—he is now beautiful, his trimmed hair and beard a dense black aureole around his beaming eyes.

Phil Lesh, Jerry's more explosive and dogmatic other half, comes right out and says that the Grateful Dead "are trying to save the world," but Jerry is more cautious: "We are trying to make things groovier for everybody so more people can feel better more often, to advance the trip, to get higher, however you want to say it, but we're musicians, and there's just no way to put that idea, 'save the world,' into music; you can only *be* that idea, or at least make manifest that idea as it appears to you, and hope maybe others follow. And that idea comes to you only moment by moment, so what we're going after is no farther away than the end of our noses. We're just trying to be right behind our noses.

"My way is music. Music is me being me and trying to get higher. I've been into music so long that I'm dripping with it; it's all I ever expect to do. I can't do anything else. Music is a yoga, something you really do when you're doing it. Thinking about what it means comes after the fact and isn't very interesting. Truth is something you stumble into when you think you're going someplace else, like those moments when you're playing and the whole room becomes one being; precious moments, man. But you can't look for them and they can't be repeated. Being alive means to continue to change, never to be where I was before. Music is the timeless experience of constant change."

Musical idioms and styles are important to Jerry as suggestive modes and historical fact, but they are not music, and he sees no need for them to be limiting to the modern musician or listener. "You have to get past the idea that music has to be one thing. To be alive in America is to hear all kinds of music constantly—radio, records, churches, cats on the street, everywhere music, man. And with records, the whole history of music is open to everyone who wants to hear it. Maybe Chuck Berry was the first rock musician because he was one of the first blues cats to listen to records, so he wasn't locked into the blues idiom. Nobody has to fool around with musty old scores, weird notation, and scholarship bullshit; you can just go into a record store and pick a century, pick a country, pick anything, and dig it, make it a part of you, add it to the stuff you carry around, and see that it's all music."

The Dead, like many modern groups, live that synthesis, but the members' past experience encompasses a breadth of idiom unmatched by any other comparable band. Electronic music of all sorts, accidental music, classical music, Indian music, jazz, folk, country and western, blues, and rock itself—one or all of the Dead have worked in these forms. In mixing all of them they make Grateful Dead music, music beyond idiom, which makes it difficult for some whose criteria for musical greatness allow only individual expression developed through disciplined understanding of a single accepted idiom. A Dead song is likely to include Jerry's country and western guitar licks over Bill and Mickey's 11/4 time, with the others making more muted solo statements, the whole thing subtly orchestrated by an extended, almost symphonic, blending of themes. Whatever it is, Jerry doesn't like to call it rock 'n' roll—"a label," he says—but it *is* rock; free, daring music that makes the good times roll, that can, if you listen, deliver you from the days of old.

It works because the Dead are, like few bands, a group tried and true. Five have been performing together for four years; Tom Constanten, though he only joined the group full-time last year because of an Air Force hitch, has been with them from the beginning. Mickey, a jazz drummer leading the straight life until two years ago, joined because Dead music was his music. After meeting Bill and jamming with him twice, he asked to join a set at the Straight Theater: "We played 'Alligator' for two hours, man, and my mind was blown. When we finished and the crowd went wild, Jerry came over and embraced me, and I embraced him, and it's been like that ever since."

The Dead have had endless personal crises; Pigpen and Bob Weir have particularly resisted the others, Pigpen because he is not primarily a musician, and Bob because of an oddly stubborn pride. Yet they have always been a fellowship. "Our crises come and go in ways that seem more governed by the stars than by personalities," says Bob. Two years ago Bob and Pigpen were on the verge of leaving. Now the Dead, says Phil, "have passed the point where breaking up exists as a possible solution to any problem. The Dead, we all know, is bigger than all of us." Subsets of the seven, with names like Bobby Ace and the Cards from the Bottom and Mickey Hart and the Heartbeats, have done a few gigs, and several of the Dead are inveterate jammers, but these separate experiences always loosen and enrich the larger group, and the Dead continue.

In life as well as music. When the acid tests stopped in the spring of 1966 and Kesey went to Mexico, the Dead got off the old bus and started their own (metaphorical) new bus. For three months they lived with Augustus Owsley Stanley III, the media's and legend's "Acid King," on the northern edge of Watts in L.A., as he built them a huge and complex sound system. The system was no good, say some, adding that Owsley did the group nothing but harm. Owsley was weird all right, "insistent about his trip," says Bob, keeping nothing but meat and milk to eat, forbidding all vegetables as poisons, talking like a TV set you couldn't turn off, and wired into a logic that was always bizarre and often perversely paranoid if not downright evil. But what others thought or think of Owsley has never affected the Dead; he is Owsley, and they follow their own changes with him, everything from hatred to awe to laughing at him as absurd. If you're going further, your wagon is hitched to a star; other people's opinions on the trip's validity are like flies to be brushed aside.

Their life, too, is without any idiom but their own: They returned to San Francisco in June 1966, and after a few stops moved into 710 Ashbury, in the middle of the Haight. It was the first time they actually lived in the city as a group, and they became an institution. "Happy families are all alike," Tolstoy said, but the happy family at 710 was different from most, a sliding assortment of madmen who came and went in mysterious tidal patterns, staying for days or weeks or just mellow afternoons on the steps bordered with nasturtiums. A strange black wing decorated an upper window, and occasional passersby would be jolted by sonic blasts from deep in the house's entrails. Like the Psychedelic Shop, the Panhandle, the Oracle office, or 1090 Pine St. in the early Family Dog days, 710 Haight was another bus, an energy center as well as a model, a Brook Farm for new transcendentalists.

With all the other groups in the city, the Dead did become a band, an economic entity in an expanding market. They did well; since the demise of Big Brother and the Holding Company, they are of the San Francisco groups second only to the Airplane, and are one of the biggest draws in the business. But the Dead were always different. Their managers, Rock Scully and Danny Rifkin, were of the family, all stoned ten-thumbed inefficiency. While other groups were fighting for recognition, more and bigger gigs, the Dead played mostly for free. Monterey Pop was a godsend of exposure to most groups, but the Dead bitched about it, arguing that it should be free or, if not, the profits should go to the hippie anarchist group, the Diggers; they refused to sign releases for the film that became *Monterey Pop*, helped to organize a free festival on a nearby campus, and stole banks of amps and speakers for an all-night jam (they equipment was, eventually, returned).

But of course they did go; maybe Monterey was an "L.A. pseudo-hip fraud," but the Dead were a rock band as well as a psychedelic musical commune, and they knew it. The problem was combining the two. The spirit that had energized the early days was changing and becoming harder to sustain. The formlessness was becoming formalized; artifacts—whether posters, clothes, drugs, or even the entire lifestyle—became more important than the art of their creation.

"The acid tests have come down to playing in a hall and having a light show," Jerry says. "You sit down and watch and of course the lights are behind the band so you can see the band and the lights. It's watching television—loud, large television. That form, so rigid, started as a misapprehension anyway. Like Bill Graham, he was at the Trips Festival, and all he saw was a light show and a band. Take the two and you got a formula. It is stuck, man, hasn't blown a new mind in years. What was happening at the Trips Festival was not a rock 'n' roll show and lights, but that other thing, and if you were hustling tickets and trying to get a production on, to put some of the old order to the chaos, you couldn't feel it. It was a sensitive trip, and it's been lost."

Yet in trying to combine their own music lifestyle with the rock 'n' roll business, the Dead have missed living the best of either. Their dealings with the business world have been disastrous; money slips through their fingers, bills pile up, instruments are repossessed, and salaries aren't paid. The group is $60,000 in debt and those debts have meant harm to dozens of innocent people. "I remember times we've said, 'that cat's straight, let's burn him for a bill,'" says Phil Lesh.

It is not that the Dead can't be commercially successful. Their basic sound is hard rock/white R and B slightly freaked—not very different from Steppenwolf's, Creedence Clearwater Revival's, or the Sir Douglas Quintet's. "Golden Road to Unlimited Devotion," the Dead's 1967 single, could quite easily be a hit single today. They would have been happy had success come to them; unsought success, a gift of self-amplification, is a logical extension of electrifying instruments. But they just won't and can't accept even the machine's most permissive limits. Their basic sound is just that—something to build from, and they know intuitively—if to their own frustration, that to accept the system would to them be fatal.

"Rendering to Caesar what is Caesar's is groovy," says Phil, "as long as you render to God what is God's. But now Caesar demands it all and we gotta be straight with God first."

The Dead see themselves as keepers of the flame. Smoking grass on stage, bringing acid to concerts, purposely ignoring time limits for sets, telling audiences to screw the rules and ushers and dance—those are just tokens. In late 1967 they set up the Great Northwestern Tour with the Quicksilver Messenger Service and Jerry Abrams's Headlights, completely handling a series of dates in Oregon and Washington. "No middlemen, no bullshit," said Rock Scully. "We did it all—posters, tickets, promo, setting up the halls. All the things promoters say you can't do, we did, man, and 'cause we weren't dependent, we felt free and everybody did. That told us that however hard it gets, it can be done, you don't have to go along."

Out of that energy came the Carousel Ballroom. The Dead, helped by the Airplane, leased a huge Irish dance hall on Market Street in downtown San Francisco and started a series of dances that were a throwback to the good old days. But running a good dance hall means taking care of business and keeping a straight head; the Carousel's managers did neither. They made absurdly bad deals, beginning with an outlandish rent, and succumbed to a destructive fear of Bill Graham. The spring of 1968, with the assassinations of Martin Luther King Jr. and Robert F. Kennedy, was hard on show business everywhere. Graham, in the smaller Fillmore smack in the center of an increasingly unfriendly black neighborhood, was vulnerable and ready to be cooperative. But to the Dead and their friends he was big, bad Bill Graham, the villain who had destroyed the San Francisco scene. So as the Carousel sank further into debt, they refused the help he offered. Inevitably they had to close; Graham moved swiftly, took up the lease, and renamed the place   113 the Fillmore West. The Dead were on the street again, licking their wounds, self-inflicted and otherwise.

Two years later they are still in the street; they are not quite failures by accepted business terms but certainly have been stagnated by their own stubborn yearning. A drug bust in the fall of 1967 and the increasing deterioration of the Haight finally drove them from 710 Ashbury in 1968; similar hassles may drive the remnants of the family from their ranch in Novato. The band members now all live in separate houses scattered over San Francisco and Marin County. They are still talking of making a music caravan, traveling from town to town, in buses like a circus. They know a new form has to be found; the "psychedelic dance concert" is washed up, but what is next? Maybe a rock 'n' roll rodeo, maybe something else that will just happen when the time comes. They don't know, but they are determined to find it. It is hard to get your thing together if your thing is paradise on earth. "We're tired of jerking off," says Jerry. "We want to start fucking again."

Seven o'clock Friday morning, Santa Barbara was deep in pearly mist, and Jerry Garcia was pacing back and forth in an alley behind the motel, quietly turning on. One by one, yawning and grunting, the others appeared and clambered into the Pontiacs. It was the start of a long day: 8 A.M. flight to San Francisco; change planes for Portland; crash in the motel until the gig; play, then get to bed and on to Eugene the next day. There was neither time nor energy for postmortems; the thing to do was to get on with it.

At 7:30 Lenny Hart was fuming. The Bear was late again. Where was he? No one knew. Lenny, square-faced and serious, drummed on the steering wheel. "We gotta go, can't wait for him. What's so special about Bear that he can't get here like everyone else?" Phil started back to the motel to find him, but then out Bear came, sleepy but dapper in a black leather shirt and vest, pale blue pants, and blue suede boots. Lenny's eyes caught Bear's for an instant, then he peeled out.

No one missed the confrontation: Lenny and the Bear, like two selves of

Jerry Garcia, 1971. © Baron Wolman

the Dead at war, with the Dead themselves sitting as judges. Lenny, a minister who has chosen the Dead as his mission, is the latest person they've trusted to get them out of the financial pit. The Bear, says Jerry, is "Satan in our midst," friend, chemist, psychedelic legend, and electronic genius; not a leader, but a moon with gravitational pull. He is the prince of inefficiency, the essence at its most perverse of what the Dead refuse to give up. Lenny and the Bear are natural enemies, but somehow they have to coexist for the Dead to survive. Their skirmishing has just begun.

The day is all like that, suddenly focused images that fade one into another.

At the airport the Air West jet rests before the little stucco terminal. It is ten minutes after takeoff time, and the passengers wait in two clumps.

Clump 1, the big one, is ordinary Santa Barbara human beings: clean, tanned businessmen, housewives, college girls going away for the holiday, an elderly couple or two, a few ten-year-olds in shorts. They are quiet and a bit strained. Clump 2 is the Dead: manic, dirty, hairy, noisy, a bunch of drunken Visigoths in cowboy hats and greasy suede. Pigpen has just lit Bob's paper on fire, and the cinders blow around their feet. Phil is at his twitchiest, his face stroboscopically switching grotesque leers. The Bear putters in his mysterious belted bags, Jerry discards cigarette butts as if the world was his ashtray, and Tom, one sock bright green, the other vile orange, gazes beatifically (he's a grade 4 release in Scientology) over it all and puns under his breath.

Over on the left, in the cargo area, a huge rented truck pulls up with the Dead's equipment, ninety pieces of extra luggage. Like clowns from a car, amp after amp after drum case is loaded onto dollies and wheeled to the jet's belly. It dawns on Clump 1 all at once that it is those arrogant heathens with all their outrageous gear that are making the plane late and keeping them, good American citizens, shivering out in the morning mist. It dawns on the heathens too, but they dig it, shouting to the quippies to tote that amp, lift that organ. Just about that time Phil, reading what's left of the paper, sees a story about People's Park in Berkeley and how the police treated the demonstrators like the Viet Cong. "But that's just what we are, man, the American National Liberation Front," he shouts, baring his teeth at Clump 1.

Ticket takers talk politely of "Mr. Bear" and "Mr. Ramrod"—the Dead's chief roadie; in San Francisco Airport a pudgy waitress, "Marla" stamped on the plastic nameplate pinned to her right breast, leaves her station starry-eyed and says she's so glad to see them because she came to work stoned on acid and it's been a freak-out until she saw them like angel horsemen galloping through her plastic hell. Tom, his mustachioed face effortlessly sincere, gives a beginning lecture on the joys of Scientology, explaining that he hopes someday to be an operating thetan (OT) and thus be able to levitate the group while they're playing, and of course they won't ever have to plug in.

Pigpen glowers beneath his corduroy hat, grunting, "Ahhh, fork!" whenever the spirit moves, and the Bear starts a long involved rap about how the Hell's Angels really have it down, man, like this cat who can use a whip like a stiletto could slice open your nostrils, first the right, then the left, neat as you please, and everyone agrees that the Angels are righteously ugly.

The Dead miss their San Francisco connection and have to hang around the airport for a couple of hours, but that somehow means that they ride first class, free drinks and all.

With lunch polished off, Mickey needs some refreshment, so he calls across the aisle to Ramrod, then holds his fingers to his nose significantly. Ramrod tosses over a small vial of cocaine and a jackknife, and Mickey, all the while carrying on an intense discussion about drumming, sniffs up like he was lighting an after dinner cigar: "Earth music is what I'm after"—sniff—"the rhythm of the earth, like I get riding a horse"—sniff, sniff—"and Bill feeds that to me, I play off of it, and he responds. When we're into it, it's like a drummer with two minds, eight arms, and one soul"—final snort, and then the vial and jackknife go the rounds. Multiple felonies in the first-class compartment, but the stewardesses are without eyes to see. The Dead, in the very grossness of their visibility, are invisible.

The plane lands in Portland. "Maybe it'll happen today," says Jerry, waiting to get off. "The first rock 'n' roll assassination. Favorite fantasy: sometime we'll land, and when we're all on the stairs, a fleet of black cars will rush the plane like killer beetles. Machine guns will pop from the roofs and mow us down. Paranoid, huh? But, fuck, in a way I wouldn't blame 'em." No black cars though, that day anyway.

Lenny has done some figuring on the plane. "Things are looking up," he says. "We ought to have the prepaid tickets for this trip paid by the end of next week." Jerry says that's boss, and the Bear makes a point of showing off the alarm clock he got in San Francisco. Lenny takes it as a joke and says just be ready next time or he'll be left behind. Danny brings the good news that they have a tank of nitrous oxide for the gig. Everybody goes to sleep.

The dance is at Springer's Inn, about ten miles out of town, and they

117

start out about 9:30. A mile from the place there is a huge traffic jam on the narrow country road, and they stick the cars in a ditch and walk, a few fragments in the flow to Springer's under a full yellow moon. The last time they played Portland they were at a ballroom with a sprung floor that made dancing inevitable, but Springer's is just as nice. It's a country and western place, walls all knotty pine, and beside the stage the Nashville stars of the past thirty years grin glossily from autographed photos: "Your's sincerely, Marty Robbins"; "Love to Y'all, Norma Jean"; "Warmest regards, Jim Reeves." "You got a bigger crowd than even Buck Owens," says the promoter, and Jerry grins. It is sardine, ass-to-ass packed, and drippingly hot inside.

The band stands around the equipment truck waiting for the Bear to finish his preparations. Someone donates some Cokes, Bear laces them with his concoction, and they make the rounds. "Anyone for a lube job?" Bill calls to the hangers-on. "Dosed to a turn," says Phil. Jerry, already speechlessly spaced on gas, drinks deep. They are all ready.

It seems preordained to be a great night. But preordination is not fate; it comes to the elect, and the elect have to work to be ready for it. So the Dead start out working; elation will come later.

"Morning Dew" opens the set, an old tune done slow and steady. It is the evening's foundation stone, and they carefully mortise it into place, no smiles, no frills. Phil's bass is sure and steady, Bill and Mickey play almost in unison. Then Bob sings "Me and My Uncle," a John Phillips tune with a country rocking beat. They all like the song and Bob sings it well, friendly and ingenuous. Back to the groove with "Everybody's Doing that Rag," but a little looser this time. Jerry's guitar begins to sing, and over the steady drumming of Bill, Mickey lays scattered runs, little kicks, and sudden attacks. Phil begins to thunder, then pulls back. Patience, he seems to be saying, and he's right: Jerry broke a string in his haste, so they pull back in unison and end the song. But Jerry wants it bad and is a little angry.

"I broke a string," he shouts at the crowd, "so why don't you wait a minute and talk to each other. Or maybe talk to yourself, to your various selves." He cocks his head with a glint of malice in his eyes. "Can you talk to your self? Do you even know you have selves to talk to?"

The questions, contemptuous and unanswerable, push the crowd back—who is this guy asking us riddles, what does he want from us anyway? But the band is into "King Bee" by that time. They haven't played it for a while, but it works, another building block, and a good way to work Pigpen into the center, to seduce him into giving his all instead of just waiting around for "Lovelight." It is like the Stones but muddier—Pigpen isn't Mick Jagger, after all. Jerry buzzes a while right on schedule, and the crowd eases up, thinking they were going to get some nice blues. The preceding band had been good imitation B.B. King, so maybe it would be a blues night. Wrong again.

"Play the blues!" shouts someone in a phony half-swoon.

"Fuck you, man," Mickey shouts back. "Go hear a blues band if you want that, go dig Mike Bloomfield."

Another punch in the mouth, but the moment is there, and the audience's stunned silence just makes the opening gong of "Dark Star" more ominous. In that silence music begins, steady and pulsing. Jerry, as always, takes the lead, feeling his way for melodies like paths up the mountain. Jerry, says Phil, is the heart of the Dead, its central sun; while they all connect to each other, the strongest bonds are to him. Standing there, eyes closed, chin bobbing forward, his guitar in close under his arm, he seems pure energy, a quality like but distinct from sexuality, which, while radiating itself outward unceasingly and unselfishly, is as unceasingly and unselfishly replenished by those whose strengths have been awakened by his.

He finds a way, a few high twanging notes that are in themselves a song, and then the others are there too, and suddenly the music is not notes or a tune, but what those seven people are, exactly; the music is an aural holograph of the Grateful Dead. All their fibers, nuances, histories, desires, beings are clear. Jerry and his questing, Phil the loyal comrade, Tom drifting beside them both on a cloud, Pig staying stubbornly down to earth; Mickey

119

working out furious complexities trying to understand how Bill is so simple, and Bob succumbing inevitably to Jerry and Phil and joining them. And that is just the beginning, because at each note, at each phrase the balances change, each testing, feeding, mocking, and finally driving each other on, further and further on.

Some balances last longer than others, moments of realization that seem to sum up many moments, and then a solid groove of "yes, that is the way it is" flows out, and the crowd begins to move. Each time it is Jerry who leads them out, his guitar singing and dancing joy. And his joy finds new levels and the work of exploration begins again. Jerry often talks of music as coming from a place and creating a place—a place where strife is gone, where the struggle to understand ends, and knowledge is as evident as light. That is the place they are in at Springer's. However hard it is to get there once there, you want to cry tears of ease and never leave.

The music goes fast and slow, driving and serene, loud and soft. Mickey switches from gong to drums to claves to handclapping to xylophone to a tin slide whistle. Then Bob grabs that away and steps to the mike and blows the whistle as hard as he can, flicking away insanely high and screeching notes. The band digs it, and lays down a building rhythm. The crowd begins to pant, shake, and then suddenly right on the exact moment with the band, everyone in the whole goddamn place begins to scream. Not screaming as they would at the Beatles, but screaming like beasts, twisting their faces, trying out every possible animal yowl that lies deep in their hearts.

And Jerry, melodies flowing from him in endless arabesques, leads it away again, the crowd and himself ecstatic rats to some pied piper. The tune changes from "Dark Star" to "St. Stephen," the song with a beat like bouncing boulders, and out of the din comes Jerry's wavering voice. "One man gathers what another man spills," and everyone knows that means that there's nothing to fear, brothers and sisters will help each other, and suddenly there is peace in the hall. Phil, Bob, and Bill form a trio and play a new and quiet song before Mickey's sudden roll opens it out to the group, and "St. Stephen" crashes to an end with the cannon shot and clouds of sulphurous smoke.

Out of the fire and brimstone emerges Pigpen singing "Lovelight," and everyone is through the mind and down into the body. Pigpen doesn't sing; Pigpen never sings. He is just Pig being Pig doing "Lovelight," spitting out of the side of his mouth between phrases, starting the clapping, telling everybody to get their hands out of their pockets and into somebody else's pocket, and like laughter, the band comes in with rock-it-to-'em choruses.

The crowd is jumping up and down in witness by this time, and one couple falls on stage, their bodies and tongues entwined in mad ritual embrace. They don't make love, but in acting it out, they perform for and with the crowd, and so everyone is acting out sexual unison, with Pigpen as the master of ceremonies. The place—one body, built in music—fucks until it comes, the cannon goes off one final time, and Mickey leaps to the gong, bashing it with a mallet set afire by the cannon, and it makes a trail of flame and sparks when it hits the gong, the gong itself radiating waves of sonic energy. Bill flails at the drums, Phil keeps playing the same figure over and over, faster and faster, and Jerry and Bob build up to one note just below the tonic and hold it until, with one ultimate chord, it all comes home. The crowd erupts in cheers, as the band, sodden with sweat, stumble off the stage.

"We'll be back, folks," says Jerry. "We'll be back after a break."

Bob laughs as he hears Jerry's announcement. "It's really something when you have to lie to get off the stage."

Because it's over, gone, wiped out. They gather by the equipment van, and all but Tom, still cool and unruffled, are steaming in the chill night air. The moon has gone down, the stars are out, and there is nothing more to be done.

Mick Jagger on stage, 1969. © Ethan A. Russell

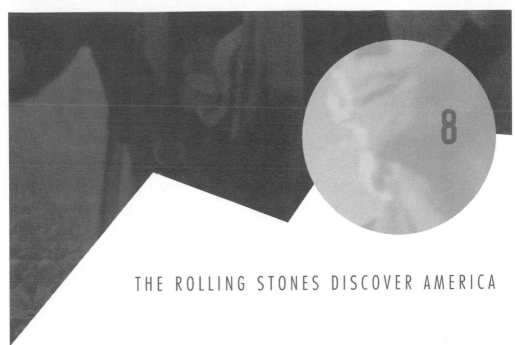

8

THE ROLLING STONES DISCOVER AMERICA

1 9 6 9

Flying across America with the Rolling Stones in 1969, riding in limos and smoking pot with them, was the apotheosis of my rock 'n' roll reporting career. My comrade and fellow writer Stanley Booth knew that we were where every hippie in America wanted to be, and we jumped into the tour with our eyes and ears wide open and with big grins on our mugs.

Yet the fun came alloyed with an unsettling tension. If in the shuffle of an airport arrival I ended up in a limo with Mick Jagger or Keith Richards, that was a good day; if I ended up in a van with the roadies that was a bad day. I can't blame my queasy ego-struggles on the Stones as people. They were all pleasant to me, and I came to like and admire them as hardworking and dedicated cats. The problem was the gravitational pull that stardom inevitably creates: no matter what they or anybody else felt about it, "the Boys" were the center of the tour universe, the rest of us minor satellites spinning about them in fixed and distant orbits.

Yet the tensions of the tour taught me a valuable lesson: stardom distorts reality. One night after a concert I was walking beside Keith down a long airport corridor. With the night's music still ringing in my ears, I said to him in sincere appreciation, "Man, you played your ass off tonight." Keith turned to me. "Did I?" he asked, his face open and uncertain. "Did I?" In that moment I knew that Keith Richards was not the impervious rock star I and other fans and rock writers had helped create. He was another guy like me, and, in his own way, just as nervous as I was. Looking back, I'm not surprised that soon after the tour was over, I began to play music myself. Keith and Mick (and John and Paul and Janis and Jerry), I had learned, were not idols to be worshipped from afar, but kids my own age who were giving their all to making music. If I did the same, no matter how my music came out, we'd be equals.

> You can't always get what you want
> You can't always get what you want,
> You can't always get what you want,
> But if you try some time,
> You just might find,
> You get what you need.
>
> —Mick Jagger and Keith Richards

Four A.M. on the first day of December—thirty more days until 1970—and it is bitter, bitter cold in West Palm Beach, Florida. Or, to be exact, at the Palm Beach International Raceway, a funky little redneck dragstrip a few inches above the waterline of a bush-league Everglades fifteen miles (plus a few thousand social light years) from the palm fringed luxury of the coast. Thirty thousand kids are huddled before a makeshift stage vainly trying to stop the insistent wind from pushing the swamp's primeval damp through every hole in their torn army jackets, dirty sleeping bags, raveled sweaters, and patched-up jeans. A few campfires make cozy orange patches in the dark, and the stage scaffolding looms skeletonlike against the cloud-flecked sky.

They've been there, this little fragment of the Woodstock Nation, for three days of music and misery (naturally it rained) that has become a ritual for a generation. "Everybody must get stoned," said Bob Dylan in the pun of the decade, and these kids, radiantly happy and hopeful in a squalor as total as it is voluntary, are living it. Even in the dark the faces are familiar: teenagers still pimpled, with their hair just barely long, clean cut but trying to be less so, adolescents awkwardly making the shift from beer and cars to grass and "love." There are a few hippies who have been doing it for years, but most of the kids—it is Florida, after all—have just begun to "do their thing." Their yearning to come together (where does it come from?), to experience that love-in, festival feeling they've heard so much about, floods up to the stage in waves of expectation so trusting and naïve as to be at once absurd and deeply moving.

It's the last night of the Palm Beach Pop Festival, the smallest, last, and least fashionable festival of the year, and it barely came to pass. Southern Florida, land of orange groves and the American Legion, had responded to a Miami festival and Door Jim Morrison's supposed self-exposure with a hysterical decency campaign manipulated by grown-ups (!) like Jackie Gleason and Art Linkletter. It wanted no more festivals. From the moment that thirty-one-year-old promoter Dave Rupp announced the organization of the Palm Beach Pop Festival, "the Establishment," as he called it, tried to stop him. He was kept in court until a week before opening day, defending himself on a dozen legal fronts. His business, Dave Rupp Auto Brokers, was burned to the ground; his wife Sheila, a kindergarten teacher, was told, "It's trash like you that's making our kids turn out the way they are"; the insurance on the drag strip in which he is a partner was canceled, politicians threatened mass drug arrests, and he and his family were ostracized by their neighbors.

But the tract-home Bermuda-shorts conservatives of West Palm Beach hadn't reckoned with Dave Rupp. Soft-spoken, sandy-haired, and a self-described "straight," Rupp is a 1950s hot-rodder who became a world champion drag racer, then a Wichita, Kansas, rock club owner (he assembled the Kingsmen of "Louie Louie" fame), then high-performance car dealer. He never forgot what it was to be an American teenager. "The cops are pigs and the kids are great," he says looking out from a corner of the light booth. "I've known that since the days when I was thirteen and outrunning the fuzz myself. I've lost $250,000 going through with this festival, but it's been worth it because of those kids."

So, with his business gone, deep in debt, and as an outcast in his own town, Dave Rupp got his show on. Despite about one hundred drug busts and a personal visit by Governor Claude Kirk, who kept the National Guard on pointless alert, it was a groove. Janis Joplin, the Jefferson Airplane, Sly and the Family Stone, and many others came and knocked themselves out. And now it is 4 A.M. and the biggest act of all, the group that should have been there twelve hours before and for whom the crowd has waited through the dark night—the Rolling Stones—are about to come on. At least some guy said ten minutes ago that they'd be on in three minutes, and . . . yes, there they are, Mick dancing out with an Uncle Sam hat on his beautiful head, and these kids shed the sleeping bags and blankets and leap up to cheer and cheer and cheer.

But that's the end of the story, or almost the end, and most often it's best to begin at beginnings, if you can find them.

> Well, it goes from St. Louis down to Missouri,
>   Oklahoma City looks oh so pretty,
> You oughta see Amarillo and Gallup, New Mexico,
>   Flagstaff, Arizona, don't forget Winona,
> Bagdad, Barstow, then San Bernardino,
> Won't you get hip to this kindly tip,
> And take that California trip,
> Get your kicks on Route 66.
>
> —Bobby Troup, "Route 66"

In 1967 rock 'n' roll, while exploding with unprecedented energy, suffered a triple loss: the Beatles, Bob Dylan, and the Rolling Stones stopped touring. The biggest draws in the business, they were also the most important musical and cultural influences on the whole rock scene. Each in a class by itself, the three together made their own class. Years before, rock's only other super-superstar, Elvis Presley, had withdrawn into films, but the near simultaneous decisions by the Big Three shocked fans who had come to expect live contact with their idols. Their retreat created a vacuum that no one since has been able to fill.

At the time it was hard to conceive of a nontouring band—stories on the Beatles assumed they were breaking up—but now the reasons seem obvious. Rock 'n' roll touring is exhausting work; for stars who have to be guarded like the atomic bomb, it is claustrophobic and monotonous. Before 1967 almost no one listened at the concerts anyway, and for young men excited by the adult possibilities of their music, the public adulation attending it seemed a childish drag, which only increased bank accounts already immeasurable. With an independence not dreamed of by earlier entertainers who feared losing popularity, they simply stopped doing what they no longer enjoyed. None did lose popularity; all established their continuing preeminence with every new record.

The rock world from which they had withdrawn changed just as they did, expanding many times over and becoming a sophisticated community that saw itself as the aesthetic and social center of its time. In live performance rock is now the greatest audience-gatherer in show business history. Provincial music when Elvis began to shake it on out in Memphis, it became a worldwide fad with the Beatles, and then, after San Francisco, an energy locus for a movement that looks like a new children's crusade.

None of the Big Three played at the Monterey Pop Festival, the event that signaled the opening of the new era, but they were missed. Woodstock—in fact, Bethel—was a misdirected pilgrimage to Bob Dylan's home, but at that remarkable convention few missed the stars because, finally, the audience was the star: any stoned kid blowing his heart out on a bamboo flute could think he was as beautiful as Paul McCartney. The Beatles had said years before that anybody could be a Beatle. On that August weekend half a million people glimpsed the grail.

Fascinating news to the stars; they had quit touring to rest from a world that suffocated them with its wants. Now that world was as far out as the stars themselves, maybe farther out. In 1966 the Beatles—all longhaired dropouts—played for hysterical and shorthaired school kids. In a 1969 audience half the kids might look as thoroughly strange as John Lennon.

And touring itself looked like it might be fun again. After a few years of settling into marriage and babies and quiet evenings, what a gas to taste again those touring pleasures, the late-night motel living, the hopped-up edge of extreme fatigue, the girls, the parties, the cities and airports flashing by! On the road again! And best of all was the thrill of playing on stage and getting the rush of moving so many thousand people to the whim of your lyric imagination. Money, too, of course. The success of Cream, Jimi Hendrix, Led Zeppelin, Johnny Winter, and Blind Faith in the spanking new civic auditoriums that dot America seemed profoundly encouraging to the money men who have always stood close behind rock 'n' roll royalty.

So in 1969 the Big Three began to talk of going out to see the rock 'n' roll army they had helped so much to call into being. The Beatles were not able to agree on a format. Dylan, encouraged by the success of his one-time backup band, made a few lightning appearances and planned a tour. But the Rolling Stones, whose tours had always set an exactingly debauched standard, were the first to do a tour in the old full-blown, one-nighter style.

Who else but the Stones? Since the days when, freezing in London flats, they argued about soloists on old blues records, when they were huffing and puffing their way through Muddy Waters tunes in raggedy pubs and at debutante parties or getting their first following at the Crawdaddy Club in Richmond, the Stones have been the very toughest essence of a rock 'n' roll band. No mean thing to be, but a precise amalgam of diverse elements: a punk craftiness and sneering narcissism, a group comradeship unspoken and total, a cynical materialism that could never be bought, and a passionate love for a music that goes back to blues and boogie-woogie through rhythm and blues and all its white modifications. There was never anything metaphysical about the Stones, nor anything frilly. As hard and homeless as their name, unvarying in a densely primitive yet sophisticated simplicity, the Stones peered blankly out from their record covers and called everybody's bluff. Performers of "(I Can't Get No) Satisfaction"—one of the few perfect rock 'n' roll songs—the Stones expressed a unique alienation that is the germ kernel of the rock 'n' roll sensibility: a profound frustration countered by an inchoate yearning for beauty.

Last spring the group conquered its final doubts and decided to plan a tour. Rhythm guitarist Brian Jones—strange, elusive Brian—did not want to go. Almost the founder of the group, he had been drifting out of its center for years. Without rancor but also without ceremony, he was replaced. In July, with new guitarist Mick Taylor, the Stones did a free Hyde Park concert that briefly held the record—250,000 kids for one sunny afternoon. Brian had drowned alone in his swimming pool two days before, but the show went on. Who ever expected the Stones to mourn? Mick Jagger read Shelley ("Peace, peace, he is not dead, he doth not sleep, he hath but awakened from the dream of life") and released a thousand white butterflies from the stage.

The concert was a huge success, and they fixed on an American tour for the fall. Mick finished up his film role in *Performance* and left for Australia to make *Ned Kelley*. Shooting ran late and then a few weeks of obstructionism by the U.S. Passport Office delayed progress again. By late October a brand new corporation called Stones Promotions had a tour itinerary: nineteen concerts in fourteen cities that would start on the West Coast and work its way east. The Stones gathered in Los Angeles to finish the new record, rehearse, and soak up American vibrations from the vantage point of three mansions high in the Hollywood hills.

Across the country the fans rushed for tickets, the most expensive for any rock concert series. Three years of incredible history, good times and bad, drugs and street fighting and growing up, and now the Stones, whose music has followed it all at a distance, were coming back to kiss off the decade. The Stones tour—say the words and you heard the sizzle of mysto excitement, and put your tickets in the safest corner of your drawer. What would it be like to see the Stones again? One morning I hitchhiked down

from the country to San Francisco, flew to Los Angeles, and joined the tour.
I had, I told my friends before I left, no idea what it would be like.

Rolling Stones HQ (plus home for Charlie Watts, his wife Shirley, baby
Serafina, and assorted tour personnel) is a DuPont family house above
Sunset Strip with a panoramic view of the city, a swimming pool, tennis
court, and a gas fireplace in the living room that burns constantly with a
steady hiss of expensive waste. Despite an impersonal rent-a-palace feeling,
the Big House, as it's called, is homey. Serafina Watts toddles about the
kitchen with her nanny, the cook, and the maid, watching everything with
wide gray eyes. Charlie talks chess with Sam Cutler, the Stones' closest aide-
de-camp ("Why does the game end when you get the king?" asks Charlie.
"Couldn't the pawns revolt and continue the fight on their own?"), while
Ronnie Schneider, head of Stones Promotions, makes deals on the dining
room phone.

The house has a cast of characters, one that with additions and dele-
tions will remain constant for the month-long living drama. The Watts
family will soon leave for England, but Charlie the ever phlegmatic drummer will stay, and so will Sam, a Cockney madman passionately devoted to
the well-being of the Boys. So will Ronnie, a small, dark, and dapper businessman of twenty-six who is never without his sleekly rounded briefcase or
his astonishingly vulgar humor; and Jo Bergman, Mick's personal secretary,
whose democratic good temper and apparently inexhaustible patience make
her an oasis of resigned sanity in times of stress.

The cast has infinite gradations, but there are essentially two groups:
Stones and non-Stones. Non-Stones serve Stones, and all, down to temporary
secretaries and groupie chauffeurs, have specific functions. While record engineer Glyn Johns must be picked up at Burbank by Mary the Driver, Doreen
the PR Lady must pilot Mick through days of interviews. Jo deals with the
calls for free tickets while Ronnie battles with Bill Graham about the Oakland
concerts and Cathy snags a car to take Shirley and Charlie out shopping.

Dour Bill Belmont ("My job is logistics and keeping the goddam expenses down") is in and out, planning the movements of the sixteen-man stage crew that will be hustling fifteen tons of sound and light equipment from hall to truck to plane to truck to hall. "The best crew in the world, run of course by Chip Monck, the best stage manager in the world," he says late one night, slouching on one of the living room's three gigantic beige sofas. "Chip, after consulting with Mick, plans a theatrical approach. No crappy light shows, but a proscenium stage backlit for a changing color ambience highlighted by six Super-Trouper spots. The sound towers will be draped in gray, and Mick will sing from the center of a white starburst on a purple carpet."

Bill's voice singsongs on about "real-time analyzers" and "acoustic voicing equipment," while Ian "Stew" Stewart, sometime piano player, road manager, and lifelong friend of the Stones, plays a deft shuffle on Charlie's drum kit to a Count Basie record. Other voices drift in and out: "I'll never forget my first Stones tour," says Ronnie's wife Jane, a girl of a vacuity as charming as it is natural. "I was eighteen, from a hick town, and did I have my eyes opened! I saw everything, believe me. Girls and girls, boys and boys, and oh, one crazy Negro girl who ran around the motel screaming she was God, for Chrissakes." Pretty Doreen (indignant): "I hung up on *Vogue* today. They asked for fourteen tickets—fourteen! Would they ask for fourteen tickets if it was the Beatles or Dylan?" Charlie (quietly): "It was different a few years ago. We were a pack then, when Brian was alive, a family in a way. But sometimes now I'm not sure I know the others."

Next day Mick comes by from the house he shares with Keith and Mick Taylor (it's rented from Stephen Stills of Crosby, Stills, Nash and Young), and is interviewed by two young rock critics from New York. Two of the best, they feel a comradeship with Jagger that they can't express, and are nervously torn between awe and skepticism. Mick, dressed in green velvet, answers them with just enough boredom to keep them tense and enough informality to keep them hoping for more.

Why the tour? "I've been on the musical stage since I was five, and I've missed it for the past few years. So I said to meself, 'Back to the boards where we belong, lads.'"

White blues? "We were never hung up about not being black. We just did imitation blues, but it was always good imitation."

Popularity? "Never thought we'd be big; thought we'd do blues for the fanatics. Then we heard the Beatles' 'Love Me Do' and figured we could do music like that and not compromise, so we did."

John Lennon and Apple Records? "The trouble with John Lennon is that he's never read Marx. If he had, he'd never have tried being a pseudo-capitalist and make such a mess of it."

Politics? "I was much more political before I started music. At the London School of Whats-Its-Name I was big on it, big arguments and thumping on tables—like everybody in college, man."

He smiles the Jagger smile at the room, making deep ridges beside his famous mouth; an ironic jester who insists his words, sung or spoken, don't matter at all. The interviewers leave, happy to have been there but sure he has danced beyond their range.

> I'm sitting here thinkin' just how sharp I am,
> I'm sitting here thinkin' just how sharp I am,
> I'm an under assistant west coast promo man,
> So sharp, so very, very sharp.
> —Mick Jagger and Keith Richards, "The Under
> Assistant West Coast Promotion Man"

"No, I wouldn't say we have a publicity strategy for this tour," says David Horowitz, the vaguely prissy PR man from Solters and Sabinson, assigned to the Stones. "The Stones, we believe, will make their own news. We see our job as facilitating the dissemination of that news as widely as possible. It's a great story and, we believe, an important assignment for the firm."

He's wearing a double-breasted blue blazer, a wide pink tie under a spread Italian collar, and sideburns an inch and a half longer than the nationwide norm for thirty-five-year-old males. His office is in a brand new building on Sunset Strip; the garage is full of Buick Rivieras and the elevators full of David Horowitzes—the sideburn set in pastel shirts and cuffless pants whose lifework it is to service the entertainment center of the Western world. The Strip, a broad snake of a street always shedding its skin for something more glamorous, is their home, the press release and billboard their language.

Old ladies are still on the corners selling the out-of-date maps to movie stars' homes, but it is rock 'n' roll, not the movies or even television, that is the "now" industry of the street. Tawdry shacks like the Whisky or Thee Experience are the public places to see and in which to be seen. Tiny boutiques with grimy dressing rooms are the centers of a fashion industry that can make yesterday's eccentricity tomorrow's old clothes. The Strip is the natural American home of the Rolling Stones. When they are not eating, sleeping, or slouching about listening to records (their major occupations), they are on it.

Never to stay, but for quick jumps out of chauffeured cars into Schwabs for vitamin pills and sunglasses, into this shop for a shirt, into that one for a belt and a pair of boots, into a club for a few drinks and a set of Bo Diddley, Little Richard, Taj Mahal, Chuck Berry, or the Flying Burrito Brothers. The visits—Keith and Mick are the most serendipitous—are always informal, yet somehow regal. What they buy and where they stop is of course accidental, but the Strip does not believe it. "The Stones were here last night," "Bill bought a vest here"—awed incantations that report a blessing from the gods.

The more adventuresome do not wait for a visit, but attack the citadel directly. The Stones' house is a temporary Versailles, and through it flow the suppliants, this one with a film deal, that one with a poster deal, another trying to get a record endorsement. One young man talks vaguely of his road management experience and offers his services for the tour if they'll just pay his expenses. Cool young ladies insist that Keith invited them up, and photographers and writers swear they were promised exclusive interviews. Some, even by the Strip's exacting standards, are important—singers, producers, promoters, and groupies—but in the Stones' house they are all   133 nervous. The Stones are in town, and all orders of caste are suddenly overturned; it's no longer Who do you know? but Do you know the Stones?

The Stones themselves are distant from most of it, protected in part by the palace guard of Jo and Sam ("Let's not bother the Boys now," Sam suggests a dozen times a day in a voice that charms as it refuses), in part by their cultivated indifference to their effect, and in part, too, by the terrible shyness that afflicts these determined seekers at the crucial moment. Groupies of every sort who spent weeks to get to the Stones suddenly turn abject and fade into the wallpaper when confronted with one in the flesh.

"All these people, what are they here for?" says Charlie one day to no one in particular.

"I finally figured out why I want to go home," replies Shirley, a slender blonde with large sad eyes. "It's because I'm tired of being in a house where everyone is a job and no one talks anything but numbers. 'Twenty thousand, 65 percent, dollars, seats.' And there are too many people who talk nicely to you and then don't say good-bye when they leave. Have you noticed that, Charlie?"

He has, but the conversation dwindles. In the dining room Ronnie is working to a climax. He's got one overambitious sideburner in a carefully laid trap, and he's springing it. What is being said is indistinct, but there is no mistaking the glow of pleasure in Ronnie's New York accent as he presses his advantage. The sideburner feints in embarrassment, looking for a safe retreat. Ronnie counters; a note of humiliation comes from the mouse in striped pants; Ronnie decides on mercy and lets his prey scurry through the kitchen to his Riviera and back to the haven of the Strip. Ronnie strolls into the living room, snapping his briefcase shut.

"Oh, these pathetic bastards," he crows. "I'll screw 'em, screw 'em all. Remember when Bill Graham came down, full of bluster, telling us he'd do the whole tour, as a favor? Listen to this, Charlie, you'll get a kick out of it. There's Graham, telling me what a big shot he is, how he built the Fillmore, how he's booked this group, that group. So I sit and wait for him to finish, and then I say, 'Well, Bill, that sounds pretty good, but what did you ever do big?' He almost fell on the floor."

A phone rings. It's for Ronnie, and he's back at work.

At long last the tour begins, an out-of-town preview, though no one calls it that, at the University of Colorado in Fort Collins. The Stones and their entourage gather in the President's Club Room, the VIP lounge of Continental Airways at the Los Angeles Airport. A motley crew, to say the least, but the President's Club Room has seen their like—Donovan's name is scrawled a few pages back in the guest register. A few businessmen stand in a corner (they call it "the ghetto"), pushed there by the strange vibrations of these millionaire hippies with twelve guitar cases and their feet up on the fake Japanese furniture. One, with a Bloody Mary clenched in a well-tanned hand, wanders over and notices Astrid, Bill Wyman's quiet wife.

"Well, lookee here," he calls to chuckling friend. "I think I'll sit down next to this pretty young girl, and what's your name, young lady?"

Astrid looks at Bill; Bill smiles.

"You the fellas who had the hockey game canceled for your concert?" says the friend. He's drinking Scotch. Bill says the game wasn't canceled, only moved to the afternoon.

"Aw, don't mind us," says the first. "We're from the Manned Space Center in Houston, drinking up a little rest and relaxation in California." He toasts them.

"You mean you guys are putting people on the moon?" asks Keith.

"That's right," says the friend, "if Nixon will give us the money. You want to go to the moon?"

"Sure," says Keith.

"Just lemme know when," says the first.

In another corner a woman with pearls and a Chanel copy suit is showing her husband Irving pictures of their furniture in *Better Homes and Gardens*. She looks up, catching the eye of Cathy, Mick's friend and chauffeur.

"Now can you tell me which one of these boys is the father of two children by two different girls? I read about it in *Cosmopolitan.*"

Before Cathy can answer, Keith strides over. He has on huge purple sunglasses that obscure the top half of his face, a floor-length leather coat over his shoulders, a dirty Irish sweater, maroon velvet pants, and lizard-skin boots. A cougar tooth earring hangs from his left ear, and his thatch of home-cut hair dribbles to his shoulders.

"Are you talking about me babies?" he demands in a piercing high camp.

"I read in *Cosmo . . .* "

"You read too many magazines, sweetie." He turns, and the lady, who must spend a lot of time with interior decorators and hairdressers, stage whispers knowingly, "I'm sure he's nobody's father." Keith whirls.

"Try me some time, baby."

Irving is still deep in the *Los Angeles Times.* "Irving," she whines, "Irving, they're so goddam hostile. Why, Irving, why are they?"

It's sixty-six degrees and sunny in Denver. The fleet of rented limousines whirs swiftly across the fall-orange prairie as the sun sinks behind the Rockies. The campus looks more like an airport or an electronics factory than a college; four hours before concert time, the kids are lining up at the doors. The Stones get there early for a sound check, and with a bored professionalism do their jobs, calling out for more gain on the stage monitors, less treble for Bill's bass, and another mike for Charlie's tom-tom.

"I don't know what it is, Chip," Mick says through his mike, "but we were loud in rehearsals, and now it just isn't loud."

Chip mumbles assent and goes back to his dials. Mick jumps down from the stage and walks to the back of the hall to listen. Coming back, he begins a little dance, a quiet hop march on the band's offbeat. His long muscular arms swing with a peculiar grace and his head is held at an angle both restful and proud. There are thirty people there, stagehands, ushers, a few girls, and they all stop to watch Mick Jagger walk. When he notices the eyes on him, he laughs, breaks stride, and then jumps back up on stage.

By eight o'clock the gym—basketball nets folded like landing gear into the ceiling—is packed. A few freaks from Denver and Boulder, but the cross section looks like a Eugene McCarthy volunteer reunion; nice-looking kids, smoking dope but still in knee socks and circle pins, plaid shirts and loafers. For the first time there is that soon-to-be-familiar tensely compressed energy, directed to the bright spot that waits for the Rolling Stones.

The Stones get dressed in the Letterman's Lounge, not nervous (though Charlie has his usual problem of shaky feet), but as expectant as the kids. "I wonder what these kids are like now," says Keith. "I mean, do they watch TV or are they turning on in the basement?" "Or watching *Easy Rider*?" says Mick. No one knows if they'll scream; maybe they'll even be disappointed. Mick picks out a slow blues on an acoustic guitar. Keith and Mick Taylor tune up together, leaning over a small amp. Sam rushes in; it's time to go. They make a procession down the halls, carrying their guitars close so they won't get knocked out of tune. They wait at the steps as the lights dim. Sam takes the mike.

"Okay, Fort Collins, Colorado, we made it, we're here, and so I want you to give a big Western welcome to the group you've been waiting for, the Rolling STONES!" Up the steps and into the light. Keith's red shirt is dotted with sparkles, his black pants have silver conchos down the side. Mick is in white, a long black scarf trailing almost to the floor. He leaps high, then bows.

"All right, Fort Collins, all right!" There's an edge of scorn in his voice, but Fort Collins is on its feet and yelping, and Keith hammers out the first chords of "Jumping Jack Flash."

I was born in a cross fire hurricane . . .

Yahoo! The Stones are here!

I was raised with a strap across my back . . .

Don't they look fine! Bill Wyman, his Fender high over his hip, standing in his customary trance. Mick Taylor bending over his Gibson, Charlie snapping at the high hat, and Mick strutting like a little red rooster.

> But it's all right now
> In fact it's a gas
> It's all right
> I'm Jumping Jack Flash
> It's a gas, gas, gas

A holy moment for ten thousand kids, but it doesn't get as high again. Mick never hits a peak, and the kids are shy. An eighteen-year-old freshman from Laramie is beside me, crewcutted and in his high-school letter jacket. He's kneeling in an aisle with his date, loving it; his girl's bright brown eyes drink in Jagger's body, but they are cautious and baffled. "Street Fighting Man" closes the show; could it be their song, now or ever?

> I was like any other kid, which is why all the rest identified
> with me. I was just the same as they were, except that I'd
> jumped the tracks a bit more, that's all. All the stuff: about my
> leading them and perverting them or whatever, it's a lot of cock
> . . . We just sort of went along together, didn't we?
> —Mick Jagger, quoted in *Playboy*

The Los Angeles Forum ("the Fabulous Forum," say the ads) is color-coded. On one side all the seats, signs, and mini-togas of the ushers are a garish yellow; on the other, all is an equally garish orange. The Forum can hold eighteen thousand at full capacity and can be adapted to suit any sport, entertainment, or convention purpose; its parking lots end only where the Inglewood racetrack's lots begin; it has no windows. Swathed at night in cosmetic lighting, dreamlike and utterly free of blemish, the Forum seems a scale model of itself. More than the new Madison Square Garden, more even than Houston's Astrodome (obviously Texas eccentric), the Forum seems a fantasy tribute to the tons of excess wealth that burden 1960s America with a Tiberian opulence.

The Stones are scheduled for two concerts on a single evening at the Forum; thirty-six thousand people, mostly teenagers, have paid an average of seven dollars a seat to see them. Scalpers are getting $50 for the $12.50 top-price seats. That is but a fraction of the money spent for this evening's pleasure. The children of Los Angeles, Pasadena, Burbank, Glendale, Riverside, and the other fabled freeway towns arrive in five-thousand-dollar cars designed by Detroit for the youth market, in clothes of suede and silk and exotic plastics, in boots from Italy and vests from Persia, sunglasses from Paris and belts from Mexico, bells from India and T-shirts from London. Levis, too, but more likely beige corduroy than blue denim; leather jackets, but of tailored buckskin with beaded fringe fifteen inches long. They don't look neat, because that's not the look. They are hippies, after all, stoned high and low on every conceivable (and therefore available) drug, but they are rich. Not everyone, yet as they drift in clumps to their orange and yellow seats, their easy acceptance of the divine right to overconsumption is as evident as their Southern California tans.

The show starts almost two hours late—the rush conversion from the afternoon's hockey game took longer than planned—but no one minds. It's the full tour concert as the Stones planned it. Nineteen-year-old Terry Reid, the latest in a long line of handsome English guitarists, opens it with his rock-blues trio, then B.B. King does his customarily magnificent set. Ike and Tina Turner follow, and their precision choreographed rite of sexual ecstasy knocks 'em dead.

On run the Stones, Mick in black tonight, waving a big hello to Los Angeles—"Has it really been three years, Los Angeles? It doesn't feel so

139

long"—and smiling back as he crests the wave of adulation that rolls up from the darkness. They lay it down, moving through the rockers, dropping back into blues, then "I'm Free," Mick going to the stage corners and telling the eighteen thousand, "I'm free, I want you to be free, we gotta be free, we can be free if we know we're free." On into the sublimely evil "Midnight Rambler," and then he stops at center stage and peers out through the spotlights.

"I wish I could see all you people," he says with honeyed wistfulness. "You can see us and we're beautiful, but there are so many of you and you're probably a bit more beautiful than we are." (Is Mick Jagger actually ceding his spotlight place to the multitude?)

"Chip, let's have some light on the people." Instantly the Forum is bright, and the crowd, freed from darkness, looks at itself, and the Stones blast into "Little Queenie," then "Satisfaction" ("Oh, we gotta find us a little satisfaction, gotta find it, and I can't find it for you, you gotta find it for yourselves"), then "Honky Tonk Woman," and the kids are on their feet, leaving the seats and pouring into the aisles, jumping over the sideburn set in the front rows, streaking to the stage, body to body, faces laughing and incredulous, Mick dancing just above their outstretched arms.

She said her name was Terri, and she appeared out of the slowly disintegrating stage-side mob, crying, shaking, and almost vomiting with fear. Shouting ushers were clearing the hall for the second show, and she dodged around them, her eye makeup smudged blackly around her tiny nose. She said she had come with her boyfriend Jim and they had been sitting up in back but had worked their way down front and then she lost him. He had her pocketbook in his jacket with all her money and she didn't know what to do.

At 1:30 A.M. poor crying Terri was a pitiful sight. Two friends and I took her out to eat (she refused everything). She said she lived in El Monte, had run away from home and was staying with friends. She didn't know their name though, and her Jim, off the next day to Vietnam with the air force, was last name–less to her too. She was scared of going home ("they'll kill me"), and every public crash pad and free clinic in L.A. was either closed for the night or for good. "You're a girl of our times," said Eve. "Like a rolling stone," joked Harry.

There was nothing else we could do, so we gave her a lecture on getting along with her parents until she could make it on her own, put ten dollars in her reluctant hand, and forced her into a cab that would take her to El Monte. I hope she got there.

Bukka White, an old bluesman from Memphis, cousin and teacher of B.B. King, is backstage at the Forum, and a young white friend takes him in to meet the Stones. Keith is sitting plucking out a tune on his National steel guitar. That's Bukka's instrument too, and he listens for a minute, then turns to Mick. "Why, that boy's pickin'!" says Bukka, genuinely amazed. "He's a star. Hey boy," and he taps Keith's knee, "you ever cut any records? You're that good, boy."

Oakland is next, and as the tour day drags to a start about 1 P.M., there arrives a singular addition to the cast, one John Jaymes, at times accompanied by his business partner Gary M. Stark, at others by his mother. John Jaymes, who is thirty, very, very fat, and whose name has been shortened from something long and Italian, is the president of a New York firm called Young American Enterprises, which in turn controls the fortunes of some nineteen other companies. John is essentially a "fad merchandiser"—"fads are my basic business material." Through his companies he creates, designs, manufactures, distributes, and sells T-shirts, bumper stickers, buttons, notepads, dolls, balloons, and toys keyed to any bit of nonsense that is currently sweeping the country. One company has a contract to merchandise *Rowan and Martin's Laugh-In* products, another makes "graffiti stationery," another is preparing to flood the country with body-painting kits. "We're

141

getting it so good now," says John, "that if there's a fad on Monday, we'll have a button and sticker for it in the stores by Friday."

Though he claims to have made and lost millions in it, merchandising only hints at the diversity of John's interests. A one-time narcotics agent (the grass we smoke, he says, is garbage), he once ran unsuccessfully for office in New York and promoted rock 'n' roll shows at Shea Stadium. He is now setting up a youth paper to be sent free to a carefully selected list of a few hundred thousand teenage consumers, serves on a Congressional youth committee, and also does "youth promotion" for various major corporations, including Chrysler, the maker of Dodge cars.

How he got on the tour is a mystery, but Dodge was his angle. With him arrives a fleet of Dodges to replace the rented cars, and for every tour city similar fleets plus trucks for the equipment are promised—and maybe a Dodge executive plane from time to time. All this comes free to Stones Promotions, as does John himself. "It's a gamble for me," he says. "It's a prestige promotion for us, plus, of course, a tie-in promotion for Dodge."

Yet John's real (or maybe apparent—such distinctions lose their meaning around John Jaymes) contributions are his chutzpah and his "contacts." John, says John, can fix a ticket anywhere, make sure nobody gets busted, find hotel rooms when none are available, make scheduled airlines wait for late equipment trucks, and bluff his way through to the man at any top. "Everything's angles and how to work 'em," he says.

He meets a test the first day out. The scene: Oakland's Edgewater Inn; time: 6 P.M. Everyone but the Stones, Ronnie, and Sam is safely in Oakland, and the Stones plane is due any minute. In the restaurant John has a phone glued to his ear, a drink to his hand. Word comes that a few reporters and maybe one hundred kids have gathered at the airport. John smells disaster: hadn't Mick said "no reporters"? His porcine face takes on a Churchillian belligerence, the table becomes war operations nerve center. Calls flash out. The airplane must land at a new spot. Impossible? He asks for a higher-up. There is none. Then the limousines must be able to drive to the airplane steps. Impossible too. He orders more drinks. David Horowitz arrives and offers hushed suggestions; John waves them away. He demands that the Stones be radioed the information that an unruly mob awaits them. No. Finally he gets permission to board the plane himself and warn them in person.

Down goes the phone; double-time through the lobby, and a 70-mile-per-hour run to the airport. No limousines. He rents a few cars: "Send the bill to me." The plane lands. John is up the steps, then down. He leads the Boys out. There is one TV crew, two kids with movie cameras, and perhaps fifty others who walk politely beside the group until they reach the cars, of which there are not enough. We all pile in, eight to a car. Screech to the motel. Mission accomplished.

The Oakland audience knows nothing of John Jaymes and his hustles. If they did, they wouldn't believe he could be connected with "their" Rolling Stones. In Oakland that night they want reality as they see it; a curious place, the Bay Area. This blessedly beautiful gathering of cities on still green hills beside a tranquil bay is, for its residents, a new Paris, the intellectual and moral center of the world youth avant-garde. To the Bay Area mentality, Los Angeles is plastic, London frivolous, New York impossible—and dirty, besides. Happy in its provinciality and passionately convinced of its superiority, it believes itself a microcosm of American problems and possibilities.

Problems and possibilities, precisely; the Bay Area, a tensely schizoid union of Berkeley and San Francisco, has never decided which is more real. Since the free-speech movement, militant Berkeley has angrily emphasized the problems. With the Haight-Ashbury at its golden peak, good-timey San Francisco embodied the psychedelic possibilities. While the Haight decayed and fled from itself, Berkeley took acid, created, fought for, and lost People's Park, and now no one knows what to do. Berkeley and San Francisco have become less geographic entities than conflicting states of mind, often existing in equal strength within the same person.

Rock 'n' roll has become the prime symbol of the paradox and a bone of incessant contention. The militant calls it a capitalist diversion and quotes Bob Dylan to prove it; the fan mocks the militant's paranoia and dances, convinced that music will dissolve entrenched and profitable inequity. Both mistrust their own feelings as much as their "enemies," and the Bay Area hasn't had a community good time in years. In a summer of rock festivals, San Francisco's effort, the Wild West Show, was destroyed before it happened by the tactless extravagance of its "hip rock" backers and the concerted spite of radicals who mistook incompetence for a plot against the people.

The incestuous battling did not cease for the Stones; if anything it got more intense and more confused. Promoter Bill Graham and *San Francisco Chronicle* columnist Ralph J. Gleason, who usually defend rock as the poetic revolution while avoiding radical attacks on rock's business ethic, publicly lashed the Stones for their reactionary arrogance and greed. "Mick Jagger may be a great performer," Graham told all listeners, "but he's an egotistical creep as a person." Jagger, wrote Gleason, had personal moral responsibility for the high ticket prices and the tour's tough contracts. The radicals, who in their hearts adore the Stones for their uncompromising toughness, did their best to forget their political doubts and scrambled for tickets with the rest of the fans. Both concerts, of course, were total sellouts.

It's all there at concert time: a community's projected doubts and wants brought together by the magic of theater into the blue-gray cavern of the Oakland Coliseum. Gathered, they focus before the stage as an invisible but palpable question that demands resolution in the music of the Rolling Stones. The Stones fend it off, avoiding questions about money and politics at a small preconcert press conference. "I think you know we're with you on Vietnam and everything," Mick says. "It's just that I don't find it a thing to sing songs about. It's music for us, and supposed to be fun. We want you to get up and dance, not sit back and be worried about what you're supposed to do."

The first concert, plagued by broken amps and erratic mikes, barely gets off the ground, but the second is a gas. Feeding on the crowd's intensity, the band plays magnificently, Keith hurling back the invisible demands in twisted, astringent lines from his transparent guitar. "I'm Free" goes dead to the crowd that's been wearing "Free Huey," "Free the Oakland 7," and "Free the Chicago 8" buttons for years—so what if you're free, Mick Jagger?—but when the lights come up, the crowd breaks loose on schedule. Some dance to the music as they once did at the Fillmore, but thousands surround the stage in a sea of upraised fists, each begging Mick's approval, each asking, Which side are you on, boy?

A few bearded kids try to climb on the stage and Mick dances back from the edge, his ironic smile suddenly gone. He sings "Satisfaction" as if possessed, his head shaking in fury, but the fists still wave in his face, unsatisfied. Into "Street Fighting Man," and Mick's right hand finally makes a fist that rises slowly above his head. A new wave of fists appears, but then his left rises in a V. There are scattered boos. A kid makes it over the edge; Sam scurries over to get him off. Bill Graham, eyes blazing, grabs Sam and knocks him down. The music rockets on and the two grown men roll awkwardly under the piano. In the crescendo Mick hurls back the question that is his only answer: "But what can a poor boy do / 'cept to sing in a rock 'n' roll band?"

He grabs a hatful of rose petals and flings great handfuls of them at the mob. A few acres of kids stand openmouthed, each on some personal brink of hope and fear, and it seems that this singing poor boy is doing just fine. It's over; the Stones run from the stage.

They are disappointed; San Francisco, they had thought, was a groovy place. "Politics like that, I don't believe the intensity," says Mick. In their dressing room, the banquet Graham had ordered for them (with special English beers and cheeses) is scattered obscenely on the floor. On one wall Graham had pinned a poster of himself giving the finger to the world at large. Now food is smeared over his face, and "This is where my head is at" is written in a balloon from his grinning mouth. The Stones will be back—they had already promised a free San Francisco concert at the end of the tour—but tonight they hurry to John Jaymes's waiting Dodges and fly back to mansioned comfort in pleasant, if plastic, L.A.

And that Mick Jagger—I wouldn't take him if the price was only $3000. . . . We guessed wrong with the Rolling Stones the last time around. It was one of our biggest financial blunders. . . . The price was a bit high but it looked like a good investment. We put in wooden horses as a barrier and put a line of policemen along with them. . . . Those kids charged and rolled over everything, police, horses, and all. We wound up with some crushed policemen.

Now the Monkees, there's an improvement. Really cooperative. They opened by telling the kids, "Sit in your seats and enjoy the show." This was really good for crowd control.

—Promoter Joe Murnick, quoted in *Amusement Business.*

A strange warning, that Oakland concert—what do these kids want so badly from the Stones? But the message, even if it were decipherable, is lost in the blur of concerts that follow. With Oakland down, the opening high moments are over. Now the body of the tour begins. Above all else, it is bloody hard work. The hours are ridiculous; bed is seldom reached before dawn, and once everyone is up, showered, fed, and dressed, there is time for nothing but getting organized and to the gig. San Diego, then Phoenix (with a 3 A.M. stop for the hell of it in Las Vegas, where we wander from club to club as startled patrons ask us if we're the cast of *Hair*), then a night off before beginning a four-day run to Dallas, Auburn, Champaign, and Chicago to wind up the first half of the tour.

Touring—how to remember its oddness? It is a trip in every sense: a decision to accept the discipline of a long and intense journey that, though known in form is mysterious in content. Normal stimuli—friends, home, and daily routine—that we all call reality are replaced by the repetitive actions of constant travel. Life on tour, while infinitely more exciting than ordinary life, is much less varied. It has no cause and effect, only sequence; you cannot ask yourself, "What am I going to do today?" because you know what you have to do even though you have no idea what's going to happen. It is a tunnel of adventure through which you fall in wide-eyed but disoriented passivity. The more experienced conserve their energy, but the powerful tendency is to get stoned and stay stoned on whatever combination of pills and powders, liquids and weeds comes your way. To leave the tour is almost unimaginable. Moments that could be snatched for walks, reading, or sight-seeing are passed up. When you get to your motel room, you turn on the TV and leave it on, never changing channels, until you leave.

Undoubtedly more bizarre in detail (do candidates sniff cocaine through tightly rolled ten dollar bills in the first-class jet compartment?), the tour is more like a presidential campaign than anything else. We leap across the vastness of America in giant bounds. To everyone on whom we descend in sloppy mass—desk clerks, Avis girls, stewardesses, porters, head waiters, and cops—we are an event ("Guess who I saw at work today, dear?"). We move in an unwieldy splendor, waiting grumpily for John Jaymes's arranged Dodges or limousines, ignoring ranks of empty cabs.

At each city is the meeting of the faithful, who have already been warmed up by the introductory acts before we arrive. The Stones come on just barely in time, deliver the prepared show, bow, then roar away through the waving hands and smiling anxious faces of well-wishers. There is no flesh-pressing. The promoter and his family, maybe a disc jockey or two, get into the dressing room to thrill for a moment in the glow of indisputable fame, but the ordinary Stones lover is kept at a distance that would appall the post-Kennedy politician. Surrounded by security men, we sweep in and out of cities, honking our way through red lights at top speed, driving as though pursued by assassins to elude the few carloads of fans who want only an autograph and a good snap for their Instamatics.

In political terms, the Stones are the candidate, Ronnie the campaign manager, Sam the go-for and court jester, and Jo the traveling secretary and liaison with campaign headquarters—the Stones' London office with which she is in daily contact. John Jaymes is the fixer and detail man; Tony, a big and nutty black kid, the strong man; and there is even a press corps: photographer Ethan Russell, Stones biographer Stanley Booth, and myself. In Los Angeles there were always extras in our cast; on the road there are none.

The cast becomes a group—not quite a team, but a band united by the uniqueness of the joint experience. The whole tour numbers perhaps forty people, counting equipment men and supporting acts, but they travel in their own casts, converging with us only at concert time. Chip Monck, Bill Belmont, and Stew—the advance men—we see often, but B.B. King, who appeared at half the concerts, barely met the Stones. (In the whole month, none of "the Boys" took the time to introduce himself and pay respects.) There were light men and sound technicians who, after working for a month in absolute interdependence, did not know each other's first names. Stanley, Ethan, and I have little to do but stay reasonably alert, take our notes and pictures, and be sure we're not left behind—a demanding task in itself. Everyone else has one or many jobs to do, and while everything gets done, nothing is done well enough for anyone to relax. That is in part due to Murphy's inexorable law, in part to the last-minute scramble in which the tour was planned, and in part because there is no chief of operations. Ronnie, John, or Bill Belmont can, for instance, set the time and means for departure from hotel to gig, and they often do, in conflicting independence. When they do agree, Sam, acting on mumbled instructions from a sleepy Keith, can insist on new arrangements that will give the Boys another hour's sleep.

So we arrive in Dallas to find that all room reservations have been canceled because Bill had forgotten to reconfirm them. While he chews at the scarred stubs of nails long since bitten away, a furious Ronnie has a tearful desk clerk begging space from every hotel in town. The plane chartered for the Dallas to Auburn leg flies away empty on instructions from an unknown culprit. Two hours of frantic calls result in the following travel spaghetti: press corps, Jo, Stew, and Terry Reid fly Delta to Atlanta and rent cars for a three-hour drive to Auburn. The equipment goes to Columbus, Georgia, while the equipment crew must fly to Montgomery, Alabama, then drive to

Columbus to get it. Ronnie, Sam, and the Boys get an ancient chartered plane to Columbus. It's a four-hour flight, and after takeoff they find there is no food, no drink, and no cigarettes on board, plus no heat and stuck-open vents under every seat that emit steady arctic winds.

Dallas to Auburn was the low point and everyone was bitching. Mick wanted Bill Belmont "carpeted," and Bill said the crew thought the Stones were "a bunch of snobs playing dull music." Rookie Mick Taylor was bewildered, and Stew, on every Stones tour since they were doing England's cinema circuit, was disgusted. "We used to just do a bleeding tour," he said in soft Scots, "get into town, get a room, hire a few local blokes to carry the gear, set up and do the gig—thirty, forty cities like that. But when you start hiring whole houses and cars and have people around like Ronnie Schneider and John Jaymes, for Godsakes, you're bound to have trouble."

The real problem, however, is not the disorganization as such, but the subtly pervasive hysteria that comes with being close to the Rolling Stones. The Stones are stars, on tour if not elsewhere, automatically the center of attention and privilege. None insist on that status, but they accept its security with an equanimity both innocent and arrogant.

The Stones' perspective on the tour is, of course, unique. They are, for instance, the only people who have old friends along for company—themselves. The whole machine, with all its delicate tunings, is caused by and devoted to them; their only job is to play. Since they do that well, they are willing to treat the rest as someone else's job and thus ignore it. All private people, they retreat as best they can from the center of attention. Charlie, like all drummers, is just the drummer; one suspects that he has opinions, but he keeps them to himself. Bill Wyman, always followed closely by Astrid, goes his own silent way; Mick Taylor, although treated with a generous courtesy by the others, is still, by virtue of his newness, on his own. Keith, the group's eminence bizarre and Mick Jagger's unsentimental alter ego, scorns any overt leadership role. Only Jagger—to all non-Stones the very center of this hierarchical solar system—takes an active interest in the overall direction of the machine; yet he refuses to lead it, and so no one does. His wishes for it are vague and unformed; as interpreted by the loyal lieutenants, they become the ultimate command: "Mick wants. . . ." But when the organization broke down completely in Dallas, he complained bitterly, "The trouble with this tour is that there is no one strong enough to run it." The irony went unremarked; the Stones, and certainly Mick, are the tour's essential premise, and therefore, if not always right, never wrong.

All non-Stones are relatively insecure and in a constant struggle to maintain their place in the graded orbits around the band. While on one hand there is an undercurrent of hostility to the Stones—why do they always get the dope first?—there is a stronger one of self-dramatization, a pressure to maximize one's importance. That in turn increases the Stones' status; everyone is more important if the Stones are more important.

John Jaymes's noisy finaglings in Oakland are a classic example of the syndrome, but almost no one is immune—Ronnie, for instance. A nephew of the Stones' business manager Allan Klein, he quit Klein's firm, ABKCO Industries, just before the tour and set up Stones Promotions as an independent company. The Stones' tour manager when he worked for Klein, he now has cautious hopes of enlarging his role, if not of replacing Klein entirely. The best means to that end is a successful tour that in his terms means, above all, substantial profits. He can do nothing the Stones do not want—that is, baseball stadium concerts, but he can drive exacting bargains. He does; he gets the whole guarantee from each promoter, rather than the normal half, before concert time. This he puts into short-term notes at 8½ percent. He cuts the booking agency's commission to 7½ percent; it is normally between 10 and 15 percent for major acts. At every concert he dogs the promoters, watching for every possible hustle, checking receipts, and bullying them when they complain of minor contract infractions. He makes sure the Stones know all of this in gleeful boasts of his prowess.

(It is not all boasting; Stones Promotions grosses approximately $1.7 million on the tour. From that figure, however, must be deducted all costs and overheads, including the fees for Terry Reid, B.B. King, Ike and Tina

Turner, and Chuck Berry, all hired by the corporation. Each Stone probably added about $50,000 to his present fortune for the month's work.)

Sam makes himself gatekeeper to the Boys and treats them with a deference due only retarded royal children. Jo worries she cannot be all that Mick expects of her. Jeff, the equipment boy, quits Terry Reid to join the Stones because "carrying Stones' amps is more fun." For myself, when I spend a day close to the Stones I feel anointed and cool; whenever I drift away from the inner circle I feel nervously out of it. We all grow tired of smiling but fear stopping. The jostling of those close to the Stones to stay close is—entirely noncoincidentally—strikingly similar to the mad rush to the stage at every concert.

All of this is a colossal bummer, but the miracle is that, despite it and even with it, the tour is an absolute gas for all concerned. That is indubitably due to the Rolling Stones; the hysteria is but the obverse of the excitement, and the coin comes up heads far more often than tails. Withal we are mates and have great fun together.

> Girl: I LOVE the Rolling Stones.
>
> *Time* Reporter: So do I, but . . .
>
> Girl: No buts for me. Mick is so beautiful. You know how he
>   can stand there with his hand on his hip, twitching his little
>   ass, and then he smiles! and falls back, pushing the micro-
>   phone away, and does little hops, I could die.
>
> Reporter: Wow, you really . . .
>
> Girl: And Keith, he's so mean and sexy—evil, my girl friend
>   calls it, but I bet he's real shy inside. And Charlie's got the
>   greatest smile, looks like a camel or a dolphin, or somebody
>   who knows just everything.
>
> Reporter: I like them in my head, but I don't know how to
>   show it.
>
> Girl: Well, take off your tie, stupid, and let it all hang out.
>   That's your story 'cause that's what the Stones are all about.

151

Night after night, the concerts themselves are a stoned perfect thrill and delight to the ear, eye, mind, and soul. No two concerts are the same; each is influenced by an infinity of variables. The Champaign hall is open and spacious, Dallas's Moody Auditorium low-ceilinged and dense; the Arizona State Coliseum is a scarred old rodeo palace. On B.B. King nights the mood is subtly spiritual; Tina Turner nights are unmistakably musky. One concert influences the next. Tired, rested, stoned, unstoned, grooving, or edgy, the Stones themselves are never the same. Among other things, the Stones are Englishmen in America; they think the cars, papers, TV, freeways, clothes, slang, and even airport shops filled with the products of a thousand "fad merchandisers" are all far out and fascinating. L.A., Dallas, Chicago—they get a buzz from just being in such exotic, storied places, and it all comes out in the music.

On the way to Fort Collins, Mick and Keith set the basic format, scribbling the names of fourteen tunes (out of thirty rehearsed) on airplane stationery. "Jumping Jack" to open, then Chuck Berry's "Carol" from their first record, "Sympathy for the Devil" and "Stray Cat Blues"—all uptempo rockers. Then Mick and Keith alone on two slow blues, "Prodigal Son" and "You Gotta Move," then the moving "Love In Vain" from their new album with the whole band. A little pickup with "Under My Thumb" and "I'm Free," then the showpiece, "Midnight Rambler," followed by another Berry tune, "Little Queenie," to open a string of their biggest hits, each building on the one before: "Satisfaction," "Honky Tonk Woman," and "Street Fighting Man." Nicely balanced between old and new, fast and slow, the show has a solid dramatic form: strong opening, introspective middle, then out to a one-two-three finale.

They never stop changing the order and balance. "Love in Vain" moves forward to the spot before "Prodigal" so they can come out of the blues straight into "Thumb." That is sometimes replaced with "Gimme Shelter." "I'm Free" is dropped after Oakland, and they start doing "Live with Me." Mick fiddles with his costume, too; sometimes in white, he most often wears black pants with silver buttons from waist to heel, a long crimson scarf, a studded belt, and a black T-shirt with the upside-down U glyph of Leo, his sun sign. The format changes less than any other aspect of the concerts. "If we keep the same tunes," explains Keith, "we can improvise within them rather than stumbling rigidly through new ones all the time."

The concerts always improve, but there are down nights. In Auburn, Chuck Berry refuses to get off the stage, letting his nightclub routine on "My Ding-a-Ling" run forever. The hall is full of Southern fraternity gentlemen and their ladies. The Stones concert is a prestige date: Friday night the Stones, then a drive to Athens Saturday to see the Auburn Tigers play the Georgia Bulldogs. They sit there, in their Ivy League suits and permanent waves, still trying to catch up with 1959. Maybe high school kids would have a better time, but they're all watching their own night football games. All over America kids are learning they can be teenagers at thirty-five, but the Auburn crowd is a comfortable thirty-five at twenty-one. When the second show closes at 2 A.M., student entertainment director Jette Campbell announces, "The dean of women students has said all girls have 'when over' permission, so don't worry about being late." It gets the biggest applause of the night.

But no, I cannot describe the shows for you, nor tell you what fun they were, nor explain the breathtaking symmetry of Chip Monck's blue spotlights cutting icelike down through the smoky air to end in golden sparkles on Charlie's cymbals in the pool of red-green light that is the stage. What is that rush that inevitably comes as Bill Wyman's bass makes its guttural run to open "Live with Me" and Mick picks it up with those masterfully slimy lines, "Well, I got real nasty habits, yeah, an' I take my tea at three." Or the kaleidoscopic flash of memories of times and dances and girls when they get to "Little Queenie"—"She's too cute to be a minute over seventeen." Every night, sometimes with the first notes of "Jumping Jack," sometimes not until Keith steps forward to do his solo on "Sympathy," Stanley Booth (a remarkable lunatic from Memphis) and I share a look of bewildered joy, know we are both insane Rolling Stones fans, and then whoop with the jolts of pleasure they give us.

They are a band, the Rolling Stones, five young men working together to

153

make that precious thing that is rock 'n' roll music—no "type" of rock, just rock 'n' roll, period. Keith, their master musician and the leader of the band, looks strikingly like Isak Dinesen in her old age. The resemblance is more than skin deep. Every night he plays his lean and keening lines, and beneath their harshness there appears suddenly a dedication to the classic elements of music—form, clarity, and grace—so intense that his wasted face, pathetic skinniness, and utter carelessness for his body will never be a mystery again. He sits to play "You Gotta Move," and his hands bring from the battered steel guitar a lyric twinging sadness and crushingly fateful chords. As Charlie keeps a muffled beat behind them, Mick sings the ancient Negro words:

> You may be high, you may be low,
> You may be rich, chile, you may be po',
> But when the Lord gets ready,
> You gotta move.

and you know that they know exactly what it means. Arrogant they may be, but their absolute knowledge of that rock-bottom blues truth gives them full right to a cynical disdain for those who haven't dared to learn it.

Interviewers ask Mick Taylor if it feels strange to replace Brian Jones, and he never knows what to stay. Of course it is strange, and Mick, with his shy and friendly face, has not replaced him. But only those who ask care. His playing gets stronger. On "Sympathy" and "Love in Vain" he shares solo spots with Keith, and by Champaign we are all listening to what he has to say—a music quieter and less sure of itself than Keith's, but fresher, more open and searching. The spontaneous applause that greets his work is a full welcome to the group.

Bill and Charlie—the rhythm section. Not very fancy, almost dull. Bill stands there like a gargoyle, his eyes blank and his fingers barely seeming to move over his baby blue Fender, one of the cheapest basses you can buy. Charlie keeps the beat and does his job as if he were a musician they had hired for the night. And yet you can't listen to the Stones without moving, without succumbing to their dark and merciless drive. Thank Bill and Charlie for the inescapable pounding that grounds each song to a dynamo.

"I'm free to sing my song, even though it's out of tune." Mick Jagger wrote those words as a twenty-year-old boy, and prancing and dancing up there in the middle of his starburst, he lives them. Leo is the lion's sign, the sign of the full golden sun of summer, of radiant self-love, and Mick is Leo incarnate. Dancer and singer, he does not interpret his songs bodily, like James Brown, but moves in independent counterpoint. He ducks, leaps, and almost falls; stamps his foot, then suddenly is still; bends out over the edge of the stage or walks petulantly away and gulps beer with his back to the crowd. He can flirt, scorn, mock, and beseech, changing mood and aspect with a dazzling and magical speed. At times he seems less himself than his archetype, the beautiful young man: Narcissus, Patroclus, David, Romeo—that ideal creature of myth beloved by all generations of men and women. Just barely graceful, erotic more than sexy, and only now becoming truly handsome, he is *free*. It seems the only word ("He does anything he wants," someone behind me murmurs in Dallas as we watch, transfixed): free as a bird, free form, free time, and fancy free. Free to sing his song, any old time.

Then all together—the combination of the sight and sound is mind-boggling. There is in the show some reference to all the arts, painting and sculpture as well as dance and drama. Mick and Keith, Keith and Charlie, Bill and Charlie, Keith and Mick Taylor; the empathetic intricacy of their relationships as they bend to one another, listen, suggest, take command, retreat, form, re-form; and all the time the lights are changing, and the terribly familiar songs are turning up new lines, new associations, until one can only bathe unreflectingly in it all.

And the Stones, of course, are but half the concert. The kids—10,400 at Fort Collins; 36,000 in L.A.; 19,318 in Oakland; 21,000 in Chicago; thousands and thousands and thousands of kids—are the other half, and are they ever fine! Of all the concert variables they are the most important. Nothing can happen without them, but with them, when they start to smile

155

and shake, to stand and shout, to forget why they came and how they got there and what they were planning to do the next day, to forget everything but being right there, then everything happens, and it's no longer a concert, but a wild high-time happiness that everyone shares.

There's a million theories about rock 'n' roll, what it is and means, but what's most obvious is most overlooked: it's music. Plain old music: rhythm, melody, and harmony; mathematical relationships of frequencies and time intervals; those pleasing combinations of vibrations that some philosophers declare to be the ultimate mystery and reality of the universe. And these kids, ordinary American kids we all know and recognize, are true music lovers. They just love music, that's all; spend vast sums on it, listen to hours of it, think about it incessantly, find their heroes among its makers, date their lives by it and, in geometrically increasing numbers, make it themselves. When I was in school, musical kids were the sissies, and we read in social studies that Italy was a musical country. What is going on here anyway? The holy rollers used to be a minority sect.

In Phoenix three girls are sitting in the front row, obviously friends who came together: a pretty girlish blonde, a rather plain brunette with glasses, and a cool beauty-queen type who smokes her cigarettes in a holder. No dates. At first they are reserved and stiff, trying to look their best—do they have fantasies that maybe He will notice them? They smoke a lot. The blonde starts to smile during "Carol"; the brunette blushes when Mick puts the microphone between his thighs on "Sympathy." She recovers during the blues, but the beauty queen's jaw sags open the tiniest bit. Her tongue flickers out during "Under My Thumb" and she drops her holder. She doesn't pick it up. By this time the blonde's neatly coiled hair has somehow come undone on one side and, never taking her eyes off the stage, she vainly pecks at it with one hand. "Midnight Rambler" is too much for all of them. In its moment of eerie silence they watch as Mick slips off his belt and falls to his knees. He raises it above his head. "Well, now you've heard about the Boston Strangler. . . ."

Bam! The belt comes down as the band hits a monster chord. The blonde almost falls back over her seat, the brunette covers her breasts, and the beauty-queen goes limp. Mick hisses: "Honey, he ain't one of those!"

They're hooked. No more cigarettes. The brunette's glasses have disappeared, and when the lights go on, the girls are on their feet. Tears start in the blonde's eyes. The stage rush begins, and a big hulking kid leaps over three rows, aiming for a gap beside the beauty queen. He doesn't make it and hits her heavily on the shoulder. She doesn't feel a thing. Her body rolls with the unexpected blow as if she were water. I lose them in the crowd; my last glimpse is of the brunette, her hands above her head, palms up and fingers spread wide, her mouth wide open, singing, "No satisfaction, baby, no satisfaction," and she is beautiful now, transformed, her eyes bright as a bride's, her hair swinging loose around her shoulders.

Faces pop out of the crowd, eyes suddenly make contact, and for a few seconds, kids who may be twenty rows apart and total strangers smile, wave, and dance together. Kids with beards, kids with mustaches; twelve-year-olds with their parents, thirteen-year-old runaways; kids stoned on acid, kids who've never touched a joint; unimaginable freaks and student-body presidents. In the top balconies, from which the Stones are barely visible but the music is still bell clear, kids dance in the aisles behind their seats as if the concert were the best sock-hop ball in the world. There are no bad dancers; the straightest-looking kids move with awesome grace, picking up on the songs at whatever level they dig best and working it on out. Some kids look scared, afraid to show what they feel, and they watch it all happen, holding their jackets and handbags tight in damp hands. But they're not having a bad time, and who knows what they'll do at the next concert?

They seem the children of some miracle. I have, I suppose, no real knowledge of who they are and what they'll become. What it means I could never say. Maybe it is as illusory as music itself, some hypnotic trick, an evening's diversion, but I do know that while I am dancing too, and singing along with "Satisfaction" until my lungs are bursting ("Gonna find some, Gonna get some, some satisfaction"), I feel a kinship with these kids, my brothers and sisters, as profound and happy as any I have ever known.

Dearest Mick I, Mick II, Keith, Charlie, and Bill,

Welcome back to America and Chicago. It's been a long time since I saw you last. Never in my life have I ever missed your concerts. Even if you gave two shows I would spend the whole day with you and enjoy every heart breaking minute.

I'm very sorry to hear about Brian. I'm a Roman Catholic and I gave Brian two spiritual bouquets. Masses are being said for Jones in America now. One bouquet in Chicago and one in Michigan, I promise that as soon as I feel I have the money I will give you all a bouquet. There are Masses also for the living. At different times I will be sending you Mass cards c/o your fan club c/o Jo Bergman. I want to help you people. I'm so worried about you and I luv you so much.

I do hope you enjoy my cookies that I made for you. They all were made each with luving care my dears. If I get my gift and letter thru, would you give me some acknowledgement that you received my letter etc. all in one piece? I still have your last letter that I got from you in 1965. I got it on May 11 and you had a concert May 10, I think Mother's Day. That concert was really great. I luv all of your concerts very much. Your records are the greatest. They make me feel good all over whenever I play them, but lately I feel a little sad.

Anyway would it be possible if you could send a heart-broken, lonely girl 21 yr old fan a word of encouragement, and acknowledgement of my gift. Thank you.

I can't sleep tonight. It's now almost 12:45 A.M. I wish somebody with real strong hands would rub my back real hard and good. I've been having back aches now for about two weeks straight. They hurt like anything. Oh well, I wish I were real tired too, but I'm not.

Well better go. Take care and may Our Lord always watch over you and protect you especially while you're touring and

crossing the ocean going from country to country. Do be good
Stones and let me hear from you. I'm so lonely.

All My Luv. Always My Dears, [signed]

This letter was attached to a plate of cookies given the Stones in
Chicago. The Stones neither saw the letter nor had any of the cookies.

Abbie Hoffman is at the Chicago concert (along with the most and loudest-
screaming girls of any show). He didn't have a ticket, but an usher who recognized his face and curly hair let him in to the $7.50 section right up front.
He had been trying to reach the Stones for days, even calling up the
Ambassador West and pretending to be Elvis ("Yassuh, I jes' wanned to see
how Mick an' the boys were doin'"). He sends a note to the Stones from his
seat; it gets through. Mick wants to see him too, and they get together in the
dressing room for a few minutes before show time.

Mick is dressing and brushing his hair; both are a little awkward. They
compliment each other on what they've been doing. "Your thing is sex,
mine's violence," says Abbie, and they both crack up. Abbie asks if he knows
that they are playing at the site of the 1968 Democratic convention. "Sure I
know," says Mick.

"Anita and I just came from the Washington moratorium," says Abbie.
"Great. There was Mitch Miller, or maybe it was Pete Seeger, leading the
crowd in 'Give Peace a Chance.'"

"Why not?" says Mick.

"I'll give peace a chance," says Abbie laughing, "one more chance."

A joint comes by and they have a few tokes. Abbie wanders over to
Ronnie, who is reading contracts.

"Hey, man, you the cat to see about money?"

Ronnie looks up guardedly at this freak in the inner sanctum.

"See, we could use some bread for our trial, you know, the Chicago 8. I
promise I'll pay you back right after it's over."

"No," says Ronnie with utter unconcern. Abbie goes back to Jagger.   159

"Could you lend us some money for our trial? It's expensive making the revolution."

"We got our own trials," says Mick. He slips on his deerskin moccasins. Abbie is left hanging. None of the other Stones seem to know or care who he is. Mick Taylor asks him for a match.

"Bunch of cultural nationalists," he says good-humoredly as he goes out the door. After the concert he says he's not sure how the Stones fit into the revolution, but "Mick Jagger sure is something else on stage." In a speech a few weeks later he calls him "our Myra Breckinridge."

With Chicago down and the tour more than half done, the Stones fly back to Los Angeles for a week's break. The first day back is for taping the *Ed Sullivan Show.* "We wanted to do Sullivan, not one of the new shows, 'cause there's nothing more far out than the *Ed Sullivan Show,*" says Keith. "It's so old it's funky." Like Ed himself, whom all the technicians in CBS's huge Hollywood studio call "Dad." The taping should be a bore—the band standing in place faking it to a record while Mick sings a new vocal track—but Dad saves the day.

Between numbers Ed is supposed to walk up to Mick, say a few words, and then retire while they begin the next tune. Out he lumbers as they finish "Gimme Shelter."

"That was great, Mick, glad to have you back on the show. What are you going to sing now?"

"We're going to . . . "

But Ed, in suit, shirt, and tie of television blue, is so precisely what he has always been and always will be that Mick starts to laugh. Keith howls and runs to hide behind the silver foil set. The audience titters.

"Cut," someone cries, and they try again. Ed says exactly the same words with exactly the same inflection, and this time everyone laughs.

"Maybe we ought to do it without you saying anything," Mick suggests, trying to be both practical and kind. That's okay with Ed. Third try. But Ed forgets not to say anything and again delivers his lines. The place erupts with laughter. Fourth time gets it, and the Stones disappear for a week of rest far from the madding crowd and public eye.

Cathy: Two years ago my girlfriend Mary and I were married and living in Ojai. It was okay, but boring, and all we ever thought about was Mick Jagger. We loved him a lot more than our husbands. So one day we decided; we'll split, get divorces, and move down to the Strip. It was great, you know, hanging around the clubs. We got to know a lot of groups but never forgot Mick. So imagine how we felt in the Whisky one night when this guy said he was Sam Cutler and asked if we'd like to be with the Stones when they were in L.A., and drive 'em around and stuff.

It was Sam who picked me up, and I felt loyal to him, but when we were up at Mick's house the first night, well, I'm only human. We were all sitting around, and Mick said he was going to bed. I was really disappointed. But he came down again and started pouring perfume on me, and sort of whispered, "Will you come up with me, then?"

I almost died, but I managed to say, "Only if my friend Mary can come too." We had been together through two years, and had made a pact not to leave the other out. He said okay.

It was funny, man, I could hardly get it on. He makes all the sexy noises in bed, like he does singing. I was laughing so hard, but know what was funniest? For two years I had been thinking with every guy, "He's great, but he's not Mick Jagger." And then with Mick, all I could think was, "He's great, but he's not Mick Jagger."

He has to work at being Mick Jagger, you know? Some mornings he wakes up and says, "I feel so fragile this morning, Cathy, be gentle," and I think, "This is the Mick I idolized?" But now I know he's a person I love him more.

Anyway I'm having the time of my life. I mean it.

A black woman cabdriver takes me in from the airport to the Detroit concert, the first after the break, and tells me she thinks it's great, all these kids getting together for music.

"It was the same when I was that age," she says. "I'd save up all my pennies, sneak out of the house if I had to, to hear Charlie Barnett. You might think he's square, but back then he was the greatest. The way I look at it is, it's all jumpin' music, and ain't nobody ever gonna stop kids from lovin' jumpin' music."

In Motor City it is jumping music indeed. The Stones play better than ever, and the kids are dynamite. Some places the kids seem to be imitating San Francisco, New York, or L.A., but in Detroit they have a funky independence, unwashed, tough, but cheery. Crazy-leaping before the stage, they're laughing at the Stones because that night it seems so funny, and the Stones dig them back, spreading out the songs, adding choruses, and building finales until it looks like they might just play all night.

But no; they run off, roar out and into a tiny plane that drones us across a bed of moonlit clouds to New York. Bill and Astrid fall asleep, Charlie and Mick Taylor stare calmly out the windows, and Mick, Keith, and Ronnie play poker on a drum case. Dozens of joints make their mellow rounds, and conversation drops to the chatter from the card game.

Keith plays, Mick plays to win, and Ronnie plays to win money, but they are three close friends, and no one really cares. Ronnie makes like a hot-time dealer ("Pair of deuces on my left, possible straight on the right, and not a thing in my hand, bet up, gentlemen"). Mick and Keith play back like titled English ladies at fin-de-siècle Monte, broken by fortune but haughty to the end.

"I'll stake my carriage," says Keith, adjusting an imaginary stole.

"My horses and one chambermaid on this turn of cards, sirrah," says Mick.

"Are you kidding me?" says Ronnie. His wad of bills is held neatly in his hand, Mick's and Keith's are crumpled heaps before them. "Okay, I'll throw in my mother and my uncle."

"And no children?" says Lady Keith, horrified.

"Sure, my kid too," says Ronnie. "Another card, ladies." It goes on like that until the clouds melt away and the lights of Manhattan are bright beneath us. The plane floats into the LaGuardia Marine Terminal; the droning stops. In the sudden silence we straggle across the wet, black macadam. It's about 4 A.M. Our only greeters are the limousine drivers shivering in the cold. The Cadillacs purr through Queens, over the bridge and on, through streets now oyster grey, to the Plaza Hotel. On little cat feet, as it were, the Rolling Stones arrive in New York.

An elegant New York groupie—a veritable Madame Pompadour at the high court of the counterculture—arranges an intimate party for the Stones in a Village apartment. By invitation only, and there are only thirty-five invitations. It's very late and very stoned. The guests, all young, all longhaired, sit or stand around the edges of the room, silent and nearly motionless, ultracool and ultra-awkward. No one knows what to say, for over there in a little group are the two Micks and Keith. A blues record is on, and they're chatting about it softly among themselves. When they get too tired, they leave. It's the only real party the Stones attend in New York, and when the gossip mills get rolling the next afternoon as the in crowd awakes, it's considered high points to have been there.

New York and Los Angeles are as different on tour as they are at anytime. In New York, gone is the open, lazy feeling of the West Coast; the four-walls feeling of hotel life replaces it. The idea of the Plaza is a gas, but as daily fact it is just another hotel. Bizarrely expensive, the Plaza stops its room service at 1 A.M. (lunch time for this crew), and the service is slower than the slowest Squaliday Inn. A sandwich and a beer is an hour wait, an elevator five minutes, and a phone call to another room a succession of "One moment, please." The cast again adds extras: cops, drivers, reporters, petitioners of every sort, buddies of John Jaymes, and then buddies of buddies.

163

Suite 969, the Plaza, afternoon. Ronnie, tie off, feet up, is on the phone. "What's this about overage in Illinois? Yeah, Champaign . . . Whaddya mean, late? We closed the show on time, didn't we? . . . I don't care what the man said. I said, not him." A shirtless John Jaymes, his chest, back, and enormous belly covered with hair, is on another line. "Yeah, I know a lotta people were promised interviews. Pope Paul, he was promised an interview, but he can't make it. Sorry, man, no show."

Four beefy security men, Italian friends of John's from the Bronx, sit around a table playing poker. In the bedroom Cecil Beaton paces about as an assistant snaps pictures of Mick. Beaton's silvered voice drifts out into the sitting room: "Great . . . great . . . excellent, marvelous . . . great . . . lower and spin . . . great . . . yes, oh, yes . . . great." A *Daily News* reporter waits patiently for the interview he is never going to get. A pretty young model named Barbara, soon to take John's body-painting kit on a nationwide tour ("my big break"), plays solitaire. Jo's on another phone to London but stops to rummage through her bag when Sam dashes in to borrow her hair dryer for Mick Taylor. "I want it back this time," says Jo.

"Sure, Luv," says Sam, "and do you have any perfume for Keith?"

"What kind does he like?"

"Joy," says Sam. "He puts it in his bleeding armpits."

Mike Quatro, a pint-sized twenty-three-year-old Detroit promoter, kibitzes the card game. A child prodigy piano player on *The Lawrence Welk Show*, Quatro has bought a house in Grosse Point Farms from the proceeds of his rock 'n' roll agency-promotion firms. He's in management too, his biggest act being the Hedonists, an all-girl group made up of his four older sisters. He's come to New York hoping to make future deals with Ronnie, deals that might affect his plans for doing some "Woodstock-type" festivals next summer. Ronnie gets off the phone, and Mike slides over to him.

"How about talking business, Ronnie?"

"Sure, kid, but listen, will you call room service again for those goddam sandwiches?"

"Sure thing," says Mike, leaping to the phone.

Around this crowded center is the New York "scene," which, from its own center at Max's Kansas City, plots incessantly on how either to infiltrate the Stone's center or at least to find out "what's happening." Max's hears that there are code names used to reach the Stones' rooms; that this supergroupie or that supergroupie has or has not made it to Mick or Keith; that Charlie is sick; that if Jimi Hendrix decides to go to X's party, Bill Wyman will probably be there too; and that perhaps, hope of hopes, the Stones will come to Max's itself.

The scenesters (a New Yorker once called them "the young elite of the communications industry") finally get a chance to see their heroes at the obligatory press conference held in Rockefeller Center's Rainbow Room, sixty-five stories above the ground. At no concert has there been such hysteria. Photographers and TV crews and reporters with tape machines press forward to the microphone-loaded table with a loudmouthed aggression that the Kodak-wielding kids in Dallas or Chicago would have found appalling. Young "rock writers," "company freaks," and scenemakers who have been ringing PR lady Doreen for days to get there, sip their drinks and tell their friends that it's such a bore. The Stones file in to a blinding splatter of flashbulb explosions. Everyone cries for everyone else to sit down. All stay standing.

Sam introduces the Stones by name.

"Can we have that again?" shouts a TV man.

"Down in front!"

"Shut up, willya, so we can hear."

Keith: "Should we scream at you like you scream at us?"

Silence. There are no questions.

Mick: "We're just sitting here, man, you gotta do it."

An interminable statement-question on marijuana legalization and on violence. Mick says something like "We gotta stop the fight between young people and their . . . " before he's cut off. What about the U.S.A.?

Mick: " . . . it just explodes all the time, it's great, you look more beautiful than ever over here."

You wrote "Satisfaction"; are you more satisfied now?

Mick: " . . . sexually satisfied, financially unsatisfied, philosophically still trying . . . "

Keith: "Wiser, wiser."

Sadder?

Keith: "No, of course not."

What about John Lennon giving back his M.B.E.?

Keith: "At last! He should never have taken it. We don't care, we'll never get one."

Hey, Mick, you were wearing an omega button in L.A. It stands for draft resistance. How do you feel about that?

Mick: "Draft resistance? I though it stood for infinity."

What about being philosopher king?

Mick: "I withdraw from the role, it's a banality."

Bill and Charlie are asked no questions and say nothing. Mick Taylor is asked about taking Brian's place. He smiles back at the questioner, then looks away.

"That's it," says Sam.

Mick: "Thank you, New York."

The consensus on the packed elevators is that it was a freak show, but then everyone knew it would be, and knew they should have stayed home. New York is disappointed. It had wanted the Stones to be the Stones of the days when the pop demimonde was taking over the columns from the café society that had run itself down twisting at the Peppermint Lounge; when Andy and Baby Jane and pill parties on the Lower East Side were the action. But this Thanksgiving weekend Max's is full of PR men, not painters, and the Stones are five young men who have been away from home for a month and a half, and who want to see friends and family, not new streams of strangers, however glamorous.

Charlie and Keith call home to London every day, and when one girl gets to Keith's room, he offers her tea and shows her baby pictures. Mick Taylor just wishes he could find a few hours to walk about the city and shop. Bill and Astrid do go downtown to see a strip show ("I'd never seen one,"

Keith Richards relaxing in the dressing room, Madison Square Garden, 1969.
© Ethan A. Russell

says Astrid, "and, oh, but she was fat!"), and Charlie slips off to Slugs, a jazz club deep in the East Village, to hear Tony Williams's Lifetime, but otherwise it's sleep and work. Jo gets them together to discuss what concerts and TV dates to do when they return to England; Mick calls Ahmet Ertegun of Atlantic Records to arrange to use their studios in Muscle Shoals, Alabama; and Keith never stops writing songs.

They are doing the tour now, still as brilliantly as ever, but there are no more surprises; Philadelphia, Baltimore, three shows at Madison Square Garden, and then Boston—the concerts are now a perfect machine. The record they were finishing in Los Angeles, *Let It Bleed* (a pun on the Beatles *Let It Be*), is a smash hit, and the crowds cheer the new tunes as much as they do the old.

In Philly I see a dozen kids charge one door, knock down the elderly ticket taker, and scatter into the crowd. A group from Students for a Democratic Society in Beantown's ancient Boston Garden rips down the American flag and then is trapped and beaten by quick-moving police. John Jaymes sprains his wrist when he tries to bash one of the kids and hits a wall instead.

Madison Square Garden is dotted with celebrities: an aging Murray the K, promoter of the Stones' first American concert ("they were scared little boys back in '64"), a tipsy Janis Joplin, who joins Tina Turner for a brief but ecstatic moment that brings the house down, and a subdued Jimi Hendrix who jams with Keith in the dressing room. Leonard Cohen, Paul Simon, Woody Allen, Viva, and the Jefferson Airplane come to see what it is all about. The Garden shows are recorded, Glyn Johns hunched over a Wally Heider sixteen-track machine in a Hertz truck backstage. Glyn wants a double album of everybody—Terry Reid, B.B. King, and Ike and Tina—if they can get contract releases. Mick doesn't like the idea.:"Double albums are so pompous; Dylan's is the only one I could ever stand." Bob Dylan, though, doesn't come to the Garden. "He doesn't do this kind of thing anymore," says a friend. "He's a family man, doesn't want to be a star making a fuss."

The tour is coming to an end. After Baltimore, Ronnie starts a count-down. Leaving Boston Garden, he shouts, "Only one more to go! "

"I don't believe it," says Charlie, "they really want us to go home, Ronnie and John do. It was fun at first, then work, now a bloody drag to have us around."

"That's right," says Ronnie. "Go home, you little limey."

"I will," says Charlie, "will do."

At 3 A.M. a seemingly endless and disorderly stream of very drunk young men and women of New York society comes flowing through the lobby of the Plaza. They've been at a ball at which twelve of their kind have come out from nowhere into what their mothers at least must consider somewhere. The boys are in white tie and tails or modish varieties of evening dress, the girls in awesomely beautiful formal gowns. Few of them are out of their teens. One tries to slide down a brass stair railing. When he falls off, his mates cheer him with a loud hip, hip, hooray. Five boys stagger along, their arms around each other's shoulders, trying to recall, then sing, that World War I song about "Hinky Dinky Parlay Voo." An astonishing vision: children of the fifties, consciously acting out, on the cusp of the seventies, a perfect imitation of the twenties.

In walk the Rolling Stones and entourage, tired and disheveled from a hard night's work in Boston. Our stream passes that of the society kids; the Stones take no notice, but a few of the Golden Youth stop and stare.

"Well, what do you know, the Rolling Stones!"

"In the Plaza? Ha, ha ha."

"You're Mick, aren't you, 'Satisfaction' and all?"

To some the Stones are just a bunch of hippies who have inexplicably swum into view, and a few V signs are flashed.

I stop to watch, and a pretty girl named Connie smiles and gives me a flower from her bouquet—is that etiquette when confronted by a longhair? Two of her friends— Lyle in a floppy blue velvet bow tie, and a dark Harvard freshman—stop, and we all talk for a few minutes.

The three apologize profusely not only for having been at the party, but also for their whole lives, then point out that they really are *high* society. "The nitty-gritty," says Lyle. Yes, they say, life's a bore, but amusing. The joints and the amyl nitrite poppers at the party were almost as plentiful as the champagne, they say, and some kids were even sniffing spoons of cocaine. Connie: "It's expensive, but so groovy if you can afford it"—which she surely can. Does she know that low class rock 'n' rollers like Mike Jagger and Bob Dylan have written songs to her?

"Oh, yes," she says. "'Playing with Fire' is my favorite Stones song, and 'Just Like A Woman' my Dylan favorite. You know the line in it, 'her fog, her amphetamine, and her pearls'? Every time I hear those lines, I think, Yeah, that's me. It feels pretty weird, I'll tell you."

The last day of the tour is a wintry gray day in New York. We clear out of the Plaza and drive to the Marine Terminal to leave as we arrived. But we are late for the chartered plane to West Palm Beach, and so, we are told, must wait for new takeoff clearance. We wait.

One hour goes by, then two. John and Ronnie dash angrily back and forth between plane and terminal. First they report engine trouble. Then a snow flurry, then President Nixon landing in Air Force One. Four hours, five hours.

After three hours all diversions have been used up. Charlie wakes up to find the plane unmoved. Bill Wyman quits his card game with Al the security man and tries to sleep. Mick and Keith have run through all their tape cassettes. The Sunday paper is scattered all over the plane, and no one has missed skimming a month-old *Sports Illustrated.*

There is nothing new to bitch about. They had planned to play at sundown, and it's already dark. Keith goes to sleep. We munch sandwiches, drink beer, and chat. I tell Mick about Connie and her favorite songs. "We make music to please all kinds," he says. "One of those kids said to me, 'You want to go to a debutante party?' and I said to him, 'There are no real debutantes in America.'"

Somehow a few of us start on politics, and for an hour carry on with the normal sound and fury. Bill goes back to his cards; Mick Taylor never joins in. Like all such conversations, it is filled with unreal rhetoric and impossible hopes. We go round in circles, all wanting some indefinable "more" and having no idea how to find it. Sam's the organization man; it should be possible, he says, to get enough people together to seize a section of London.

"But what'll you do with it when you've got it?" asks Charlie.

"Just run it the way we want to run it," says Sam, "whatever comes of it. We can't do worse than the bastards in power now."

"I think we should, too," says Mick, "but in England you never will. Nobody's interested. In America there is at least a sense of change, people willing to try things, but England's dead."

"What do you want to knock off the old thing for when you've got nothing to take its place?" says Charlie.

"I'd put nothing in its place," Mick shouts. "Just subvert it, do away with it because it's irrelevant and should be wiped out. But in England people like the system. With our so-called socialism, you couldn't believe the rules we've got, and people obey them just like they did the aristocracy. I wish things were more capitalistic, and less restrained."

"I don't know," says Charlie, by now the only quiet voice. "I like my house and horses and land."

"You're nothing but a bleeding liberal, joining all the preservation societies," says Sam.

"Another Cockney turned English gentleman," says Mick.

"I'll admit I'm materialistic," says Charlie.

Sam corners Charlie and runs down statistics on land use and population, and the conversation falls dead. "I'd do anything political I thought would work," Mick puts in as a parting shot, "that would really shake things, but I still haven't found anything as good as what I'm doing, or anybody to do it with."

By 10 P.M.—almost eight hours late—we're off the ground, for some reason in another plane. Mick had almost decided to call it off. "We could send a helicopter down there with the money and drop it on the crowd." By 1 A.M. we land in Florida, and after a few helicopter rides and another long wait in a beachfront hotel, we get to the dragstrip and those cheering kids.

The Stones come on wrapped in jackets, but when Keith sees the crowd he strips his off in witness and plays in a skimpy shirt that leaves his stomach bare. He plays like a demon, fighting the cold that stiffens his fingers and detunes his guitar. The others, even Mick, look like they want to do a quick set and split, but Keith pushes them on.

After "Sympathy," Mick apologizes for being late. "May we be forgiven?" he asks with a smirk. It's not good enough, and Keith cuts him off and starts "Stray Cat." Mick seems to get the message and steps forward to speak at the next break. "We think it's really amazing to be here, you and us," he calls out, "because to get this all together after all the hassles and find you all here at four in the morning, is fantastic."

There's a small burst of cheers. Mick waves for silence. He is dead serious.

"You're all pretty special people, yes you are, and this moment is pretty special. It matters that you are here, but I guess you know it matters, because you stayed through the night, and you're here. We're all here."

For the first time since Oakland he calls for "I'm Free," and the kids are dancing as best they can. What lights there are go on the audience, and now, bathed in orange, they at least look warmer. Chip Monck, his long blond hair plastered down by intercom earphones, stops jumping to the music for a moment, and shouts a command into his mike. The spotlights on the high towers suddenly swing from the stage and swoop over the crowd, catching briefly, as if in deep blue pools, hundreds of happily shrieking kids.

The band builds to the finale, which is now the finale of finales. It is almost a disaster. An amp blows out and is replaced. Mick Taylor breaks a string, Charlie's hands are blue, and Mick keeps sniffling to clear his nose. Bill's bass is awesomely out of tune, and no one knows what the audience is hearing. But they drive on, Keith always taking the lead, and halfway through "Street Fighting Man" Chip, on some inspiration, calls again to the spotlight crews. The lights leave the crowd and turn to the sky, crossing and recrossing in triumphant arcs. Mick grabs the whole basket of rose petals and, not stopping for the normal handfuls, leans back and flings it as far as he can. Red petals are still falling as the last note dies away.

The helicopters take us back to the beach. In the east the sky is turning pink, the night's clouds disappearing to the west. The Stones walk to the water's edge and watch until streaks of crimson dart deep into the darkness, then, turning their backs, trudge to the hotel before the sun is fully risen.

The chartered plane will take them to Muscle Shoals in a few hours and, forcing themselves to stay awake, they eat a desultory breakfast. John Jaymes comes over to the group of sofas and chairs where they are sprawled. He's carrying a 1970 Dodge catalog and will, he says, take orders for whatever models they desire. It's all on Dodge, and they can renew every year. They huddle excitedly to look at the catalog, then give their orders as if John were a waitress in a hamburger joint: "I'll have mine silver, a hardtop," says Charlie, "with the biggest engine and all the extras."

"And that includes air-conditioning, AM-FM radio and stereo tape deck," says John.

"Great," says Keith, "I'll have the same, but can I have lavender?"

John takes notes, makes a few suggestions, rechecks all the specifics, and walks away.

The Stones share a look that if not guilty is slightly furtive. Keith shrugs and laughs. Mick's eyes follow the wide sport shirted back of his benefactor.

"Christ, I can't stand that man," he says with a condescending sneer.

They hit him . . . I couldn't tell whether it was a knife or not . . . but on the side of the head. And then . . . he came running towards me, and then fell down on his knees and then the Hell's Angel, the same one I was talking about, grabbed onto both of his shoulders and started kicking him in the face about five times or so, and then he fell down on his face. . . . And then one of them kicked him off the side and he rolled over, and he muttered some words. He said, "I wasn't going to shoot you."

We rubbed his back up and down to get the blood off so we could see, and there was a big hole on his spine and a big hole on the side and there was a big hole on his temple. A big open slice. You could see all the way in. You could see inside. You could see at least an inch down and stuff, you know. . . . All of us were drenched in blood.

—An eyewitness account of the stabbing of eighteen-year-old Meredith Hunter, killed by Hell's Angels at Altamont; from *Rolling Stone*

It all came down at Altamont on that strange day. A cold sun alternated with bright clouds, and 300,000 young Americans stepped into the future (or was it?), looked at each other, and were frightened by what they saw. It was the biggest gathering in California since the Human Be-In three years before, not only in numbers but in expectation. In common with all the voluntary mass events of the sixties—was the Sproul Hall sit-in the first?—it would, all believed, advance the trip, reveal some important lesson intrinsic to and yet beyond its physical fact. The 300,000, all in unspoken social contract, came not only to hear music, but to bear living testimony to their own lives.

The Stones as well as the audience, and whether such a distinction should or could be made was one of the day's questions. They had wanted the free show to be in San Francisco's Golden Gate Park, their gift to the city and its culture. As their long hair, outrageous manners, and music had helped make San Francisco possible, San Francisco had helped make the past three years possible. Like thousands before them, the Stones were coming to say thank you. They hoped it would be in all senses a free concert, an event spiritually outside the commercial realm of the tour. It both was and was not. Neither the tour's footnote nor quite its denouement, that long Saturday was the drama's second and enigmatic ending, one that proved all endings as false and hard to mark as beginnings.

When the Stones left for Muscle Shoals, first Sam, then Jo, Ronnie, and John flew to San Francisco. Rock Scully, a long-time manager of the Grateful Dead, met Sam at the plane, and concert planning began at the Dead's office and communal ranch. The Dead, hosts of more free concerts than any other band, are still the best embodiment of the San Francisco spirit that in 1967 captured the imagination of the world. True if harried believers in the psychedelic revolution, the Dead promised full cooperation, and the concert seemed to be in good if freaky hands. On Tuesday no site had been secured; by Wednesday morning the director of the Sears Point Raceway promised his grounds free of charge. Chip and his crew, aided by the Dead's extended family, started moving tons of equipment to the drag strip north of San Francisco. Then came the problems.

An essential element of free concerts is simplicity. You want to hear music? Okay, do it! Get a place, a source of power, a flatbed truck, a few bands, spread the word, trust God, and have the thing. But this free concert was also a Stones concert, free or not, and everybody wanted a piece of the action. Hustlers of every stripe swarmed to the new scene like piranhas to the scent of blood.

The Sears Point man got cold feet or itchy palms or both and asked for $6,000, plus $5,000 to be held in escrow against possible damages. Costs mounted on a dozen fronts; fearful of huge losses, Ronnie decided on a film designed for a TV special to be made by the Maysles brothers, who had already been shooting the final stages of the tour. Any profits would go to charity—"as yet unspecified," said John. The actual owners of the raceway, a Hollywood-based company called Filmways Corporation, which had promoted two of the tour's concerts, heard about that and demanded film distribution rights as part of their fee. Ronnie refused, and Filmways, overriding their local management, responded by upping the fee to $100,000.

That was late Thursday. The San Francisco papers and radio stations were announcing Sears Point as the site, and a large volunteer vanguard had already encamped. The blatantly colorful attorney Melvin Belli offered his help in the fight with Filmways, and Ronnie accepted it. The Dead office was abandoned as the HQ, and was replaced by Belli's office in San Francisco's financial district and Ronnie's suite in the posh Huntington Hotel. Managers of local bands started calling to get their groups on the stage for the priceless exposure; the city's rival Top 40 stations, KFRC and KYA, started running hourly bulletins, each trying to be the unofficial "Stones station." Underground KSAN-FM, which had had the best coverage early in the week, was slowly edged out. Communes of ordinary hippies offering their services were rebuffed. The radical community, suspicious from the start, started talking about the festival as "one more shuck."

By midmorning Friday, Filmways was still adamant, but then got left when another track, this one a stock car oval called Altamont, offered its several hundred acres of rolling hills. Track director Dick Carter thought it would be "great publicity." The half-built stage at Sears Point was dismantled, and radio stations blasted the new directions with frantic assurances that, yes, the Stones concert was still on.

By late Friday afternoon the concert was the sole and obsessive topic of hip conversation, and Altamont a familiar name. KFRC had on-the-spot reporters on every spot worth being on, and KYA's deejays bemoaned the fact that "some stations are trying to turn something that should be free and groovy into a commercial event." Both stations carried hi-fi store ads for "all new stereo tape recorders so you can make the Stones concert more than a memory." The scores of equipment trucks got to Altamont, fifty miles east of Berkeley, by early Friday evening; a huge volunteer crew worked like ants under blue floodlights amid a growing tangle of wires, planking, and staging. "No one will be allowed on the grounds until 7 A.M. Saturday, so stay home," was the broadcast word, but by midnight there were traffic jams miles from the site. The Stones got to the Huntington Hotel by 10, exhausted. In Alabama they had heard only the confusing rumors, but were determined to go ahead. "We'll have it in a bloody parking lot if we have to," said Keith. He and Mick flew out to see Altamont. Mick went back to get some sleep; Keith stayed all night.

As the stage crew labored, a few thousand people who had missed the roadblocks slept before the stage or stood by campfires; other thousands waited behind a fence for official opening time. I wandered from fire to fire; place was immediately made for any stranger, and joints steadily circled the impromptu hearths. I made scores of friends I'll never see again.

One girl told me solemnly that it would be a heavy day "because the sun, Venus, Mercury, and some other planet are all in Sagittarius, and the moon's on the Libra-Scorpio cusp." Another presented me with a grotesque doll made by her dead husband. "He lives in the doll; I know it," she said, nodding her head uncontrollably. "He sees everything." I said I was sorry. "Oh, that's okay, he was shot through the heart and lungs and the liver, but I really don't mind,

176

'cause he must have been meant to die, and anyway, I have the doll." Still nodding and smiling, she took it back and wrapped it in her shawl.

They came from everywhere. Two boys boasted that they had seen the Stones in L.A., Chicago, Philly, and Palm Beach without ever buying a seat; someone countered by saying he had been to fourteen festivals plus Woodstock. A girl said she was from Akron, had run away to New Orleans, got an abortion in Houston, and had been on her way to Seattle ("I heard it's groovy there"), when she met a dealer in Phoenix who took her to San Francisco, then split to avoid a bust. "It's all so far out," she said. Somebody with a phonograph played *Abbey Road* over and over. The spindly light towers grew tall, generators roared, helicopters clattered overhead, and as night became gray dawn, Altamont looked strikingly like the mad consummation of Federico Fellini's *8½*.

At 7 A.M. the gates are opened. Over the hill and down into the hollow by the stage comes a whooping, running, raggle-taggle mob. From sleeping bags peer sleepy heads that duck back as the mob leaps over them and dashes between them. In minutes the meadow is a crush of bodies pressed so close that it takes ten minutes to walk fifty yards. Only the bravest blades of grass still peep up through the floor of wadded bedding. On and on comes the crowd; by 10 A.M. it spreads a quarter mile back from the stage, fanning out like lichen clinging to a rock.

There are the dancing beaded girls, the Christlike young men, and smiling babies familiar from countless stories on the "love generation," but the weirdos too, whose perverse and penetrating intensity no camera ever captures: speed freaks with hollow eyes and missing teeth, dead-faced acid heads burned out by countless flashbacks, old beatniks clutching gallons of red wine, Hare Krishna chanters with shaved heads and acned cheeks. Two young men in filthy serapes and scraggly beards lean against a crushed and brightly painted derelict veteran of the demolition derby. In the brims of their cowboy hats are little white cards: "Acid $2." A shirtless black man stands in the center of a cheering circle. "I have in my hand," he barks, "one

177

little purple tab of 100 percent pure LSD. Who wants this cosmic jewel?" A dozen hands reach out eagerly. "Who really wants it?"

"I do, I do, I want it, me, me, me."

"Going, going, gone to that freaky chick with the blue bandana." He tosses it to her, and reaches again into his leather bag. "I have in my hand one cap of mescaline, guaranteed organic. . . ."

Two middle-aged men with pinched Okie faces set up a card table and hawk Rolling Stones programs left over from another tour. They've only sold a few when a milling crowd of radicals surrounds them. "It's free, man, nothing is sold today." "Better give the stuff away, man, or we'll rip it off in the name of the people."

The men are frightened. A kid dashes up and grabs a handful of the glossy books. The table collapses. One man scoops the programs from the dirt, the other brandishes the table in wild-eyed defense. They retreat, walking backwards, as the brave guerrillas search for other targets.

Face by face, body by body, the crowd is recognizable, comprehensible. An ugly beautiful mass, it is bewilderingly unfamiliar—a timeless lake of humanity climbing together through the first swirling, buzzing, euphoric-demonic hours of acid. Is this Hieronymous Bosch or Cecil B. DeMille? Biblical, medieval, or millennial? Are we lost or found? Are we we, and if we are, who are we?

Whoever or whatever, we are here, all here, and gripped by the ever-amazing intensity of psychedelics, we know that this being here is no accident but the inevitable and present realization of our whole lives until this moment. One third of a million postwar boom babies gathered in a demo-lition derby junkyard by a California freeway to get stoned and listen to rock 'n' roll—is that what it has all been about? And someone, thinking maybe to help feed us, brought a split-open crate of dirty, wilted cabbage heads. They got kicked around in the dust until they rolled under cars and were forgotten.

Some call us Woodstock West, but we are not. Woodstock was a three-day encampment at which cooperation was necessary for survival; it was an event only because it became an event. The Altamont crowd is demanding that an event come to pass, be delivered, in a single day; should it go bad, well, it'll be over by evening. And it's four months later, and it's California, where inevitably everything is that wee but significant bit less known, less sure, less safe.

And more political; if *concert* isn't the right word for the day, *festival* isn't either. The week's maneuverings, still known only by rumor, have raised a hard edge of suspicion; the day's vibes include aggressive paranoid frequencies that demand self-justification. Some come in bitter mourning for two Chicago Black Panthers shot to death just days before; a concert without confrontation would be frivolous escapism for them. But it is more than the radicals; large segments of the crowd share a dangerous desire to tighten up that festival idea a few notches, to move to a new level: just how weird can you stand it, brother, before your love will crack?

It isn't that the morning is not a groove; it is, friendly enough and loose. But ... but what? There is too much of something; is it the people, the dope, the tension? Maybe it is the wanting, the concentration, not just of flesh, but of unfulfilled desire, of hope for (or is it fear of:) deliverance. ("There must be some way out of here, said the joker to the thief / there's too much confusion, I can't get no relief.") What is our oppression that in escaping it we so oppress ourselves? Have we jammed ourselves together on these sere hills miles from home hoping to find a way out of such masses? If that is our paradox, is Altamont our self-made trap? And yet might we just, in acting out the paradox so intensely, transcend it?

The Jefferson Airplane are on stage, knocking out "$^3/_5$ of a Mile in Ten Seconds" with a mad fury—"Take me to a simple place / where I can easily see my face," but that place is not Altamont. Suddenly all eyes rivet on an upraised pool cue. It is slashing downward, held by a mammoth Hell's Angel, and when it hits its unseen target there is a burst of water as if it had crushed a jellyfish. A wave of horror ripples madly across the crowd. The music stops and the stage is full of Angels in raunchy phalanx. The music starts, falters, stops. Thousands hold their breath and wave pathetic V signs. No one wants the Angels. A few scream, "Pigs, pigs." The odds against the

179

Angels are maybe 5,000 to one, but the crowd is passive and afraid. The Angels stay on stage, sure of their power.

Now something is definitely wrong, but there is no time or space to set it right. The Angels become the villains, but why are they here?

They just came, of course, as they always do, but, we hoped, as friends. Since Ken Kesey faced them down and turned them on, San Francisco has had a sentimental romance with the Angels: the consummate outlaws, true rolling stones, street-fighting men: they're so bad they're good. It turns out later that they were actually hired by the Stones on the suggestion of the Dead; their fee, five hundred dollars worth of beer. But now their open appetite for violence mocks our unfocused love of peace; their grim solidarity our fearful hopes of community.

Community? It doesn't feel like that anymore. Though participants in the whole rite, we are not actively engaged in it; we are spectators who came to "see" the Stones, voyeurs hoping, like all voyeurs, that "something" will happen. But since we're just watching, we can say we're not to blame—it's the Stones and the Angels, the stars, they did it all, so they're to blame, right? The *I Ching* says all communities must have a leader, but every community member must be willing to become that leader at any time.

So we're all voyeurs, but what do you have to do in late 1969 to get 300,000 people to watch it?

> Now the rovin' gambler he was very bored
> He was tryin' to create a next world war
> He found a promoter who nearly fell off the floor
> He said, I've never engaged in this kind of thing before,
> But, yes, I think it can be very easily done
> We'll just put some bleachers out in the sun,
> And have it on Highway 61!
>
> —Bob Dylan, "Highway 61 Revisited"

The day drags on. Many leave, as many more arrive. Invisibly and inevitably the crowd squeezes toward the stage until the first fifty yards around it are suffocatingly dense. Occasionally it becomes too much for someone, and while twitching in the grip of some apocalyptic vision ("We are all going to die, we are all going to die, right here, right here, we've been tricked!"), he is carried by friends to the medical tent for some Thorazine and, if he's lucky, some thoughtful attention.

Darkness begins to fall. "The Stones are here." "I saw their helicopter." "Somebody said they're not gonna show." The lights come on, and a new wave sweeps thousands more toward the stage. The stage itself is so full that it is sagging in the center. The Angels continue their random attacks. "The Stones are here." "That's why they turned on the lights."

In fact, they are—packed into a tiny trailer filled with stale smoke and spilled food. Charlie's happy; he needs only to get through this final set and he can go home to Shirley and Serafina. Mick is upset; as he got off the helicopter a freak had rushed him, screaming, "I hate you, I hate you," then punched him in the face. For all his presence, Mick Jagger is not fearless; on tour, when the engine of one small chartered plane had flamed briefly as it coughed to a start, Mick leapt from his seat, crying that the plane was about to explode. Keith, up all night and in the trailer all day, is exhausted. Crying girls peer and shout through the small screen windows. Jo Bergman is huddled in a corner waiting for it to be over. Ronnie cracks nervous jokes.

It is time. Surrounded by security men, they squeeze the few yards to a tent directly behind the stage. Mick Taylor, Keith, and Bill tune up. A dozen Angels stand guard, punching at faces that peek through holes in the canvas. They are ready. The Angels form a wedge; they file between two equipment trucks, up four steps, and they are there.

It is fully dark now but for the stage; in its incandescence, the Rolling Stones are as fine as ever. Mick bows low, sweeping his Uncle Sam hat wide in an ironic circle, and on Keith's signal, the band begins "Jumping Jack Flash." That incredible moment is there again.

In those first seconds when Keith's shirt is sparkling, and Charlie has set his big cymbal shimmering with a snap of his right wrist, and Mick bends forward biting out the first defiant words, that enormous pressure of wants, material and spiritual, dissolves—phisst! like that—in thin air. For it is just that moment, that achievement of perfect beauty after impossible trial, that is the object of all those longings.

> 'Cause it's all right now,
> In fact it's a gas,
> It's all right
> I'm Jumping Jack Flash,
> It's a gas gas gas!

And then the moment is irrevocably gone. Four Angels flash from behind the amps, one vaulting almost over Charlie's head. One jumps from the stage, and the crowd scatters into itself in total panic. There appears to be a fight. Then it seems to be over. The music goes on. Again: more Angels, this time wandering around among the Stones. They stop playing.

"Fellows, fellows," says Mick, "move back, won't you, fellows?" His sarcasm gets him through, and they start again. Trouble for the third time, and this time it's serious. Two Angels (I saw two) wade deep into the crowd. There are screams. Rows of faces fishtail away before these thugs from some very modern nightmare. Boos rise from the mass of the crowd who can't see what's wrong and who just want the show to go on.

The band starts again, but something unmistakably weird is still going on down in front. A few kids escape to the stage, streaking to the safety of its far corners. Sam comes out. He has been begging this crowd all day for cooperation; his voice is flat and hoarse.

"This is an important announcement. Someone has been hurt and a doctor is leaving the stage right now; that's him with his arm raised, he's got a green jacket on. Will you please let him through? Someone has been badly hurt."

Security men are begging that all those who do not absolutely need to be on the stage leave it. I leave, not unhappily, and walk through the burnt-out campfires, small piles of trash, and rakishly tilted motorcycles behind the stage, then up a slope where the kids are standing on cars, maybe thirty to a car. A girl comes by asking for her friends; she has cut her leg on barbed wire and wants to go home, but she lost her friends with the car at noon.

The Stones are going again, and the crowd is with them. We can't see them, but the music sounds good—not great, not free-festival great, but no one hopes for that anymore. It is enough that it is here. Around me a few people are dancing gently. The morning's dope is wearing off; all the trips are nearly over. We do glimpse the basket flying through the air, trailing petals. We all cheer one last massive cheer.

Friends find friends; the crowd becomes fragments that get into cars that back up on the freeway for miles and for hours. Luckily it is only about eight; but it feels like the very end of the night. The only want left is for rest. I realize that the Grateful Dead did not get a chance to play and figure that I won't go to any more of these things.

In the days that follow, the free concert becomes "the disaster at Altamont." There is wide disagreement on what happened and what it meant; everyone, it seems, had their own day, and that was, we all say, one of the problems. The only common emotion is disappointment and impotent sorrow. "If only . . . if only . . . " The papers report that there were three births (though later the figure cannot be substantiated) and four deaths. Mark Feiger, twenty-two, and Richard Savlov, twenty-two, friends who had recently moved to Berkeley from New Jersey, were killed when a car on its way out to the freeway plowed into their campsite hours after the concert was over. A young man with long hair, moustache, and sideburns, with a metal cross through his pierced right ear, still listed as John Doe, stumbled stoned into an irrigation canal and drowned. Another, a young black man, Meredith Hunter, was stabbed, kicked, and beaten by Angels right in front of the stage while the Stones were playing. His body was battered so badly that doctors knew, the moment they reached him, there was no chance to save him.

So far no murder charges have been brought. It was not until a week later, when someone asked me about it, that I even considered the possibility that the police, whom no one would have wanted at Altamont in the morning, would actually investigate the horrendous act that closed it and bring any person or persons to trial. We all seemed beyond the law at Altamont, out there willingly, all 300,000 of us, Stones and Angels included, and on our own. And anyway, the tour is over.

Dontcha panic, dontcha panic
Give it one more try
Dontcha panic, dontcha panic
Give it one more try
Sit down shut up don't dare cry
Things'll get better if you really try
So dontcha panic, dontcha panic
Give it one more try
Try on!
  —Mick Jagger and Keith Richards, "One More Try!"

Aretha Franklin at the Fillmore, 1971. © Ellen Mandel

ARETHA FRANKLIN AT THE FILLMORE WEST

1971

Aretha Franklin may be the greatest of all the many musicians in this book. She's not a songwriter on a par with John Lennon and Paul McCartney or Bob Dylan, though she's written excellent songs. She's not a master instrumentalist like B.B. King, though she plays superb piano, and though she can move multitudes, she's never attracted huge crowds like those that flock to Rolling Stones concerts. Aretha's greatness comes from her God-given gift of music, music that lives in her like a fountain deep inside the earth, music that gushes out of her every time she opens her mouth to sing. On one record, after singing a pyrotechnical cadenza that would leave Joan Sutherland gasping for breath, using only the syllables "la-la," Aretha comments, matter-of-factly, "That's 'la-la,'" as if she had an entire repertoire of such cadenzas for "mi-mi," "re-re," and every other singing syllable, and she probably does. Before such gifts, other musicians can only bow—no, not bow, for to hear Aretha is to share her glory and her passion, to be ennobled and enriched by her faith and her beauty.

It was a night of nights. Tower of Power set the mood—"You got to funkify"—and then King Curtis and his Kingpins and the Memphis Horns and Billy Preston, and after that, Aretha Franklin and the Sweethearts of Soul for an hour and a half. And then if your soul could stand it, Ray Charles and Aretha and all of the above on one stage gathered, rocking, reeling, rolling, and tumbling with the spirit of music. It was Sunday, March 7, 1971, the excited eve of the Muhammad Ali–Joe Frazier fight, at the Fillmore West in San Francisco. The moment was recorded forever on inchwide magnetic tape and released as *Aretha—Live at Fillmore West.* It happened simply.

Aretha was closing her third and final show, leading out of "Dr. Feelgood," as she had on the previous two nights, into a long yeah-saying call and response with the crowd; then slowly, as if she were building a sermon, she began "Spirit in the Dark." This song Aretha made the title tune of an album; it suggests that a good cure for whatever ails you is to cover your eyes with one hand, cock the other hand on your hip, and wait until the spirit in the dark comes pulsing inside you and you are dancing and feeling good again. Try it sometime.

This night she spread the song out forever, then walked off the stage and came back with Ray Charles on her arm. She led him carefully to the microphone, sat down at the piano, and the song went on. Ray stood beaming, then, encouraged by Aretha, started to sing. The band soul-stewed as never before, the whole crowd boogied, and Ray and Aretha traded shouts, licks, breaks, jumps, and howls, suggesting that everybody get, keep, feel, and cherish that spirit.

The music didn't stop. We danced, clapped, hugged, kissed, and finally wept, sweating, eyes open and closed, arms above our heads—and they sang. Aretha found Tower of Power's lead singer and danced with him. She got Ray to sit down and play. Play he did, dazzlingly. In perfect a duet, each seemed more individual than ever: Ray a more weathered and older spirit, Aretha a brown blossom, unquenchably feminine youth. Ray's heavy head is touched with gray, Aretha's skin is as clear as a Polynesian's. She was a girl beside him. Their selves seemed commingled.

Finally Ray went off waving to the crowd, leaving Aretha to close her own show. She sang a soft song about reaching out your hand to a friend—"making this a better world if you can." She bowed to all sides, spoke thanks to the band and to the crowd. She said good-bye, good-bye, good-bye. "I love you, I love you." She was gone. The lights went up.

Moments of perfect beauty are brief, impossible to repeat, and ultimately inexplicable. I did that night feel joined in musical-spiritual exultation with Ray Charles, Aretha Franklin, and many hundreds of other humans. I cannot say how or why. The moment, though part of sluggish time, was instantaneous and spontaneous, and seemed to transcend and illuminate the confluence of processes, large and small, that created it.

Aretha Franklin is now thirty. Music has been her life all her life. A performer since childhood, a professional since her teens, a success for nine years, and a star for six, she is the most successful black woman singer ever. Dutiful daughter of the Reverend C. L. Franklin, a preacher who has recorded sermon LPs for Chess, Aretha first sang gospel. She was not yet twenty when she struck out on her own, determined to be a star. For several years she sang and played piano in the supper clubs of Manhattan, recording ballads for Columbia. As she and her listeners began to recognize her talents, they realized she was too fiery for those cool musical settings. Atlantic's Jerry Wexler wooed her, signed her, and put her together with the company's most dependable rhythm-and-blues hit makers. Her first Atlantic single, "I Never Loved a Man the Way I Love You," was an instant smash. So was "Respect," which had also been a hit for Otis Redding; he said gallantly that Aretha had topped him.

At twenty-six Aretha became the Queen of Soul, on the cover of all the magazines, every ambition fulfilled beyond expectation. Her crown, though proffered in apparent tribute, was heavy and hollow. It drove her to drink and demanded as its price an unqueenly slavery to the hit machine of "the charts." Aretha did her best—two handfuls of million-selling singles and

189

four smash LPs in less than two years—but she couldn't keep the inhuman pace. Her marriage fell apart. The "Natural Woman" of 1967 found that "Eleanor Rigby" fit her mood in 1969. She recorded and performed erratically; her popularity and sales suffered. Cynics readied their I-told-you-sos, pointing out that she was falling back on pop tunes like "This Girl Is in Love with You" rather than the surging R and B that had made her famous. Then she had a hit with the plaintive "Call Me"—not quite a million, but big. Atlantic released *Aretha's Gold*, which summed up her early years. She remarried happily, let her hair go natural, defended Angela Davis as a beautiful black woman, and in 1970 put out *Spirit in the Dark*.

This album, with Aretha shrouded in darkness on the front and looking expectantly into the light on the back, is an absolute triumph, a creation of a strength and grace that few artists ever achieve. Aretha Franklin's voice has always been as supple and brilliant as brook water, its expressive clarity always magical. Yet until *Spirit in the Dark* she was a young woman artist moving in a world directed by middle-aged white men whose smiles did not disguise their power. While they needed her voice to make the product they sold, they, not she, determined the essential limits of the product. In 1967 Aretha worked within those limits. She knew no other possibility. All she did know was that she could sing. "My music is me," she said in an interview for a news weekly, "but I'm not sure what that is." Her voice could bring fame, jewels, and white fur. She worked hard like a good girl, quelling her shyness and doing what she called "the uphill thing."

Spirit in the Dark, more mature musically than anything she had done before, was a dramatic declaration of independence. The generosity of her self-delight illuminates every song. "Hopes up to the skies," "nobody gonna turn us around," "think I got a winning slip," "I'm pullin' on in," she sings. Five of the twelve tunes she wrote herself; the rest she chose boldly from the hits of bluesmen Jimmy Reed, and Kings B.B. and Ben E. She makes them all hers. Not once do the band or strings cloud her presence. She plays the piano as she never played it before, striking the keys as forcibly as Thelonious Monk. The background vocalists, singing arrangements she created, do more than underpin her fervor—they complement it as subtly as perfume.

With this record Aretha seemed to have become an entirely new artist if not a whole new person. Her position had not changed, nor had the soul show-biz limits dissolved. Yet it began to be clear to her that she no longer had to act as others wished her to act. She cut another album, unreleased at the time of the Fillmore concert, which she titled *Young, Gifted, and Black*. *Spirit in the Dark* was selling well but had not won back the huge audience she had had three years before. So she decided to mend fences, and in the winter of 1971 began appearing outside the coliseum circuit to which her Queen of Soul–sized fees had driven her. She wasn't playing clubs, exactly, but she did go out after an audience. She scrapped the ponderous Donald Townes Orchestra, which had accompanied her in concert, in favor of tight combos of rhythm-and-blues studio musicians—often the same men who had accompanied her on record.

The Fillmore weekend was one of a series of promotional dates; on others Aretha starred at a record-industry convention, and played the Apollo and Fillmore East and some benefits. How much of this she personally planned I don't know. Bill Graham and Atlantic's Jerry Wexler worked out the Fillmore arrangements. The main obstacle was Aretha's own business advisor Ruth Bowen, head of Queen Booking, one of the biggest and most conservative black-run management companies. Bowen thought the Fillmore was dangerously declassé. Aretha is, after all, a preacher's daughter. Would Lena Horne play to a mob of unwashed teenagers sitting on the floor? Moreover, Bill Graham could not pay the twenty thousand dollars per show that Bowen demands on Aretha's behalf. But Aretha was becoming impatient with such high-tone stuffiness. Once Bowen was assured the money (Atlantic agreed to underwrite the three days by recording the concerts), she went along with the plan.

Jerry Wexler got a solid plug inserted in *Rolling Stone* to put the word out (San Francisco would be blown into the Bay, Wexler promised), and the three nights sold out immediately.

•

Music results from taking enjoyment in the creation of sound. It requires discipline and patience, but no self-denial. When I was in school, music meant playing from books, years of study, memorization, and cruelly hard work. Even after all that you could never be as great as people who had been dead for centuries. An aura of reverence surrounded the gods of classical music. One was not supposed to put false gods before them. Now, as I am more open to the beauty of "classical music," I feel it was not that music but an incomprehension of all music that originally created that repellent aura.

Sensing a fear of human equality in the exaggerated respect for a "bunch of dead Germans," I was attracted to the "everybody welcome" feeling of black American music. Since I first heard the double album of Benny Goodman's 1937 Carnegie Hall jazz concert and began to respond to music with enthusiasm, black music has been a beacon and inspiration. What I hear in it I want to hear more of.

The growth of black American music has been synonymous with the growth of a consciousness. Wedded to electricity, the music has communicated that consciousness with a contagious excitement. The idea it expresses has emerged in the classic way new ideas, like Protestantism, emerge. Everybody, both for and against, knows what this idea is. The idea of black American music is:

> Boogie boogie boogie boogie
> Boogie til you're done
> Boogie boogie boogie boogie
> Boogie 'cause it's fun
> Boogie meat boogie soul
> Boogie now an' then some mo'

Jerry Wexler, his pajamas royal blue, was in bed with the flu at the Huntington Hotel, San Francisco's equivalent of New York's Carlyle (Aretha was at the brassier Fairmont, across California Street). It was a pleasure to meet him, for Wexler, executive vice president of Atlantic, is indisputably one of the powers of the black music industry and has been for nearly twenty years. As right-hand man for Ahmet and Nesuhi Ertegun, who owned the company until they sold it to the Kinney-Warner conglomerate in 1969, Wexler helped make Atlantic the most important of the R&B-jazz independent record companies.

The "indies" had always competed fiercely among themselves and also fought an often losing battle against the "majors"—the record companies whose money, prestige, and power could lure away the most successful talent painstakingly developed by the little companies. Only the fit survived; Atlantic flourished.

While most of the indies were run by scrappy businessmen whose horizons were only a bit wider than those of the black artists they had under contract, the Erteguns and Wexler were at home both in the rough-and-tumble indie world and in the drawing rooms of the rich and polite. Mongo Santamaria plays at Ertegun parties that are photographed for *Vogue*, and Wexler can growl "listen, motherfucker" to a deejay on one line as he keeps a countess on hold. Likewise in sound: the "Atlantic style" melds unquestionable funk with sophistication and flawless musicality. "We like a little bel canto on our stuff," says Wexler. The company has had its share of unexciting talent, but all its products are finely crafted.

Atlantic has also had more than its share of exciting talent. The company officially designates Ray Charles and Aretha as its two "geniuses" (though Aretha has not had a "genius" LP), but it has also had John Coltrane and the Modern Jazz Quartet. Atlantic brought Otis Redding and the whole Stax-Volt roster from Memphis to international attention, and since the mid-sixties has scored spectacularly with its first forays into white pop-rock. Eric Clapton may someday be a "genius," and Iron Butterfly, Led Zeppelin, and Crosby, Stills, Nash, and Young have been among the biggest earners in the sixties music boom. The key to success in the record business, says producer Ralph Bass, is "finding the bodies"—recognizing talent, getting it signed and in the studio. Atlantic has this key, plus salesmanship. The company pushes its product with a determination so dogged that it must spring from devotion. Wexler is a businessman "with a heart for the music." The label is known as a good label; musicians and listeners tend to trust Atlantic as a company that keeps its side of the bargain.

Wexler shook hands and brought out a joint. His face was friendly, greyly leonine, his voice gruff. A one-time journalist (at *Billboard*) and still a would-be writer, he likes to talk to reporters. Today there were three at his bedside. He spoke of the weekend ("We want these longhairs to listen to this lady; after that there'll be no problems"), of why the Erteguns and he had sold Atlantic to the Kinney Corporation ("It comes down to, unless you sell, you can't realize what you worked your life to get in a form you can pass on, like to your kids"), and said that we shouldn't be talking to him but to Art Rupe of Specialty Records or Saul Bihari of Modern ("They were the cats who did the hard work to get the music out of the ghetto. It wasn't the big companies that were hip to black music, man, it was the indies. Dedicated guys like Georgie Goldner, he found Frankie Lyman, dig?"). He said the American music-buying public is still racially prejudiced, consistently preferring white imitations to the real thing. "You can sell black stuff now, sure, but you gotta fight for it."

Wexler's combination of cynicism and nostalgia, anecdote and innuendo, was captivating—we were getting the straight dope from the man who knew. His charm is famous; one reason for Atlantic's high critical esteem is that there are few music writers who do not consider it an honor to know Jerry Wexler.

The conversation drifted from subject to subject. Ray Charles, Wexler said, had been Atlantic's greatest artist. Why had he left Atlantic for ABC-Paramount, a move that created a watershed in his career? Wexler, the man at Atlantic who most closely handled Ray's recording career, said he did not know. "I followed Ray all around the country with a contract in my hand," he said, but to no avail. Why? "For one thing, as you know, Ray is blind, so he has aides, dig, and for them the status quo means nothing's happening. They like change. So they got Ray's ear—maybe they inflamed suspicions in his mind, who knows?—but they were saying 'go for money.' Maybe Ray wanted to be on a major label, to 'make it,' get away from the indie background." Was there any conflict between himself and Ray, any bad feeling? "No, absolutely none. Ray and I have never fallen out personally."

Wexler spoke of Aretha's drinking ("though she's got it under control now, I think"), added that he'd speak to her about giving interviews, but that maybe she'd be difficult, and then he started hyping Donny Hathaway, a young black singer who might be "another Ray." If we came back the next day we could hear a dub of his new record. He was full of praise for King Curtis, who after years as a regular Atlantic studio man was being groomed as a producer. Curtis, said Wexler, "has a sense of organization, of getting things done sensibly," and the company had high hopes for him. "He's not your standard big-name artist who's a hopeless egocentric about how important he is." I asked him what and who he might mean. Wexler looked surprised, as if to say, Doesn't everybody know that artists are basically egotistical? "I'm not naming names," he said, "that's a whole can of worms I won't open."

I did not interview Aretha Franklin that weekend. Not that I was refused; the three times we spoke, Aretha was polite. The second and third times she pointedly remembered my name. The interview didn't happen because at heart I did not want to sit, pad in hand, asking her questions. A reporter for ten years, I have been interviewing musicians for seven, drawn to them by an uncontrollable love of their music. My reporter's mask got me closer to them than the average fan in the street could get, yet it left me stuck in a frustrating "role." I seldom felt I could be myself with those whom I queried and wrote about. The awkwardness of it all seemed to contradict the spirit of the music.

A few months before that weekend I had started playing the guitar myself, and from this new vantage point of musicianship, however lowly, I had less desire to ask Aretha about influences and plans. Her music was what she was saying that weekend. I wanted to listen, not question. It was a disappointment not to interview her, but there were compensations. When I told

195

Rehearsal at the Fillmore: King Curtis, Aretha Franklin, and two of the Sweethearts of Soul. © Ellen Mandel

Cornell Dupree, who had been playing guitar with King Curtis for twelve years, that I knew three chords, he said, "Blessings upon you," and shook my hand.

Cornell Dupree plays guitar like an angel. Gangly and boyish, he's got a big grin and long fingers. All weekend I seldom saw him off the stage: he was the first to start playing, the last to stop—except perhaps for bassist Jerry Jermott, who is taller and more somber. King Curtis, as bandleader, was often in conference with arranger Arif Mardin or Bill Graham, but he too was playing every available minute. So was drummer Bernard Purdie, when he wasn't talking with pretty girls. King Curtis and the Kingpins were men ready to make music at a moment's notice, falling into it as smoothly as sleep. They smiled a lot—particularly organist Billy Preston—never showed bad temper, and got along together with a male camaraderie that was sure and relaxed. This was a gig and a good one. They worked it the best they knew, but the work was play, and they could whistle on the job.

> Ahmet Ertegun announced this week on behalf of Kinney
> Services Inc. that Kinney has obtained world-wide rights to
> recordings by the Rolling Stones. . . . These records will be
> released world-wide on a newly created label called Rolling
> Stones Records . . . [and] will be distributed by Atco Records,
> of the Atlantic-Atco-Cotillion group in the United States and
> by Warner Bros. in Canada. Marshall Chess, on behalf of
> Kinney, will coordinate the activities of the new label and will
> handle liaison among all of the companies involved. Mr.
> Ertegun said, "It is one of the most important moments in the
> history of the Kinney group (which includes the Atlantic,
> Warner Bros./Reprise and Elektra companies) to be associated
> with this most outstanding rock and roll band."
>
> —Kinney news release, April, 1971

Back in the 1940s, when the WASPs still believed in their divine right to rule America, movies were the national entertainment as surely as baseball was the national sport. Vaudeville was dead, Broadway had begun its decline, and the nightclubs and dance halls were not doing the massive business they had done before and during the Depression. *Hollywood* was a byword the world over; at home and abroad, movies commanded the big money, the big audiences, and the big talent. The most American art, it was also a most American business. The major studios, by controlling their own theaters and distribution networks, divided the bulk of the take among themselves, just as the giants of Detroit controlled the profits of the national vehicle.

Movies no longer hold that position. Television robbed them of their automatic audience, and the studio system broke down. Films could be made cheaper in London and Rome; Los Angeles became one film capital among many. Although much of Hollywood is now making television shows, it is not the once-dreaded TV that is taking the silver screen's place at the top of America's entertainment pyramid, it is popular music.

In the 1960s the recorded-music industry experienced a growth of business and profits that staggered its own imagination. "We've become a billion-dollar industry," Jerry Wexler says often and incredulously; one hears the same self-reminder intoned by other record execs. The trade has been able to sell more and more records at higher and higher prices, complete the switch to stereo and start on quadraphonic, and simultaneously push taped music in reel-to-reel, cartridge, and cassette form, as well as marketing ever more exotic player systems and paraphernalia like headphones. A new broadcast outlet—FM stereo—is now airing the record industry's products in a velvet-gloved version of the high-pressure AM sell, and a whole field of journalism has been created to review, generally glorify, and publicize records. Records were once sold from behind counters in small record stores; now they are stacked six feet high beside ringing registers in discount sound supermarkets.

The billion-dollar turning point came in 1967. Until then the 45-rpm disc was the most important medium for rock 'n' roll; LPs were still associated more with musics that sold to smaller markets. But in the 1960s, just as books in paper had found their way out of the bookstores and into the drugstores, LPs got onto "the racks"—the trade's name for all non–record store sales outlets—at supermarkets, discount centers, and at department stores in the new shopping plazas. *Sergeant Pepper* was crucial. For three years the Beatles had been on top, but their market, although bigger than any rock market before them, was still primarily the teen 45-rpm market. The new wave of interest in rock generated by San Francisco and psychedelia was the first real challenge to the Beatles and the British movement. Would the Beatles sink or swim? They triumphed with a masterpiece that lent all of their prestige to psychedelic and electronic music, summed it up, and then transcended it. Their record established the "album" as the new expressive unit for rock 'n' roll, and joined the rock market to the pop market to create a new "youth" market, the upper age limit of which was now thirty-five, not nineteen. Since then, sales of 45s have declined relative to album sales, and rock-pop figures like Carole King are selling to an audience so diverse as to be virtually uncategorizable.

By riding all of that, Kinney, with its parking-lot origins, is now in an aesthetic-economic relationship to its time not unlike that of a major film studio in the 1930s and 1940s. Kinney makes money from the Stones, Aretha, the late Jimi Hendrix and Otis Redding and Jim Morrison, Eric Clapton, Woodstock (records, film, and name on T-shirts, kites, etc.), Little Richard, Stephen Stills, the Grateful Dead, Judy Collins, Paul Butterfield, Roberta Flack, Randy Newman, the Incredible String Band, Wilson Pickett, Alice Cooper, Dr. John the Night Tripper, and many, many more. Only Columbia is as big, and Columbia, the very model of a modern major "major," *is* big: Bob Dylan, Barbra Streisand, Santana, Johnny Cash, Johnny Mathis, Taj Mahal, Earl Scruggs, and Miles Davis. All these stars are horses in the conglomerate stables. Records by the stars, or by combinations of the stars, are like the MGM and Warner Brothers films of thirty years ago: they can be seen as the shifting collaborations of artists under studio contracts. The Joe Cocker–Leon Russell LPs are like the musical comedies that featured one or two stars against a foil of familiar faces. Mick Jagger has compared his life to Cary Grant's.

The history of the movie-to-music evolution is complex, but Kinney's growth suggests it well. Warner Brothers entered the 1960s as a great studio, 199 yet not the power it had been. Frank Sinatra, a pop star who had to go to Hollywood to make it really big, made it even bigger by starting Reprise Records. Its success attracted Warner, which was looking for new entertainment resources to offset the insecurity of movie profits. Warner bought Reprise. Then in a David-and-Goliath deal typical of 1960s financing, little Seven Arts, a film production company, bought Warner/Reprise. The next series of purchases happened so fast that even company employees were unsure of who was selling what to whom. In the end, Warner added Atlantic to itself in a deal that gave Atlantic's Ahmet Ertegun more power than the head music man at Warner. Another series of moves brought in Ted Ashley from the Ashley Famous Agency (which became Marvin Josephson's International Famous Agency) to reign as entertainment tycoon for the whole of Kinney, which bought Warner and Atlantic. This show-biz empire-building was so earthshakingly immense that its tremors reached even me—my agent, who was with Josephson, moved a few blocks to the IFA offices, and her stationery changed.

All that had barely settled when I heard Kinney had also bought Elektra, rounding out its consolidation of the independents. The companies remained distinct labels, but their distribution systems and many internal company services were pooled. The addition of Marshall Chess to their executive roster was the final and perfect ironic touch: Marshall is the beloved son of the late Leonard Chess, founder of Chess Records, the prototypical independent and home of the Chicago blues upon which the Rolling Stones based their music. Meanwhile Chess was bought by the GRT Corporation, a tape conglomerate, and its offices moved from Chicago's South Side to Manhattan. The one-time majors—Decca, Capitol, and RCA-Victor—have continued with catalogs little changed since Eddie Fisher and "How Much is that Doggie in the Window?"—the point when, borne by the indies, black American music entered the white popular market.

Aretha Franklin is short and round. Her clothes—high boots, short knit dresses, sunglasses, and costume jewelry—are stylish and expensive, but, though they suit her, they are not glamorous. She is a lovely black sister, not a willowy show-biz singer like Diana Ross or Dionne Warwick, whose well-earned successes have in part depended on their stunning faces and figures. Aretha's beauty, while no less apparent than theirs, is more internal. At rehearsals her movements were restrained, her demeanor quiet. The Sweethearts of Soul, her backup singers, with curly wigs and patent leather bags, flirted and carried on like schoolgirls; Aretha stayed in the background when she wasn't singing. Her eyes took everything in but gave little back.

She was, of course, working hard, preparing not only for three shows in an unfamiliar and challenging milieu, but also to make a record—which, in her art, is the medium of permanent statement. Yet how much was it her record? It would be called an Aretha Franklin record, and all depended on her, but all was not directed by her. Wexler, Bill Graham, King Curtis, arranger Arif Mardin, and Ruth Bowen were, however subtly, more in charge than she. They deferred to her every spoken wish; when she did not speak, they decided.

The tension between Aretha as a black woman singer and Aretha as an adventurous artist in the popular music medium was palpable. She was not making her record the way her white male contemporaries Bob Dylan, John Lennon, and the Stones make theirs—on their own with friends, delivered as tapes to submissive corporations. On the other hand, she was far freer than in her days at Columbia or when she was Atlantic's brand new success in 1967. Here she was this weekend, the ranking black singer of the day playing the Fillmore, in much the same position, four crucial years on, that Otis Redding had been in at the Monterey Pop Festival in 1967. Where might Otis's music have gone after "Dock of the Bay," written on a Sausalito houseboat during a Fillmore engagement? The Fillmore audience had certainly changed B.B. King's music and career; how would it change Aretha's? Might it help her break the constrictions of race and sex that still webbed her in?

Her quietness that weekend suggested determination. As photographers came close to snap and snap at her again, she looked deeply into their lenses and did not smile. Wexler kissed her on the cheek when he arrived on stage Friday afternoon, but Aretha was unmoved. When no one could figure out the words of Stephen Stills' "Love the One You're With," Aretha listened to all suggestions, then said she'd sing it the way it made sense to her. Her short natural hair revealed a strong neck. She was smoking, not chain smoking but almost, menthol cigarette after menthol cigarette. Blues singers have never tried to save their voices—the idea would be nearly incomprehensible to them—and Aretha is a blues singer. Yet an opera singer with Aretha's voice would take care of her throat as a delicate and irreplaceable musical instrument deserves to be taken care of. I found myself wishing that Aretha would stop smoking. Her cigarettes seemed part of her guard; why should she turn the tensions of her struggle against herself?

Black American music has had many names. Blues, boogie-woogie, jazz, R and B, rock 'n' roll, soul, gospel, work songs, swing, funk, bop, be-bop, the Mashed Potatoes, the Swim, the Jerk, the Fly, the Twist. It is, says Chuck Berry, "Music that is inspiring to the head and heart, to dance by and cause you to pat your foot." The great ship of Western music has in the past twenty years drastically altered its course. Chuck Berry saw which way it was headed, for it was he and his friends who had slipped up out of steerage and seized the helm.

Friday night went off well. Tower of Power was exuberant and earnest, and nearly dwarfed by what followed them. But they were part of the Bill Graham-Fillmore empire, and the weekend was good promotional exposure. King Curtis and the Kingpins were a knockout, Aretha superb. The song order got mixed up at one point, King Curtis calling one tune when Aretha wanted another. Aretha did Curtis's song and seemed mildly miffed, but it was just a first-night rough spot, and the crowd went home satisfied.

Saturday afternoon I went back to the Huntington to hear the new Donny Hathaway LP that Wexler had hyped to the skies. Again a group of writers, out came the joints, on went the record; otherwise, a respectful silence. I found myself not liking the record, pulled out my notebook, and wrote:

"Jerry Wexler is saying this guy is a fit and possible inheritor of the mantle of Ray and Aretha. I hear him as a supertalented musician, backed by brilliant instrumentalists, but an unsure young man, inclined to sentimentality and to a little-boy appeal that lacks the manliness that Ray had at nineteen and the pride and striving for freedom that characterizes every note that Aretha ever sang."

As he flipped the record, Wexler said, "He's conservatory trained." That I could hear, but little else. If this was Wexler's third genius, Hathaway sounded like his first false genius. Genius 1 had gone to another label, Genius 2 was asserting herself; was Hathaway a genius who would stay Wexler's genius? The record ended.

Wexler said he had a tape of *Young, Gifted, and Black*, Aretha's latest work in progress. It was still a rough mix, and most of the horn and string tracks had not been added, but he'd play it anyway. It was beautiful. The arrangements she had worked out for the background vocalists were smooth as smoke. Her piano tinkled like Errol Garner and rang with the authority of classical harmonies. "I see a brand new girl," she sang in one song; that's how she sounded. I couldn't just listen and sang along. (When released in 1972, the record exceeded the promise of that afternoon's foretaste.)

As I was leaving, Wexler spoke to me at the door: "You know, I didn't really mean it about Donny." Aretha's voice was still coming out from the little tape machine. "Wow," he said, "the music pours out of her!"

Saturday night was, well, stupendous. There are many ways for an R and B horn section to play a phrase, but it sounds best if they come in absolutely on time and full strength from the first instant, so that there is no ragged fade-up from silence but a sudden punch of sound. Wayne Jackson's Memphis Horns were as crisp as karate Saturday night. Wayne is small, plays trumpet, runs the Horns as an extremely successful business, and says that "playing music is 99 percent confidence." The group was once known as the Mar-Keys and can be heard on almost every Otis Redding record and on the records of every singer who wants soulful brass and who can afford to hire them—plus many TV commercials. They are all Southern boys; several, including Wayne, are white. For some reason they ended up blowing in Memphis, not picking in Nashville, but it's all music from the same part of the world.

Bernard "Pretty" Purdie is as good-natured as the beat he keeps. The demand for his propulsive drumming has kept him shuttling in taxis between studios, morning to night, for a decade. King Curtis is the master of the stuttering sax. He has played ballads with a surprising tenderness and loves to howl uptempo. He is *the* R and B saxophone player, responsible for most of those rocking sax breaks you remember from the fifties, composer of "Soul Serenade," and a New York City session man of the first rank. Curtis is big, at least six feet three inches tall, and with the heavy gut of a muscular man living the life of steaks and imported beer. All weekend he wore a black leather jacket with a white leather horse's head coming through a horseshoe on the back. (Curtis, born Curtis Ousley in Fort Worth, Texas, was stabbed to death in New York less than six months after the Fillmore weekend. Witnesses said he was outside on the sidewalk arguing with tenants of a building he owned when one attacked him. Aretha sang and the Kingpins and the Horns played at his funeral, which was attended by everyone in soul music show business.)

Jackson, Purdie, Curtis—complete musicians. Their idiom is rhythm and blues, technically more sophisticated than in its raucous early days in the late forties and early fifties, but with the same funky power. The point of it is to entertain, make people dance; there's not much thought about art. Yet the idiom in no way restricts the musicians; they love to play and they play the music they love. It comes out R and B. Fun, for an R and B cat, is to find ways to increase the dramatic contrasts within a song, to create ever more intense rhythms. That's what people like: colorful songs with drive, songs you can get the feel of and feel with.

Curtis and company came on stage Saturday night and started out with "Knock on Wood," a Stax-Volt classic. They sounded the way they looked:

the trumpets gleaming in the stage lights, Purdie rocketing away, his eyes seldom leaving Curtis's swaying back, Jermott's fingers bounding up and down the long black neck of his bass, Dupree light and pretty on guitar. After three bars you realized what fun it was to be there, one of those paradises everyone hopes will dot their lives. (Atlantic has released *King Curtis at Fillmore West*, recorded that weekend. It is as powerful as Aretha's record.)

It was pleasant to be in the crowd that night. The grassroots that Aretha drew were not hippies but black teenagers, most of them, like Aretha, in the Fillmore for the first time. They were kids like none I ever knew—with Afros, self-assured, smoking grass and drinking wine. Some were overdressed for sitting on the floor (I saw guys worrying about the crease in their slacks); they weren't Negroes, but something new.

Aretha herself was in a trailer parked outside the stage door. A waiter from one of San Francisco's better restaurants took in a meal on a silver tray. She was the star, and when she came on stage she earned her position all over again. There were no rough spots Saturday night. At some point I scribbled in my note book, "Billy Preston–INSPIRED!"

I took a rough poll of the musicians that weekend on how they were betting the Ali-Frazier fight. Without exception they were betting on Ali. The Kingpins were to play at his postfight party. About half called him Muhammad Ali; the other half said Cassius Clay.

Aretha and Ray sat together at the Sunday night dinner party before the show, their table right beside the line waiting for ribs and greens. It was as much a receiving line as a food line. They both shook dozens of hands, and everyone with an Instamatic got a snap. The two didn't appear to talk much; they hardly could have in the circumstances. When not being spoken to, Ray was quiet, even withdrawn. Wexler waved me over to shake hands with him. Introducing me, he told Ray I was writing an article and was "into your music." "I'm glad of that," Ray replied.

•

In 1971, Ralph J. Gleason, who has been following the growth of black American music for thirty years, wrote a reflective column on the mysterious and virtually unpublicized death of Albert Ayler, a jazz musician whose body was found in New York's East River. The low significance the American public accorded Ayler's death angered Gleason. As if in defiance, he made the strongest prediction of his career: that soon, in the near future, there would be a "coming together of all musics." What could he mean? Wouldn't it be something!

Sunday night—I've already described that. Listening to the record now, I can hear what happened as I did not hear it then—we were too busy making it happen. I remember that when Aretha shouted something about, "Every now and then you gotta sit down, cross your legs, cross your arms, and say, 'Yes, Lord,'" I had an image of a middle-aged black lady like Rosa Parks on that bus in Montgomery, Alabama, or maybe Beulah, and I figured that feeling like them would feel fine.

Aretha, in white and gold, was so beautiful that night, her voice soaring, her energy awesome. "You have been more to me than anything I could ever have expected," she called out toward the end. "You too, you too," we tried to tell her back. She came down the runway. Hands reached up to touch her, she reached down to touch them. When it was over, it felt like a new beginning.

If Ali had won the next night, you could have convinced me we were about to enter the promised land.

Bob Dylan on tour, 1974. © Ellen Mandel

1974

By 1974 my music had progressed enough that I already had a couple of years under my belt singing and playing guitar in Berkeley and San Francisco coffeehouses. I had even started playing harmonica in a holder while strumming my guitar—tons of fun! Bob Dylan, the iconic young man with a guitar, was of course a prime inspiration for me and my colleagues/competitors on the Bay Area's folk circuit: the tiny Seventh Seal coffeehouse, one room in a Lutheran youth center just off the University of California campus, was the local Gerde's Folk City. There, with Ellen Mandel singing and playing piano, I played my first professional engagement in September 1973. We took home $7.50 for two forty-minute sets.

When we heard a few months later that Dylan was going out on tour again for the first time in years, we were dying to go and learn all we could by hearing the maestro in person. No backstage press passes this time—Dylan as always played his cards close to his chest—but Bill Graham did allow us to buy tickets for the Oakland and Los Angeles shows from his private reserves, and we got to all five concerts, sitting lost in the huge crowds, drinking in the music like welcome rain from heaven.

Since I gave every spare minute in those days to practicing, I finished my report a year later, long after Dylan's 1974 tour had become yesterday's news, and it lay buried in my "done but unpublished" pile for twenty-eight years.

The air was filled with music.

—Raymond Chandler, *Playback*

A four-car caravan—two back Cadillac limousines, one pale yellow camper with the decal of a smiling duck in a rear window, and a cream-colored station wagon—moved at a swift and even pace across the Bay Bridge from San Francisco to Oakland, then down the Nimitz Freeway to the Coliseum. It was a cool, almost bleak afternoon, February 11, 1974. Bob Dylan sat at one of the camper's windows. He had a gray scarf around his neck and a duffel coat over his shoulders. His eyes, which looked blue-gray, stared out at the flow of cars on the freeway, the roofs and billboards and factories and houses and warehouses that lie low on the flatlands beside the bay. His curly hair and strongly curved profile were immediately distinctive. His lips rested together, his face quiet. When he observed that two excited fans had spotted him from a car beside his, he turned his face, without change of expression, to his companions in the back of the camper. The caravan, amber lights blinking fore and aft on each car, rolled on down the road.

Bob Dylan was on his way to the six o'clock Oakland concert, the first of two that evening and his thirty-sixth in forty days. Oakland was the twentieth city, and only one more—Los Angeles, with its three concerts on February 13 and 14—remained. The tour's beginning in Chicago was already the distant past, and the complex skein of people, places, plans, and events had suffered no snarls. "Yes, there's been one surprise," said Bill Graham the next day, "nothing went wrong." A huge map of the United States covered one wall of his San Francisco office. The twenty-one cities were neatly pinned and flagged. Graham's seventeen-man FM Productions had booked and staged every concert, built and run the custom light and sound systems, and moved the tour from city to city. "No subcontractors. We were there, the planes were there, the equipment was there, and the crowds were there."

The last is understatement. That a larger audience existed for Bob Dylan than one tour could reach was presupposed. "Attention Bob Dylan fans," said a November headline in the *San Francisco Chronicle* announcing the tour; that did it. The few ads in that and other papers did no more than notify fans of the tour and give information about ticket-ordering procedures; these ads disappeared after December 2, the first, last, and only day of public ticket sales. One wave of mailed checks, bundled in fat canvas sacks, swamped twenty-one box offices. Had the concert halls no walls, Bill Graham guesses that five million people would have paid to see Bob Dylan on this tour. "Roughly 658,147," he said, did get a chance to buy tickets at a top price of $9.50, low of $4.50, indicating a gross of over $4 million in the bank before the tour began. After that no publicity was sought; most reviewers bought their own tickets. Interviews, press conferences, and backstage access were denied to reporters as a matter of policy; nevertheless, the concerts were widely covered as news and reviewed favorably as cultural events.

We entered the brightly lit bowl of the Oakland Coliseum on the evening of February 11 looking for a good time. We found our seats, took a stroll, greeted friends. On the stage stood a grand piano, an organ, two drum kits, a variety of medium-to-small amplifiers, many microphones, large piles of public address horns and speaker boxes, and a table with a silver vase filled with flowers and a few short candles; above the stage rose a black metal frame from which hung dozens of small spotlights, still unlit. When the crowd had found its seats, the bowl became dark and the spotlights turned the stage blue. The five members of the Band—Robbie Robertson on guitar; Rick Danko on bass; Garth Hudson on organ; Richard Manuel on piano; Levon Helm on drums—and Bob Dylan came up to the stage and moved from the rear through the amps and mikes. While the roar of the crowd's reception still thundered, Dylan began sweeping his hands over the strings of his tan Telecaster. Out boomed the opening chords of "Most Likely You'll Go Your Way and I'll Go Mine." In seconds the Band was with him, and through the driving rock 'n' roll came Dylan's voice.

> You say you love me, always thinking of me,
> but you could be wrong!

His voice was full, ending each phrase with a big shout.

> You say you told me, you want to hold me,
> but you're not that strong!

He stood close to the mike, staring straight before him, and sang. He wore a close-fitting black suit, a black vest, and black boots with cowboy heels. Against the wide lapels of the jacket the long collar points of his open-neck white shirt stood out bright and sharp. His legs, boyishly thin, were spread wide, and the intensity of his stance made them bowed. His heels lifted alternately for each beat.

> I'm gonna let you pass!

The huge audience whooped and cheered as the lyrics built to the end of the chorus.

> Time will tell just who has fell
> and who's been left behind

Dylan held a long note on "behind," Levon Helm underpinning it with a rocketing rat-a-tat-tat-tat that ended with a whap—

> When you go your way and I go mine!

"Thank you!" said Bob Dylan, ending with a final flourish across the strings. He stepped back from the mike and began the second song with a steady, contemplative rhythm. Then he sang again. "Lay, lady, lay, Lay across my big brass bed . . . "

The audience, which had barely stopped cheering the first song, let out a long "yeah" of happy recognition and sat back to listen.

Begin playing the guitar, and you will soon encounter the word "chord." Your teacher, instruction book, or the musician offering a few tips to get you going will show you the simplest way to hold down some of the strings with one hand so that, however awkwardly you may strike them with your other hand, an A (or C or E or G or D) chord will sound. That hand position is that chord: you hit it, you got it. Why that position makes that chord and even what a chord is comes later. First is the struggle to get unruly fingers on the proper strings for the delicious harmony of a strummed guitar chord.

To the new guitarist, his or her first chord positions—the neck-spanning G chord, C's long diagonal, the backward L shapes of E major and A minor, the reversed diamonds of D and D7—are hard won and valuable tools. To practice, the guitarist makes one chord, strums it, makes another, and strums that. It is fun. Songs one already knows appear out of these simple combinations. Many songs, "Down in the Valley," for example, need only two chord positions; "You Are My Sunshine," "I Can't Stop Loving You," "Bye Bye Love," and thousands more use only three. Every variation of rhythm in the strumming or when the chords change can bring new elements of the harmony into relief. As an infinite number of shapes can be created by varying the positions of a circle, rectangle, and triangle, so too can a lifetime of songs be created using these basic chord positions as building blocks.

The songs of the Carter Family, Woody Guthrie, Hank Williams, the Weavers, Don Gibson, Felice and Boudleaux Bryant, Johnny Cash, and Joe Tex are a parade of these first-position guitar chords in different groupings. The chords structure these songs like the legs of a three-legged stool and color them boldly with their primary colors. In contrast, songs by Cole Porter and Duke Ellington are filled with exotic minor sixth, augmented fifth, and major seventh chords, pastel harmonies that melt into each other like gossamer.

Such differences of composition are as evident to the ear as styles of architecture are to the eye. Often what makes one songwriter distinctive is what chords he likes to use to make his songs. Dion DiMucci wrote hit after hit, "Runaround Sue" among them, with the same C–A minor–F–G progression repeated ad infinitum. Bill Haley doesn't like bluesy minors; he insists that his lead guitarist play rockabilly solos with a solid major chord feel. B.B. King says he likes to use ninth chords, but to him, anything more exotic is "jazz, not blues."

Bob Dylan makes songs (with many exceptions) from the elemental chords put together with the bluntness of a brick wall. The logic of his progressions is unornamented. Chord follows chord in a steady forward march. D, A, G, E minor, C and C7—in concert his left hand, rooted to the far end of the neck, is as readable as the finger positions diagrams printed above the melody stave in his song books. His right hand, swinging supplely from the wrist, booms them out in rhythms tender and fierce. The structures of his songs are both plain and purposeful; the songs are as clear harmonically as his lyrics are verbally specific. He builds excitement more by repetition than by variation; over and over the same progression will underpin the long lines of his verses, building a cumulative, compelling power climaxed by the snap accents of his line-ending rhymes.

The textures and colors of Dylan's voice create the drama of the story each lyric tells, and flesh out his logic with emotion. At driving uptempos he hurls out his lines in devil-may-care flashes. Staccato bites of sound yield to curves of yearning. Smooth whoops bring a crooner's charm to his late-night love songs; the rasp of a sudden shout keeps the edge of his defiance keen. Quirky twists of humor punctuate cadences of loneliness. The flow of his phrasing and inflection is that of a most urgent conversation. The clarity of his diction makes every word count. The invisible panorama Dylan presents in song is varied, bold, and touched with the fantastical; the viewpoint is highly individual and grounded in his own adventurous experience.

> When you're lost in the rain in Juarez
> and it's Easter time too . . .

The Oakland crowd greeted the third song, "Just Like Tom Thumb's Blues," with an ovation as great as they gave the first two. "Tom Thumb" tells the story of a Kerouackian trip into the seamy side of Mexico that strips the bluff from its diminutive hero, leaving him walletless, friendless, and scooting back across the border and home to New York City. When it was over Dylan sipped from a water glass on the table, then began "Rainy Day Women #12 & 35." This was a big hit for Dylan in the summer of 1966 (concurrent with Ray Charles's similarly themed "Let's Go Get Stoned"), and in eight years the truth of its pun had lost none of its tickle: you're gonna be stoned, so get stoned! Dylan and the Band played it as a stomping blues, and the whole place screamed, in goofy unison, "Everybody must get stoned!"

Dylan's microphone was just right of stage center; drummer Helm sat behind him. Guitarist Robertson and bassist Danko, whose bouncy playing had a loose abandon, stood close together often using one mike left of center for singing supporting harmonies. Pianist Manuel sat at the grand piano far left, and organist Hudson seemed to preside over the others from an elevated spot, center rear. They were six attractive young men. When Dylan sang, he had the spotlight, its bright blue-white keeping his face and figure in sharp focus. The Band's members remained a distinct ensemble in a reddish ambience. When Dylan stepped back from his mike to pound out the rhythm chords for instrumental choruses, the whole stage brightened, and the spotlights followed the sound's focus—crackling, wiry solos from Robertson, meaty slamming from Helm, sudden booming runs by Danko.

After "Rainy Day Women" came another singalong from further back in the well known repertory—"It Ain't Me, Babe." Babe would like the singer to be a person cast in the mold of her own needs, but Dylan finishes

215

detailing the precise features of the mold and then concludes, "No, No, No, it ain't me, babe / it ain't me you're looking for, babe." The descending "No, no, no" is as exuberantly infectious as the "Yeah, yeah, yeah" of the Beatles' "She Loves You." Helm had his head back, howling the nos as he accented them with deep thuds from his blanketed bass drum.

Then "Ballad of a Thin Man," the story of the frightfully out-of-place Mr. Jones. The progression of this song is stark and oblique, and its melody is among Dylan's most haunting. Mr. Jones does not speak; the singer informs him with chilling clarity that he has stepped into a gargoyle party of the put-up or shut-up world. The lyrics deftly sketch shifting scenes—sexual and dreamlike—that may or may not be the play of Mr. Jones's own fantasies. For this Dylan put down the Telecaster and sat at the grand piano, Danko crossing to the second drum kit beside Helm. Dylan sat, his back straight, his head angled up to the mike and slammed two-handed chords into the keys.

You walk into the room,

The audience was caught. However familiar, the song's story had a shiver for all. Hudson's organ spun out webs of sound, long sustained minors that shifted a measured half-step downward at the end of each phrase.

You've been with the professors
They all liked your looks

Dylan sang the words with a stiletto insinuation. The ensemble sound was bluesy and eerily restrained. Strangers accost Mr. Jones and find him wanting.

Give me some milk or else go home!

At sudden moments Dylan broke the pace of his heavy chords into wild bunches of rock 'n' roll triplets at either end of the keyboard, splashy ripples and offbeat breaks that evoked whoops of excited laughter from the crowd. Steadily each chorus built to its climax in a question without an answer:

> You know something is happening here
> but you don't know what it is,
> Do you, Mr. Jones?

Self-determination has ever been the hallmark of Bob Dylan's musical career. The memories of his acquaintances, chronologically collated in Anthony Scaduto's biography, *Bob Dylan*, evoke a man constantly deciding for himself what to do next. "He learned things quickly and tried everything," said one friend. "That's one of the reasons Bob was so colorful, all the different things he was trying on for size," said Jack Elliott. "He always said he didn't know anything," remembered another. A girl named Sue Zuckerman said, "It was pleasing to watch him move." Dylan has said about himself, "I knew whatever I did had to be something creative, something that was me that did it, something I could do just for me. And I made up my mind not to have anything. I was about seventeen, eighteen, and I knew there was nothing I ever wanted, materially, and I just made it up from there, from that feeling."

Music is the immaterial something Dylan did want. Through the countless emotions of which his songs speak so graphically, this desire to be a great musician runs as a lifeline. Dylan's ambition upon graduation from high school was to play with Little Richard; like the four Beatles and many others he wanted to be "as big as Elvis Presley." Little Richard Penniman is a musician of indefatigable razzle-dazzle, a crowd-worker and a crowd-pleaser, a singer high and low, and a wild-wristed piano player. Elvis had all the grandeur one could imagine, making music that excited everyone who heard it, that presented the full force of his handsome youth in sound. He sang with a pleasure so sensual that it made his body shake, fascinating his listeners who, wide-eyed and often screaming, shook in happy response. My older brother John came running into the kitchen to tell me about "Heartbreak

Hotel" when he first heard it on the radio. "This guy has something different, he's good," he said. That throbbing blues—it became Number 1 on April 21, 1956—began Elvis's two-year single-handed domination of the record sales charts, during which time those pop charts became rock charts and, with the 45-rpm disc, a new mass market for music on record sprang into being. Little Richard and Elvis *were* rock 'n' roll.

From nothing he began with a name—Bob Dylan. To this he added a guitar, a harmonica and its holder, and a cap. Guitar and harmonica he played in a punchy style that proclaimed his presence without doubt; his cap he played with winsome insouciance. There were stages in New York City's Greenwich Village for such one-man acts. He got on them. Working single-mindedly on his own behalf, he got a lot done. In little more than a year after getting to New York in January 1961, he had become a friend and protégé of Woody Guthrie, been a featured performer with week-long gigs at major clubs, gotten a rave review in the *New York Times*, been signed to Columbia by John Hammond, and gotten his first LP out. He also signed a seven year contract with a professional manager, Albert Grossman. Duchess Music published his first songs; shortly thereafter he switched to M. Witmark, "the Tiffany of music publishers," and ASCAP (the American Society of Composers Authors and Publishers) began logging the instances of their public performance.

Dylan saluted the audience with a high toss of his right arm, then left the grand piano and the stage. It was the Band's turn. They began with "Stagefright," Rick Danko telling of the terrors of the spotlight with eloquent earnestness. His electric bass swung between his arms, and his comrades accompanied him at a cooking tempo. Then "The Night They Drove Old Dixie Down," an anthem of the sadness of a people defeated in war, and after that, "King Harvest is Surely Come"—the same people, their spirits quickening with the hopes of labor unionism.

The Band play like barnstorming rustics; led by Robertson, their chief songwriter, they've molded a sound that powers compelling lyrics with funky rhythms. Their songs create characters alive in song worlds. "Olley told me I'm a fool," begins the narrator of "When You Awake." His lyric is cheerily disjointed, but right or wrong, "I'm not gonna worry all night long." The audience's cheers for that were mixed with cries for "The Weight," the big hit from the Band's first album, *Music from Big Pink.* Instead the group swang directly into "Up on Cripple Creek," one of the biggest of many hits from the second album, the self-told tale of a truckdriver mooning over his Bessie down in Lake Charles, Louisiana, as he piles across a lonely mountain. "A drunkard's dream," that woman, loyal in times of trouble, laughing in the face of luck. Levon Helm sang, his red beard jutting out over his cymbals, the band catching the throb of his love-tickled heart. Everybody was whooping at the finale; silence hadn't come when Dylan reappeared:

There must be some way out of here . . .

Two men conversing on horseback, a windy night, a castle wall—"All along the Watchtower." The images flicker; Dylan lights his scene as if by torch light. As the song first appeared on the *John Wesley Harding* album in 1968 it had a dramatic flatness; Jimi Hendrix's recording gave it an electric howl. In concert, with Dylan strumming an uptempo rhythm, Robertson shiny and keen on his Telecaster, and Hudson rich on organ, the song suggested majesty and menace. "The Ballad of Hollis Brown" came next, the story of a despairing farmer who spends his last dollar for the shotgun shells that will end life's misery for his family and himself. This dispassionate shocker was the second song, after the title tune, on Dylan's third album, *The Times They Are A-Changing.* The black-and-white photo on the cover did show a changed Bob Dylan. He wrote the liner notes, entitling them "11 Outlined Epitaphs."

With that done the ensemble began "Knocking on Heaven's Door," Dylan's latest hit from his soundtrack for Sam Peckinpah's excellent film *Pat Garrett and Billy the Kid,* released in the summer of 1973. In it Dylan also made a stunning debut as a featured player in a dramatic film, creating the   219 character of Alias, a quick-witted printer's apprentice who joins the hunted Billy. His role grows with the story; Peckinpah shows his still face as the final image. "Knocking on Heaven's Door" is the song for Garrett's reluctant deputy (Slim Pickens) who is shot in a gunfight. The song plays as he realizes that he is dying, and his wife comes to his support. Three chords play over and over in a steady rhythm; the melody is sad and lonely. At Oakland the crowd sang along, moved by the music expressing a good man's death. "Knock, knock, knockin' on heaven's door." Dylan ended singing high. Then with a quick wave he left the stage. The Band followed him. Intermission.

Bill Graham was present at and supervised the details of all the concerts. During this month and a half on the road he continued his day to day business booking musical shows at a variety of venues on both coasts. How? "The golden weapon," Graham said, holding up an office telephone that was indeed gold-plated.

In the years since he closed the Fillmores East and West, the houses where he forged his promotional name and style, Graham's business has grown. Success with the influential Fillmore audiences meant national success for so many musicians that now in stadiums, arenas, and auditoriums Graham reaps the reward of having boosted the careers of acts like the Grateful Dead, the Jefferson Airplane, Santana, B.B. King, Eric Clapton, Frank Zappa, the Who, Led Zeppelin, the Staples Singers, the Allman Brothers Band, Boz Scaggs, Elton John, and many, many more. His consistent delivery of good shows for the money has won him the respect he battled for in the 1960s. His staff is well-trained and organized. "My value to the company," he said, "is booking and negotiation. I know who to sign, where to play 'em and when, and how much to pay 'em." He estimates that his gross business income could be $10 million a year. After a decade as an imaginative independent, he is no longer a controversial comer but a promoter in his prime, capable of gestures like a banquet-length ringside table for himself and his friends at the Fairmont Hotel's Venetian Room on Marlene Dietrich's opening night. His cantankerousness has diminished as his wealth and operations have expanded. He makes more splash and fewer waves.

Bob Dylan had often come to the Fillmore East as a guest of the house, and on those occasions Graham brought up the idea of presenting him in concert. Nothing had come of it, and in September 1973, several years had passed since they had spoken. "Then an intermediary called," Graham remembered, "'Bob's gonna go out,' the guy said, 'Do you want to do it?' 'Yeah!' I said, but I didn't believe it. I couldn't believe it." When he did, he began laying out the cities and the halls to be played. Graham presented the basic options of routes, dates, prices, sound, lighting, and staging; after discussion, "the final decision was Bob's." Then the crews began their jobs of assemblage and transportation, and Graham began making his bargains with hall managers.

Graham had never done anything bigger, either in gross receipts for a single project, in extent (the tour took him to ten new cities and to every region of the country), or in the value of his contribution to the presentation of a star performer. In record business parlance, Graham was Dylan's "one stop," combining the roles of promoter and tour manager. The organized variety of complementary services he offered minimized hassles, cut overhead, and maximized net profit and the enjoyment of audience and performer alike. As he gathered together notebooks and papers from his desk for the tour's final leg, a happy satisfaction was mingled with his weariness. To present Bob Dylan nationwide in 1974 was a challenge, and Bill Graham had met it with success.

On a sunny February 12, the tour moved to Los Angeles, as we did also on highways empty because of the "gas shortage." Midwinter Los Angeles weather was clear and balmy. In the parts of the city where show business is big business—Sunset Boulevard, Beverly Hills, Westwood, Bel Air, and Malibu—the glistening Rolls Royces, Mercedes, Jaguars, and Bentleys in eye-catching profusion, the pink and gold lobbies of the Beverly Hills and

Beverly Wilshire hotels, the bright executive office towers of Century City, the bustle of Universal Studio's back lot, the polished brass of the doorway to Chasens Restaurant, and the spotless white wall surrounding Mary Pickford's Pickfair mansion and its grounds all proclaimed the prosperity and excitement of Hollywood.

Young hopefuls waited in the sun before the Troubador on Santa Monica Boulevard to sign up for hoot night; English rock bands and American soul groups staying at the Hyatt Continental House on the Strip hung out in the coffeeshop over long lazy breakfasts at two in the afternoon. The horses were running at Santa Anita, where the tall palms of the infield wave against a backdrop of green mountains. Walter Matthau announced one race. Clint Eastwood was off to a celebrity tennis tournament at La Costa. Stevie Wonder, Gladys Knight and the Pips, Roberta Flack, and Bette Midler took top honors at the Grammy awards, televised from the Palladium. Ray Charles was hard at work recording at his RPM studio on West Washington Boulevard. James Cagney was fêted at the American Film Institute. At the many movie houses of Westwood there were long lines for *The Sting*, *The Exorcist*, *Sleeper*, *Blazing Saddles*, and *Serpico*. *Variety* reported that similar lines across the country added up to an entertainment boom that had not let up since it began, over the Christmas holidays.

Dylan's concerts were at the Forum in Inglewood, the first on the evening of February 13. As the lights dimmed after the intermission Dylan came out on the stage by himself. He held a small Martin guitar of blond wood handsomely inlaid with abalone shell; a wire holder sat around his neck, bracing a ten-hole harmonica before his lips. Midway back in the hall, on the left where the first rows sloped up from the floor, two young men, employees of FM Productions, sat at a twenty-four-channel sound board, headphones on, their hands on small knobs, waiting for Dylan to begin to play.

One spotlight shone on Dylan standing before a microphone. Otherwise the stage was dark but for the lamp and candles. The quiet instruments and amplifiers behind him were in shadow, revealed only by glowing reflections of the spotlight. As at Oakland, Dylan wore a black suit and open-necked white shirt. After a brief moment to check his guitar's tuning, he began strumming a song's chords. The Martin's bright finish scattered light over the upturned listening faces; a microphone directly before its round sound hole took the clanging of its bright brass and steel strings to the arena's furthermost upper level.

> She's got everything she needs,
>
> she's an artist, she don't look back . . .

The song was "She Belongs to Me," the portrait of a perfect lady who collects lovers like antiques, shrinking men into kneeling Peeping Toms. The lyric indicts with understatement, and Dylan delivered it with sangfroid. Alone, his concentration on what he was doing was, if anything, more intense. He pushed his voice into the mike. His tones changed timbre often—rough, piercing, sinuous, always vibrant—and created sharp, dramatic contrasts. His strumming beat, its variations matched to his voice, was quick and to the point.

Next came "The Times They Are A-Changin'." Josephine Baker performed this song at a recent concert at the Circle Star theater wearing a tight-fitting denim pants suit embroidered with glitter, and sitting on the glossy leather seat of a motorcycle with ape-hanger handlebars and chromium resonator pipes. Her lithe body expressed youthful vigor, and her voice carried the burning certainty of the words. Dylan sang the song with a similar ardor, making the song itself the call he demanded be heeded. He sang, his lower jaw jutting forward earnestly, his words conjuring up bold images of revolution, an irresistible flood tide of change tumbling the pillars of the powers that be. For many in the hall the song had long been a proudly personal anthem. Each time Dylan reached the end of the choruses, the Forum swelled with the repeated refrain sung by thousands:

For the times they are a-changin'!

The last refrain was the biggest. The hall rang with cheers as Dylan stopped his strumming hand. Then expectant silence—what next? The pleasures of the concert had already been great, the attention of the audience on the young man in the spotlight become a receptive fascination. The candles burned. The microphones in their slender stands stood poised and seemingly alert. Dylan began strumming again. "My love she speaks like silence . . . "

This song, "Love Minus Zero/No Limit," appears on the first side of the *Bringing It All Back Home* album, where it contrasts with the ironies of "She Belongs to Me." The woman in "Love Minus Zero" is soft-spoken, a winker at arguments. While the world goes its talkative, disputatious way, she comes to the singer like "a raven at my window with a broken wing." Dylan sang it evenly, articulating each word of the picturesque images:

> The cloak and dagger dangles,
> Madams light the candles . . .

With that done Dylan swung with barely a pause into "Don't Think Twice, It's Alright," one of his best-known and best-loved songs. Peter, Paul and Mary (Peter Yarrow, Paul Stookey, and Mary Travers), a trio then also managed by Albert Grossman, popularized the song on their 1963 hit album, *In The Wind.* That and their solid gold 45-rpm single of the Dylan tune "Blowin' in the Wind," first brought Bob Dylan's songwriting talents to a national audience. His own recorded version is on his second LP, *The Freewheelin' Bob Dylan.* He fingerpicks through the changing chords, delivering the lover's farewell with a stoicism that is fitting—he's heading down a lonesome road before dawn—and also wry; he's got the last word:

> You just kinda wasted my precious time,
> But don't think twice, it's alright.

It is a song honest and humorous, "a statement," Dylan told Nat Hentoff for the album's liner notes, "You can say it to make yourself feel better. . . . As for me, I can make myself feel better sometimes, but at other times, it's still hard to sleep at night."

Dylan drove through it at a rocking tempo at the Forum, taking, as he had in the songs before it, chorus-long breaks featuring the squealing melodies he played on his harmonica against the rhythmic harmonies of his strummed guitar. The ubiquitous ten-hole harmonica—Hohner's Marine Band and similar Blues Harp models are the most popular—differs in two ways from most wind instruments. It does not have "all the notes" in chromatic sequence across its range, as does a clarinet or saxophone; its design emphasizes the major scale and the basic chords of song building. This simplicity becomes an advantage when the harmonica is used to play the multitude of songs—including most of Dylan's—that are constructed on the same principles: there are no "wrong" notes to hit. Plus, the harmonica's sounds are made by sucking air in over the reeds as well as blowing out over them. The note-bending that such inspiration allows gives the harmonica player many of the in-between notes and a wide range of exciting textures

Made of the same wood, brass, and steel, the harmonica makes sounds highly sympathetic with the acoustic guitar. Many bluesmen—Walter Jacobs, Sonny Boy Williamson, and Sonny Terry in particular—have made the harmonica a powerful instrument in American music. Jesse Fuller used it as part of his one-man-band of instruments, and the great Jimmy Reed created a series of hot hits—"You Got Me Running," "Big Boss Man," and others— combining piercing harmonica wails with his thumping electric guitar. Dylan's harmonica-guitar sound is one of his most distinct styles. Often on his records his harmonica introduces the melody and sets the mood. Middle and concluding harmonica passages echo and vary his lines as wordless equivalents of his lyrics. Sometimes the harmonica comment is parenthetical, at others exclamatory; it is always continuous with the flow of his ideas and feelings.

225

"Dazzling harmonica and guitar on 'Don't Think Twice,'" I wrote in my notebook, "had the place standing." Dylan bounced harmonica phrase off harmonica phrase, quick curls from the middle holes, long scree-like sounds from the high end, and tunnel-like low sucked-in notes that curved downward until they ended in smooth gurgles—and all the while his strummed guitar kept the song's harmonies in forward motion. Dylan's swinging wrist brought out first the brightness of the treble strings, then the deeper tones of the wrapped strings, constantly changing the emphasis of the beats to match the free-form rhythm of the harmonica melody. The result, miked with electric clarity to the whole Forum, caused ripples of laughter to run through the audience. Unexpected delays and offbeat jumps evoked grunts of approval. The harmonica dashed through the final chorus like a football player running back a kickoff into a ninety-yard touchdown; Dylan had not gotten a metaphorical twenty yards before the crowd began to feel the suspense—would he make it? Everyone followed the shifts of accent and direction, saw the same openings, cheered the bold seizures of possibility, and then stood to acclaim the success of a thrilling venture.

Dylan bowed, then did a little dance, spinning in place before the microphone with both arms held above his head. The crowd cheered happily. He began to play again, and the hall quieted. The even cadence of the guitar chords was sweetly familiar, then the melancholy of the harmonica left no doubt—"Just Like a Woman." The hall welcomed the songs with shouts and sighs, many singing the opening lines with Dylan: "Nobody feels any pain, Tonight's the last night inside the rain."

"Just Like a Woman" is a song of parting; its amber harmonies frame the aching feelings of the singer as he tells Baby, "it's time for us to quit." Baby, the lyrics suggest, is rich, the singer not; her cool at first gives him refuge, then freezes him out. He hopes she will keep what was between them between them only, basing his plea on his own plaintive admission: "I was hungry and it was your world."

The song stood out on *Blonde on Blonde*, Dylan's 1965 double album; nine years later at the Forum he made it even more persuasive. Women in

Levon Helm, Robbie Robertson, and Bob Dylan, 1974. © Ellen Mandel

the audience sat on the edges of their seats as they listened, moved by an empathy with the girl-woman addressed, and a willingness to provide that cute guitar player with all the warmth Baby was silly enough to withhold. Everytime Dylan dipped his voice or held a syllable over an extra beat, at every sibilant, tongued harmonica twist, a thousand coos and giggles of feminine appreciation rose in the darkness. Men shouted "Yeah!" beside them. "She breaks just like a little girl," Dylan sang ending the choruses, stretching his deep note on "girl" each time until it had become "gu-urr-url," an intimately growled melisma.

Then "It's Alright Ma (I'm Only Bleeding)." For this, Dylan's strumming hand ripped over the strings in a rapid-fire rhythm—brrumm da da da da, brrumm da da da da; his singing voice was sharp and even. Word

227

followed word in crisp telegraphic sequence. The pace of his delivery was that of a wire service typewriter beating out a breaking news story:

> Darkness at the break of noon
> Shadows even the silver spoon . . .

The singer is bringing Ma up to date with his recent experiences, mixing his report with observations and conclusions. Slings and arrows fly all about him, the cannons of purse-lipped hostility roar in his ears. He is, as my father often said, "bloody but unbowed." Tears wet his cheeks, yet he keeps on alertly spotting and sidestepping the snares laid by hypocrites. "Pointed threats," "words like bullets," "advertising signs that con"—like "people's games" and the false promises of "teachers" and "preachers," they're "phony." What is real to the singer are his feelings. He belongs to no one and will live for no one else. At times he loses his way and even himself. He is but one man. He'll take on all that comes with Houdini's contempt for handcuffs—"What else can you show me?"—and the confidence of self-inspired optimism:

> It's alright, Ma, I can make it!

As Dylan sang the crowd responded with excited sympathy. Perhaps only he knew all the words, but it seemed that everyone present knew one phrase or another because of its absolute aptness to their own experience. One listener, or two together, or a group, having heard a series of lines with pent-up breath, would suddenly scream or sing in agreement with an idea they knew to be true. "It's easy to see without lookin' too far that not much is really sacred" pulled out howls of approval; a chorus of "Right on!" greeted, "Meantime life outside goes on all around you." Thousands sang, "He not busy being born is busy dying." For months the laborious fact-finding that slowly stripped the veils of duplicity from Richard Nixon had made fascinating headlines. When Dylan sang:

> Even the president of the United States
> sometimes must have to stand naked . . .

the hall resounded with thunderous affirmation. Dylan kept pounding the beat on his guitar, inflecting his words with an upward lilt. Between sung choruses he played short harmonica breaks that built and then faded as he began to sing again. Cheers of encouragement filled the air. As he leaned away from the mike, his strumming hand still flying, a wide, dazzling smile came to his face. "Okay, Bobby, okay!" voices cried. His eyes brimmed with pleasure. He looked like a man having a good time and glad of it.

It seemed sudden when the song was nearly over. "It's alright, Ma," Bob Dylan sang with an emphatic shout that indicated finale:

> It's life and life only!

A few quick strums and he was done. He bowed low facing front with both arms extended, his guitar held high in his right hand, then turned and bowed similarly to those seated behind the stage. The applause was tremendous. Another bow, a wave, then he handed the guitar to a stagehand, picked up his extra harmonicas, and exited. In moments the Band had assembled and began boppin' out "Rag, Mama, Rag."

Twelve years and more have gone by since Columbia Records released *Bob Dylan*, his first LP. In those years he has produced fourteen more albums, plus one single and one double album of his "greatest hits." His own prose and poetry have been the liner notes for many of the albums; his paintings and drawings have adorned the covers of several, as well as the cover of the Band's *Big Pink* album. He has published one book of writings, *Tarantula*, one book of lyrics and accompanying sketches, and many songbooks, shorter ones to accompany specific albums and larger collections that have included compositions he has not recorded. Much of his conversation has

229

been published by others in magazine and book interviews. In the early and middle sixties he played in public frequently. He starred in *Don't Look Back*, a documentary film based on one of his English concert tours, and was a major attraction in *Festival*, a movie collage of several years of the Newport Folk Festival. His concert appearances in the later sixties and seventies up to this tour were few and memorable—a Woody Guthrie memorial concert in Carnegie Hall, the debut of Johnny Cash's TV show in May 1969, festivals in Missouri and on the Isle of Wight that summer, and the Concert for Bangladesh at Madison Square Garden in the fall of 1971. (The last also became a movie.)

In all of this work Bob Dylan presents interesting ideas and emotions in striking ways. He insists that what he tells is the truth of his own story. What he tells is absorbing in itself; the many perspectives he offers continually renew the liveliness of his narrative. The passing parades of experience and imagination are his raw materials; the finished products reflect that variety. He loves, he hates, he walks, talks, and crawls. He projects a personality active in its own struggles, competitive, fierce in self-defense, humorous, hopeful, and heartfelt.

His paintings seem experimental, done to satisfy curiosity. There is something downright silly about *Big Pink*'s cover: the sitar player has a teacup on his head, the piano player is being boosted up over the top of an upright, and a grinning elephant, its rear in the wings, observes from stage right. The pink and blue painting on the *Self-Portrait* cover indicates, as does the album's sounds, that Dylan's view of himself is less settled than the view others have of him.

"People make fun of me because my monologues don't follow any definite line," says Henny Youngman, the comedian billed as the King of the One-Liners. "Neither does life." Neither does *Tarantula*, Dylan's longest prose writing. The point of view jets about like a hockey puck through a succession of more or less brief fast-action episodes. In between these are funny notes from characters like Willy Purple, Froggy, and Louie Louie who leave messages and explain things. Dylan rings all the bells in his celebrity shooting gallery: Sam Snead, Henry Miller, Jack Parr, Debbie Reynolds, Charlie Starkweather, Grace Kelly, James Arness, Murph the Surf, Ted Kennedy, Donald O'Connor, and many more get plinked in cameo appearances. Aretha Franklin, "juke box queen," is muse. Walter Cronkite is seen telling the police that he needs candles to listen to Little Richard records, Zeke the Cork recommends Jerry Lee Lewis for a book about artists, and Bo Diddley is just the man for Justine. Herold the Professor writes his students:

> I take it for granted that you've read and understood freud—
> dostoevsky—st. michael—confucius . . . all right then—what
> my work is—is merely pickin up where they left off.

The guitar-playing author is also keeping a close eye on his peers:

> dear puck, traded in my electric guitar for one you call a
> gut one . . . you can play it all yourself—dont need a band—
> eliminates all the fighting except of course all the other gut
> guitar players.

Tarantula appeared widely first in several photo-offset editions printed from typewriter copies of galleys taken from Dylan's publisher, Macmillan, in New York. The book had been ready for publication and copyrighted in 1966, but was released in 1971 when the sales of the unauthorized editions had already brought it into general and well-publicized circulation. The typewritten copy I have seen is zesty and informal; the Macmillan edition, black and formal, bears the inscription, "This is a work of fantasy and imagination." There were three printings in the first year; a publisher's note mentions in the same breath John Lennon's two popular books of stories, rhymes, jokes, and drawings, *In His Own Write* and *A Spaniard in the Works*.

In one *Tarantula* note Snowplough Floater writes,

> Look you asshole—tho I might be nothing but a butter sculp-
> tor, I refuse to go on working with the idea of your praising as
> my reward—like what are your credentials anyway? except for
> talking about all us butter sculptors, what else do you do? do
> you know what it feels like to make some butter sculpture? do
> you know what it feels like to actually ooze the butter around
> & create something of fantastic worth?

Bob Dylan has sculpted vinyl into forms of great worth. His records are central to his music; he is the center of his records' sounds. He has stamped each album with a sonic impression all its own; each, with its jacket, is individual and memorable. *Bob Dylan* is the first, and it's Bob Dylan play-ing and singing all out. On the cover is a color close-up photo of his face, hands, and the neck of his guitar. He has on a corduroy cap, sheepskin coat, and a yellow T-shirt. His face looks smooth, his eyes direct. On the back is the prominent credit "Produced by John Hammond." The notes declare Columbia "proud to introduce a major new figure in American folk music—Bob Dylan," and includes Robert Shelton's *New York Times* re-view, which in September 1961, had said Dylan was "bursting at the seams with talent."

Dylan followed his solo debut with *The Freewheelin' Bob Dylan*. He's looking at the ground in the cover picture: a young lady, holding one of his arms tightly in hers, smiles at the camera; jazz critic Nat Hentoff wrote the notes. Dylan wrote his own notes for the third album, *The Times They Are A'Changin'*, and the three that followed it: *Another Side of Bob Dylan*, *Bringing It All Back Home*, and *Highway 61 Revisited*. The notes have a swinging connection with the platter they cover; in them Dylan talks about his childhood, tells stories, and on the back of *Bringing It All Back Home*, makes a comic comment on record making:

> am standing there writing WHAAAT? on my favorite wall
> when who should pass by in a jet plane but my recording engi-

neer. "i'm here t pick up you and your latest works of art do you need any help with anything?"

Then follows, after "(pause)," a whirlwind description of his new songs. At "(end of pause)" he says:

an so i answer my recoding engineer "yes. well i could use some help in getting this all in the plane"

Tom Wilson is credited as producer of that album. *Planet Waves*, Dylan's album on Asylum released as this tour was in progress, credits Robbie Robertson for "special assistance"; most of the songs were produced by Bob Johnston. On all the albums the sound is as straightforward as on the first: playing and singing clearly miked and balanced; overdubbing, editing, and special effects at a minimum. Only the increasing depth of the polish indicates the elbow grease. Dylan began adding other musicians on his second record. First he used a bassist, drummer, and melodic guitarist—the last often being Bruce Langhorn—then building to rock 'n' roll bands, the Band (once known as the Hawks) among them. Guitarist Michael Bloomfield and organist Al Kooper stand out on *Highway 61 Revisited*. There are fifty musicians beside Dylan listed on *Self-Portrait*. This 1970 double album—a collage of his own songs, songs by contemporaries Paul Simon and Gordon Lightfoot, and pop standards, taken from home, concert, and studio recordings—has the most varied sounds of all the LPs, including strings and choral voices. These, perhaps, offended some critics: *Self-Portrait* is the only album that was panned on release. Before the criticisms had a chance to stick, Dylan released *New Morning*, all new songs played with a danceable lilt by a small combo; the album became an instant smash.

Nashvilleans Charlie McCoy, Kenny Buttrey, and Pete Drake are featured on *John Wesley Harding*, released in the winter of 1968, and on the album that followed it, *Nashville Skyline*, in the spring of 1969. On both the sound is compact and rhythmic, yet as different in mood as the records' covers. The gray formality of *Harding*'s cover matches the astringent sound of the disc; Dylan's sunny smile on *Skyline*'s cover matches the warmth of the love songs within. *Skyline*, bearing a stirring endorsement from Johnny Cash, was instant gold, selling to many who previously thought Dylan's music a bit too rough and tumble.

All of Dylan's albums are widely available. Joseph Murrells, in the *Daily Mail Book of Golden Discs*, says that Dylan "established a brand of seemingly uncommercial music into a commodity that the public really wants." The "folk protest" tag may have spread his sound first only in specialized markets; but since the Top 40 success of the single "Like a Rolling Stone" in 1965 and the long 1966 to 1968 chart run of the magnificent double album *Blonde on Blonde*, Dylan has been singing directly to a world of avid fans. They play the albums over and over; old, new, all phases hold songs of interest. Hours of rejected, rehearsal, or informal tapes have been pirated, pressed, and sold as bootleg records. Dylan sounds so lively, so personal on disc that even "Is it rolling Bob?" a snippet of studio conversation, is full signature.

The words and music of the records go to the heads and hearts of Dylan's listeners, coming out again at countless moments to express their own strong feelings. Many have been inspired to play by his example, and there is hardly a popular musician today who hasn't included one or more of Dylan's songs in his or her repertory. Together with his contemporaries, the Beatles and the Rolling Stones, Bob Dylan has helped move modern music into a bold era of exciting, electric sound. His drawing power on records and in concert, and his ability to exert the same magnetism from the movie screen, make him a show business triple threat, well-funded and well-placed for whatever he plans next.

"'The Weight'!" "'The Weight'!" "Play 'The Weight'!"

Cries for the Band to play the *Big Pink* hit that launched them as a headline act in 1968 rose in happy chorus from the Forum crowd. It is

Valentine's Day night; the Band had just finished "The Shape I'm In." The concert, the tour's last, had been two hours in progress, each minute filled with the special thrill of near completion. Bill Graham, in a plain gray shirt and dark pants, had stepped to a stage-center mike for an announcement just before the lights dimmed.

"We're gonna wait five minutes so everyone can get in their seats. This is our last one, we want everybody to see all of it. I want to ask you a few favors. Please, no film"—he meant movies—"and no flash cameras. Regular cameras, take all you want. No tape recorders. We don't want bootlegs, let's wait for the real one. And please, keep out of the aisles, take your pictures from your seats. Do that and we'll give you a great show."

At the opening Dylan had greeted everyone with a shouted, "We're glad to be here," acknowledging the welcoming ovation with a wide grin, holding up his arms like a prizefighter entering the ring. The concert had gone in quite the same order as the others. Dylan had played and sung with particular vivacity. His backbone was straight and proud, his untucked shirttail hung down below his jacket. He broke a string on his electric guitar during "Rainy Day Women #12 & 35," sang Mr. Jones's name as a two syllable scream—"Mr. Jo-ones!"—and "drove 'em wild," I scribbled in my notebook, "with his high piano triplets." Our brains were so loaded we nearly exploded.

The Band played "The Weight." Everybody loved it, singing along with "Take a load off Annie," holding a long " ... and ... " in barbershop harmony before belting the release of the last chorus line:

You put the load right on me!

Bob Dylan again stepped quickly from darkness to the light of center stage. He lifted the strap of his electric guitar over his head, settled it over his back and shoulders, turned to the members of the Band, got set with them, and began to play. The song was "Forever Young," released in two contrasting versions as the end of side one and the start of side two of

Planet Waves, and therefore a new one to his listeners. It's a song of good wishes: may the listener, the singer sings, be blessed with courage, strength, a joyful heart, busy hands, swift feet:

> May you build a ladder to the stars
> And step on every rung,
> May you stay forever young!

In the Forum the song created a palpable wave of encouragement. Not for the first time that evening, many eyes filled with tears and many faces churned with emotion. Who could withhold their "Yeah!" to such hopes? "Oooh, oooh, oooh," I wrote listening to the swinging band, Dylan's steady shouting, and the foot-stamping and screams from all around me.

After that came the acerbic "Highway 61 Revisited," a point-blank blues at full throttle tempo. The actual Highway 61 runs along the Mississippi River from Minneapolis to New Orleans. The song highway, likewise, covers a lot of ground with dramatic scenes—Abraham sacrificing Isaac and a Third World War among them—at each bend in the lyric. The song was well-known to all from many years of playing it on the 1965 album named for it, and the responsive noise built around me to a pleasurable din.

> God said to Abraham
> Kill Me a son . . .

Dylan's voice swung through sweeps of emphasis, cresting the waves of voices that sang his words with him. The Band had that "highway sound" of Chuck Berry catching Maybellene in his V-8 Ford; audience screams created the same effect as the police car siren Dylan played on the original recording.

> Where do you want this killing done?
> Out on Highway Suh-ix-ty One!

The buzz of anticipation that followed the applause for "Highway 61" seemed like silence. In it the house lights suddenly brightened. The audience looked at each other. People, with faces expressing many varieties of elation, filled row after row of yellow and orange seats. Everybody whooped approval. Dylan and the Band began to play "Like a Rolling Stone."

> Once upon a time
> You dressed so fine
> Threw the bums a dime
> In your prime
> Didn't you?

Acres of clapping hands took up the song's heavy beat. Many people jumped up and down, grinning and singing the telling words that describe, as Joseph Murrells puts it, "a girl's decline from boarding school to streetwalker." The singer hurls his analysis of the lady's collapsing illusions directly at her. She has used others; now others use her. His precise knowledge of her situation indicates that his experience has been similar; he's glad that she now sees life as he has long seen it. He feels for her, and in the circumstances his unsparing vision, filled with cruel detail, is sympathetic—comfort less cold, if she can take it, than she will receive elsewhere. Like "The Ballad of a Thin Man," the song's repeated refrain is a question:

> How does it feel
> To be without a home
> Like a complete unknown
> Like a rolling stone?

Dylan slipped the guitar off his shoulders, waved and walked off the stage. The members of the Band followed him. The audience vented wild acclaim, sure of an encore. Through a few moments of suspense the cheering continued, then grew again as the musicians returned to the stage and again took up their instruments:

I ain't gonna work on Maggie's Farm no more . . .

The singer of "Maggie's Farm" had a job doing the dirty work for a family of liars, bullies, and vicious nuts. The pay was lousy, the hours terrible. He's quitting, so glad to be done that his relief is comic. After a month and a half on the road Dylan sang it with feeling—a few more choruses and the tour would be over. His voice rang out strongly:

> I try my best to be just like I am
> But everybody wants you to be just like them
> They say sing while you slave
> But I just get bored—
> I ain't gonna work on Maggie's Farm no more!

When done, he waved for and got (relative) silence.

"We're gonna do one more," he said as the hall listened, "but before we do, we need to bring out the man who brought us to you, Mr. Bill Graham."

Bill Graham stepped out to the stage. He and Dylan saluted each other. Suddenly a stagehand grabbed Graham, lifting him off his feet while a few others leapt from hiding places, seltzer bottles at the ready, and began dousing him. Blushing deep red, Graham struggled in vain against a solid soaking. The audience flipped with delight.

Dylan began "Blowing in the Wind." This was his first big hit, the opening track of his second record. Marlene Dietrich, Duke Ellington, and many others have recorded it. Muzak plays it frequently. The lyric is all questions: how long until men can be free and live in peace? How long until a mountain become sand washed into the sea? The only answer is the sound of the song.

When done, Bob Dylan bowed deeply several times, to the Band and to the whole hall. He stepped to the microphone one more time.

"We had ourselves a ball," he said. "Thank you for coming out. Good night."

PERMISSIONS

Grateful acknowledgment is given to the following for their permission to reprint the lyrics of songs in this book:

Author Michael Lydon in 1968 with his trusty Smith-Corona. © Baron Wolman

Michael Lydon today. © James J. Kriegsmann Jr.

Michael Lydon, a writer and musician who lives in New York City, is the author of three books on pop music, *Rock Folk*, *Boogie Lightning*, and *Ray Charles: Man and Music*, and a book on literature, *Writing and Life*. A founding editor of *Rolling Stone*, Lydon has also written for many periodicals, including the *Atlantic Monthly*, *New York Times*, and *Village Voice*.

Lydon is also a singer, songwriter, and guitarist. Brite Records has released his two CDs, *Love at First Sight* and *Mike on Mike*. With Ellen Mandel, he has composed an opera, *Passion in Pigskin*. A Yale graduate, Lydon is a member of ASCAP and of the AF of M, local 802.

INDEX

This index, compiled by the author, aims to include the names of significant people, places, and works of art mentioned in the text. The subjects of each chapter are not indexed within their own chapter: Jerry Garcia is not indexed within the Grateful Dead chapter, nor are Mick Jagger or Keith Richards indexed within the Rolling Stones chapter.

Individual song titles are in quotes: "Just Like a Woman"; album, book, and movie titles are in italics: *Abbey Road.*